W9-AMC-312

"An essential guidebook for navigating our time. Bourne concisely articulates the elements of our collective emergence to the next stage of cultural evolution. *The Aquarian Conspiracy* comes of age in this volume with inspiring clarity."

> —Anodea Judith, Ph.D., author of *Waking the Global Heart* and *Eastern Body-Western Mind*

"A masterful overview of the shift in global consciousness and how it transforms our personal lives."

> —Duane Elgin, author of *Voluntary Simplicity* and *Promise Ahead*

"A truly holistic view of changes now occurring—from global to local and personal. In this book, Bourne combines rare insight into the multiple paradigm shifts due to humanity's expanding awareness with a comprehensive, sensible set of tools for personal alignment and action."

> —Hazel Henderson, author of *Ethical Markets* and coauthor of *Planetary Citizenship*

"*Global Shift* offers a roadmap for the new consciousness—a sweeping survey of the key ideas and books of the last few years that describe an astounding shift in paradigms. It provides a wonderful overview of holistic trends emerging in all fields, from quantum physics to transpersonal psychology, and includes practical tools for transforming yourself and creating a more sustainable world."

> —Corinne McLaughlin, cofounder of The Center for Visionary Leadership and Sirius Community and coauthor of *Spiritual Politics* and *Builders of the Dawn*

"*Global Shift* is a bold and practical work, calling us all to address our global crises at the level of consciousness. Bourne covers an ambitious amount of ground—from concise summaries of the leading thinkers who have shaped our postmodern worldview to implementable steps we can take to reduce global warming—in an entertaining, informative, and easy-to-grasp manner. Not only a summary of causes and indicators of paradigmatic changes, *Global Shift* is a hopeful and welcome push to pick up the challenges of our times and create a significant shift in our world."

—Jeff Carreira, director of education at EnlightenNext
and host of the EnlightenNext Weekly Webcast

"*Global Shift* provides the first comprehensive template for massive evolutionary change in the twenty-first century. It is not only thorough, but also so convincing you will breathe one great sigh of relief for the entire human enterprise. After you have read this book, you will have your finger on the pulse of these challenging times and appreciate the part you are now called to play in this epic story of transformation."

—James O' Dea, consultant to Global Systems Initiatives
and fellow of the Institute of Noetic Sciences

GLOBAL SHIFT

HOW A NEW WORLDVIEW IS TRANSFORMING HUMANITY

EDMUND J. BOURNE, PH.D.

NOETIC BOOKS, INSTITUTE OF NOETIC SCIENCES

NEW HARBINGER PUBLICATIONS, INC.

Publisher's Note

"The Cosmological Situation Today," from Cosmos and Psyche: Intimations of a New World View by Richard Tarnas, copyright 2005 by Richard Tarnas. Used by permission of Viking Penguin, a division of Penguin group (USA) Inc.

Agent-approved adaptation of pp. 32-35 from Voluntary Simplicity (revised edition) by Duane Elgin, copyright 1978, 1992 by Duane Elgin. Reprinted by permission of HarperCollins publishers

The excerpt from *Voluntary Simplicity* is used by permission of the publisher and the author. Copyright 1992 Duane Elgin. Published by William Morrow and Co. (now HarperCollins), 10 East 53rd St, New York, NY 10010.

A copublication of New Harbinger Publications and Noetic Books

Distributed in Canada by Raincoast Books

Copyright © 2008 by Edmund J. Bourne
New Harbinger Publications, Inc.
5674 Shattuck Avenue
Oakland, CA 94609
www.newharbinger.com

All Rights Reserved
Printed in the United States of America

Acquired by Catharine Sutker; Cover design by Amy Shoup; Edited by Amy Johnson

FSC

Mixed Sources
Product group from well-managed
forests, controlled sources and
recycled wood or fiber

Cert no. SW-COC-002283
www.fsc.org
© 1996 Forest Stewardship Council

Library of Congress Cataloging-in-Publication Data

Bourne, Edmund J.
  Global shift : how a new worldview is transforming humanity /
Edmund J. Bourne ; foreword by Matthew Gilbert.
       p. cm.
Includes bibliographical references.
ISBN-13: 978-1-57224-597-6 (pbk. : alk. paper)
ISBN-10: 1-57224-597-2 (pbk. : alk. paper)
  1. Philosophy--21st century. 2. Culture. 3. Civilization. 4. Social
change. 5. Spirituality. I. Title.
B805.B68 2008
190.9'0511--dc22

                          2008039787

10 09 08

10 9 8 7 6 5 4 3 2 1   First printing

Contents

Global Shift: A Preview

Transformative Practices: An Introduction

Foreword

by Matthew Gilbert

As I write this, a barrel of oil approaches $150; floods, droughts, tornadoes, and typhoons wreak unprecedented havoc in certain parts of the world; and the global economy seems poised on a downward spiral. Perhaps by the time you read this, things will have improved; perhaps they will have become worse. Either way, it seems clear to more and more of us that we have collectively created an unsustainable way of life for most of the world's people and jeopardized our very existence as a species.

I first found out about Ed Bourne's book when it was submitted to a colleague at New Harbinger. The company had recently entered into a copublishing relationship with the Institute of Noetic Sciences, where I'm director of communications and acquisitions director of our new imprint, Noetic Books. I was stunned by how closely Ed's narrative mapped onto a new study we had just released, *The 2007 Shift Report: Evidence of a World Transforming*, and further impressed that he was inspired to write this book by Willis Harman, the late former president of IONS and a renowned visionary thinker.

We wrote that report to help answer the questions we kept hearing: What is going on? Why is all this happening? Where is all this leading? We began by noting the influence of a powerful worldview—scientific materialism—that arose in response to the religious fanaticism and conflicts of the seventeenth and eighteenth centuries. It elevated reason, objectivity, and the primacy of the physical universe, and focused on the study of parts instead of wholes. While providing an abundance of impressive advances in such areas as technology and medicine, it also promoted a separatism that has been encoded into many of our institutions. This has led a majority of people to prioritize their own needs over the good of the commons, to disassociate their own well-being from that of the world around them, and to see nature as nothing more than an inert source of raw materials and a vast receptacle for the garbage and toxins of an industrial and consumptive lifestyle. All of this is underwritten by a deeper story that human life is a random accident and human beings are basically no more than complicated machinery run by genes and neuronal programming. As for religion and spirituality, they are merely evolutionary adaptations to keep us interested in staying alive.

It's a dismal scenario, to be sure, but then look at the stories that feed us every day. For anyone who reads the papers, scans the Internet, listens to the radio, or watches the nightly news, the world seems relentlessly hopeless and complex. Economic uncertainty, ecological collapse, ethnic conflicts, religious extremism, heartbreaking poverty—these harsh realities depict a world filled with fear, pain, and fragmentation while reinforcing a belief that there is little we can do about it. No wonder sales of antidepressants keep spiking upward.

Yes, the evidence is compelling that the arc of human existence is on a self-destructive decline, but it's vitally important to distinguish between breakdown and *emergence*, because once the pieces are put together, there is no denying that another reality is fighting through the cracks of the dominant narrative. It is this story that Ed Bourne rigorously presents in this homage to our potential.

In calling our current moment in time a "rite of passage," Ed shows readers a landscape of fundamental shifts that are broad, deep, and ultimately life-affirming. He presents some dominant themes of a new overarching worldview—a conscious universe, multidimensional realities, interconnected minds, and life beyond physics—and describes the shift as "a movement away from a materialistic to a humanitarian-spiritual orientation toward life." These are awfully big ideas, pushing the boundaries of our conditioning and beliefs, but our collective future is at stake and this is not a time to be reticent. Braving the currents of postmodern malaise, Ed, and the Institute, and many others believe that we are just beginning to tap into our potential as human beings despite, or perhaps because of, the multiple crises that we are facing.

This new story remains largely unreported. It reflects not an evolutionary model of randomness and survival but an evolution of human capacities that may alter the course of history and that a growing body of data from psychologists, paleontologists, neuroscientists, and quantum physicists are beginning to acknowledge. It's also a story that was further explored in the Institute's second worldview analysis, *The 2008 Shift Report: Changing the Story of Our Future*.

Over the past several decades, new scientific discoveries, along with a surge in grassroots initiatives addressing social and economic injustices, have begun calling into question that view of the universe—and in essence ourselves—as ultimately cold and mechanistic. Credible studies are finding that we're as hard-wired to connect and collaborate as to compete; that genes—as well as the brain—are malleable; that altruistic behavior enhances our immune system; and that at a subatomic level, everything is connected—literally. On the field of daily human endeavor, thousands of groups and millions of people are saying no to the madness of our time—a tacit acknowledgment that we have been sold a bill of goods about our potential and who we are. The story being told of a conniving, selfish, survival-driven species is in fact a small part, perhaps even a footnote, of a larger story in which the wisdom of our spiritual traditions and the findings of new science are finally beginning to converge.

As science and human progress are inextricably linked, the twenty-first century is finding a way to bring the highest potential of both back together. While changing paradigms is never easy, an evolutionary acceleration seems to have been unleashed, and worldview is at the center of it. Worldviews both large and small shape how we see the world, how we structure our institutions, and how we find meaning in what we do and where we're going, individually as well as collectively. The influence of modern science on worldview—the assumptions we make about how the universe works and the means we use to test those assumptions—is significant. How we've internalized this paradigm into our own being is also significant, perhaps even more so. So while marching on the World Trade Organization and confronting misuse of power remain necessary acts of defiance, marching against the dominant paradigms that live in our own hearts may have even more far-reaching effects. For the ultimate change will be a change in our consciousness and in our assumptions about the best way to live in this complicated world.

This is the gift of Ed's book. It provides a road map for how to get from where we are to where we need to be and why such a journey is both vital and inevitable. A metaphor often used to describe the development of our species is that we are struggling through adolescence, slowly groping toward adulthood. In drawing the lines between new scientific research and spiritual exploration, we may just be uncovering the nascent signs of a collective maturing, perhaps foretelling a coming Age of Reenlightenment.

Matthew Gilbert
Institute of Noetic Sciences
June 16, 2008

Grateful acknowledgment to:

Catharine Sutker of New Harbinger Publications, whose enthusiasm and support are largely responsible for making this book possible.

Matthew Gilbert of the Institute of Noetic Sciences, whose suggestions helped give shape to the final structure of this book; and

Those visionary authors whose ideas both inspired and helped to provide a foundation for this book: Willis Harman, Richard Tarnas, Christian de Quincey, Ervin Laszlo, Duane Elgin, and Ken Wilber.

Introduction

Concern about the future is widespread these days. On some level all of us know that we live in a time when our earth and civilization stand at a crossroads.

This book describes a fundamental shift in humanity's consciousness—our way of both perceiving and acting in the world. Such a shift has been developing over the past few decades and will continue to develop through much of the twenty-first century. The shift accompanies a profound rite of passage that the earth and its people are going through now as well as in the future.

What is going to change? The prevailing societal trends of unlimited economic growth and material consumption will not continue, as they are not sustainable. On a global level, humanity will outgrow its adolescence, learning to become better stewards of the earth and its resources. Nations and cultures will increasingly come to honor each other as part of a global family, regardless of differences in race, religion, or nationality. Cooperation among nations will, out of necessity, begin to supersede conflict. Such values and inclinations are prevalent now among perhaps 10 to 20 percent of the population. They may not achieve a broad base, however, until the challenges humanity faces reach a critical mass. Increasing problems posed by climate change, ecological disruption, diminishing resources (especially oil and water), population growth, and poverty are rapidly reaching a point where dramatic worldwide changes in priorities will be *required* to forestall global chaos.

The change in worldview coming about at this time can be described from multiple perspectives, both conceptual and practical. Chapters 4–16 of this book outline an emerging new perception of reality—how we perceive the world. This new perspective is taking the place of the old scientific-materialist worldview that has dominated Western society for more than four hundred years. Some of the dominant themes of the new worldview include:

A conscious universe: The universe as a whole is a conscious, coherent, and creative process, not a purely mechanistic object. Every whole system, from atoms to galaxies, has an *interiority*—a subjective aspect that exhibits attributes of consciousness such as self-organization and intentionality.

Multidimensional reality: Reality—the sum of all that is—exceeds the bounds of the physical universe and contains multiple "subtle" or transcendent dimensions. The more subtle dimensions form the matrix of the physical universe that we see.

Interconnection of all minds: Though we appear to exist in separate bodies, our minds, at the deepest level, are joined in a collective consciousness. At the level of our deepest soul, we are all one.

Complementarity of science and spirituality: Both science and spirituality lead to an understanding of the Cosmos: science of its outer, objective aspect, and spirituality—along with humanities and the arts—of its inner, subjective/symbolic aspect.

Radical empiricism: Intuitive and visionary forms of knowing are as valid as sensory-based forms of knowing, even if less subject to interpersonal and cross-cultural consensus.

Consciousness has a causal influence: Consciousness has inherent properties—such as a capacity for self-organization, intentionality, and meaning—that cannot be explained in terms of the material laws and processes of the natural sciences. Yet it has a causal influence on physical processes.

Natural ethics: Ought reduces to is. Ethical behavior—what we ought to do—follows acting out of authenticity to one's innermost nature rather than culturally relative standards.

It's clear that this new image of the Cosmos differs radically from the materialist one most of us grew up with. It is as radical a change from what has gone before as the Renaissance worldview was relative to the medieval one. Such an image exceeds the bounds of present-day science, although it's not inconceivable that science itself could eventually evolve to embrace it.

The emerging shift in worldview is accompanied by a corresponding shift in values—what we deem to be important. These new values share a common feature: *a movement away from a materialistic to a humanitarian-spiritual orientation toward life.* Greater self-awareness, spiritual growth, and a sense of responsibility to the environment are seen as equally important as—if not more important than—economic success and consumption. Among these new values are:

Reverence for nature and the earth: We are vitally dependent on the earth, the matrix of all life. Living in a cooperative, sustainable relationship with the earth is more important than exploiting it for material gain.

A sense of inclusiveness toward all humanity: We look beyond self-interest to recognize that all human beings are part of the same family, regardless of racial, ethnic, national, or religious differences. All human beings have equal rights to health, livelihood, safety, and prosperity.

Compassion: An awareness of the suffering of other human beings subjected to poverty, disease, and inhumane living conditions, regardless of who they are or where they live. A desire to help.

Integration of the feminine: A movement away from traditionally "masculine" values of hierarchy, autonomy, top-down control, and exploitation toward "feminine" values of inclusiveness, cooperation, interrelationship, nurturance, and love.

Valuing intuition: Trusting one's deeper intuitions or hunches as good guides for making decisions (along with reason).

Voluntary simplicity: Cultivating a simpler life, both for the sake of inner peace and to leave a lighter footprint on the earth.

Respect for being present: Living mindfully, or "in-the-now," is given value equal to left-brained analysis and the demand to predict and control the future.

The primacy of unconditional love: Unconditional love and forgiveness are the highest values in our relations with others. If we are all one, then to harm another person is to harm ourselves. The operative question in all situations of interpersonal conflict reduces to "What is the most loving thing to do?"

Shifts in our values ultimately lead to shifts in the way we act. Already, many of us are beginning to change the way we behave toward ourselves, each other, our communities, and the larger environment and humanity of which we are a part. The final seven chapters of this book take a practical focus, describing a number of personal transformative practices. Many of these practices foster personal healing. Others contribute to the planet's needs, such as reducing carbon dioxide emissions and conserving precious resources. Most of the practices described are quite specific, such as reducing meat consumption, embracing forgiveness, setting aside time for meditation, recycling waste, and giving time and money to nonprofits. All of them lead to a greater alignment with the shift happening on the planet at this time. In choosing to engage in these practices, we become part of the solution to the challenges that humanity faces rather than part of the problem. Not surprisingly, often what is healing for ourselves is also healing for the planet.

Vision and practice are inseparable. A shift in the collective worldview is likely to accompany (though not necessarily cause) the types of fundamental changes in values and actions required by humanity at this time. This worldview shift is part of a broader change that includes a far-reaching cultural, economic, and political restructuring of society. Such a shift happened in Europe during the Renaissance and also much earlier in ancient Greece. This time it is happening globally and, unlike the past, it may occur rapidly, over several decades rather than one or two centuries.

This book emphasizes *personal shifts* in worldview, values, and actions that are taking shape at the present time. It does not consider shifts that are happening at the institutional level, affecting fields as diverse as business, politics, education, media, healthcare, and the arts. Many good books describe the shift emerging at the more inclusive cultural and institutional level. Some of these books are listed in the resources section at the end of this book. The annual *Shift Report* published by the Institute of Noetic Sciences is also good place to get a grasp of the shift at this level. Of course, widespread changes in perceptions, values, and actions at the personal level may also help facilitate new priorities and actions at the collective level. Ultimately, world peace and planetary healing begin with the personal healing of ourselves as well as our relationships.

Questions are often raised about whether the present shift in consciousness can reach a critical mass in time to avert major upheaval for humanity. There seems to be a general consensus that time is running short. The window of opportunity for major changes in how we relate to the environment and one another is thought to be at best a decade or two. The intent of this book (with the exception of chapter 1) is to describe aspects of the emerging worldview rather than focus on the prospective breakdown of the old world order.

Each of us can take specific actions now to become more conscious—to heal ourselves as well as to help the planet. Our actions are vitally important, yet the fate of the earth over the coming decades ultimately rests in the hands of the government leaders who decide on national and global policies. Fortunately, as public opinion shifts, leaders are likely to respond.

Some degree of deconstruction of the old world order is likely necessary for a new consciousness to emerge. Decay and rebirth are characteristic of all forms of evolution, whether biological or cultural. A global shift in worldview, values, and actions is inevitable. Whether it *precedes* and redirects humanity away from chaos or *follows* an epic global breakdown remains an open question. Either way, the shift is destined to come about.

Reading This Book: An Overview

This book approaches the emerging global shift from several distinct perspectives.

Chapter 1 presents a summary of the global crises that have brought humanity to its current crossroads. Problems such as global warming, diminishing resources, loss of biodiversity, deforestation, worldwide poverty and disease, and the potential for future global conflict are described in some detail. Given the current situation, there are two alternative scenarios for the earth's future: pervasive global breakdown or significant breakthrough—a genuine shift in planetary consciousness.

Chapter 2 takes a historical perspective, describing the rise and fall of the scientific-materialist worldview that has contributed to an overemphasis on exploiting the earth rather than preserving it. Though this view of the world still prevails in many places, it has been questioned and challenged to the extent that a space has been cleared for a new worldview to emerge. Readers who are not particularly interested in this historical account may choose to skip ahead to chapter 3, which details numerous indications of an emerging new consciousness. Many of these trends—such as the environmental movement, the feminist movement, holistic medicine, an interest in Eastern spirituality, the new physics, and an increasing acceptance of paranormal phenomena—have been developing for a few decades. Collectively, these signs point to the birth of a new way of perceiving ourselves, our relationships with each other, and our relationship to the larger universe in which we live.

This new global paradigm—this new way of perceiving reality itself—is the subject of chapters 4–16. These chapters sketch various dimensions of a new worldview expected to increasingly replace the materialistic paradigm that has been dominant in the West for the past four hundred years. The content of these chapters tends to be more conceptual, describing aspects of the new paradigm that transcend conventional science. These aspects include the idea of a conscious universe, a synthesis of science and spirituality, and the notion that all minds are deeply interconnected. A brief introduction to these chapters can be found in the section, Global Shift: A Preview.

In the last seven chapters (chapters 18–24), the focus shifts from vision to action. What does the global shift mean in terms of how we live our daily lives? What can each of us do to actively promote a better world? Chapter 18 raises the question of how each of us can make the shift toward a more global perspective, one in which we begin to see beyond our own personal lives to the needs of the human community and the planet. As previously mentioned, chapters 19–24 describe a number of specific practices and actions each of us can take to align ourselves with the emerging shift in consciousness. For those readers interested in practical aspects of what to do to make a difference, these chapters will be most relevant. In brief, the latter part of the book speaks to how each of us can embody the vision described in the first part.

1

Global Crisis

Humanity is looking for a new story. The one it has embraced since the Renaissance is no longer viable. Despite all of its positive contributions to modern life, three hundred years of scientific-technological development has left our civilization in an untenable position—at odds with its natural environment and ultimately its own deeper, collective soul. Only a global shift in fundamental perceptions, values, and corresponding actions will allow humankind to resume an evolutionary path in alignment with nature and the larger cosmos. This book represents one attempt to explore the dimensions of what a new story for humanity might look like. It concludes with practical actions each of us can take in our personal and collective lives to promote the emergence of a new story.

This book took root in the year 2000. Some of the seminal chapters were written at that time—before September 11, 2001, and before the onset of eight years of political conservatism in America. In its first conception, this book was influenced by the more optimistic current of thinking in the late 1990s, when many people were envisioning a new century of positive social transformation. Bookstores at that time featured many popular books on spiritual transformation, from authors such as Neale Donald Walsch, Deepak Chopra, James Redfield, Wayne Dyer, and Miguel Ruiz.

At this writing, several years later, consciousness continues to expand around the globe, but the context has changed. The collective mood is more serious, if not somber. It appears that the last three decades of the twentieth century were a time when the world was seeded with an enormous variety of spiritual teachings and a new holistic perspective. Now, in the new century, humanity has entered a time of increasing global distress when such teachings—and the values that go with them—need to be applied on a large scale if the earth is to avoid a progressively downward path.

Gone is the plethora of spiritual-growth books and the vision of a new age. In their place is a growing awareness of an unprecedented planetary crisis on multiple fronts: global warming, environmental degradation, massive loss of species, dwindling natural resources, difficulties in switching to sustainable forms of energy, rapidly increasing population, and widespread poverty, hunger, and disease. At mid-decade, the year 2005 saw three major natural disasters: the Indonesian tsunami, the inundation of New Orleans and the Gulf region by Hurricane Katrina, and a catastrophic earthquake in Pakistan. New disasters of equal proportion took place in 2007 and 2008. Human suffering is widespread in third world countries, while an increasing subjective malaise affects many people in more technologically developed nations. There is more insecurity and uncertainty on the planet, especially with reference to the future, than there was when this book was first conceived.

Global shift—a basic shift in perceptions, core values, and priorities—is beginning to happen for people throughout the world at this time. More than ever, there is a belief that such a shift is urgently needed to forestall an unraveling of the fabric of civilized life as we know it. Though many predicted world crisis ten and even twenty years ago, the crucial moment has now arrived. Without a fundamental shift in beliefs, values, and consequent actions of a large number of people, the earth seems headed toward an era of increasing darkness.

Twenty years ago, visionary philosopher Willis Harman spoke of the "world macroproblem"—the interrelated series of challenges that the earth is facing—in a book far ahead of its time called *Global Mind Change* (1990). This book follows in Harman's footsteps and owes much to his work. What are the dimensions of the world macroproblem twenty years later?

Global Warming

For many, the term "global crisis" means the deterioration of the earth's environment, mostly as the result of adverse human impact. As this time, global warming appears to be emerging as the most critical of these man-made environmental problems. Consider some of the facts: The Intergovernmental Panel on Climate Change (basically most of the world's leading climatologists) reports that in the past fifty years human activity has raised the average temperature on earth about 1 degree Fahrenheit (with the Arctic area seeing an increase of 4 degrees). If this trend continues unabated, the average temperature is expected to rise precipitously—another 3 to 10 degrees—over the course of this century. Some of the possible outcomes of such a drastic increase in temperature include the displacement of up to a *billion* people due to floods and rising seas in some of the earth's most fertile regions; dramatic climate destabilization, with droughts and floods playing havoc with harvests and the habitability of large areas of the world (including the United States); increasingly larger, more violent, and more frequent hurricanes; drastic cooling of Great Britain and northern Europe; desertification of presently fertile areas; the spread of tropical diseases into temperate zones; and a rapid dwindling in the oceans' supply of edible fish. The reality of global warming is no longer seriously questioned in the light of multiple lines of evidence:

- In the past thirty years, the number of Category 4 and 5 hurricanes has doubled, with Katrina's devastation of New Orleans and surrounding areas in 2005 being the most blatant example in the United States (increased hurricane intensity is caused by warmer oceans).

- Of the twenty-one hottest years on the planet since measurements began in 1860, twenty occurred in the last twenty-five years.

- The Arctic polar ice cap lost a record amount of ice cover in September 2005; in September 2007 this record was surpassed by an additional 23 percent (2008). In the summer of 2007, an area of ice twice the size of Britain disappeared in one week. Greenland's summer ice melt has similarly increased dramatically in the last few years, with glacial ice moving into the sea at the rate of six feet per hour in some areas. If all of Greenland's ice were to break up and melt, global sea levels would rise eighteen to twenty-three feet (Kunzig 2008).

- Approximately 30 percent of the world's coral reefs have died due to bleaching, with another 40 percent in imminent danger. *Bleaching*, the exposing of the white calcium-carbonate skeleton of the coral, occurs when microorganisms supported by the reef die due to rising ocean temperatures.

- In the northern hemisphere, the growing season has been extended by eleven days, allowing more organic material to decay and emit carbon into the atmosphere. Shorter winters and longer summers have also upset many delicately balanced ecological cycles. For example, massive areas of pine and spruce forests in North America are being killed by bark beetles whose range and number used to be contained by colder winters.

- The earth's seas are becoming more acidic as a result of rising carbon dioxide levels. By 2050 the seas may be acidic enough to dissolve the minute aragonite shells of phytoplankton. If large amounts of phytoplankton die off, the earth will have lost one of its major resources for absorbing greenhouse gases as well as the primary foundation of the entire marine food chain.

What is most alarming is that warming appears to be accelerating faster than many scientists anticipated. While immediate action is needed, the United States, currently responsible for 25 percent of global carbon emissions, has (at this writing) done little to cut back (Stix 2006). The effort of the United States to reduce its dependence on oil by increasing ethanol production as a source of fuel is unlikely to have significant impact on its total carbon output. In fact, a recent article in *Time Magazine* suggests that production of corn-based ethanol may actually have a larger carbon footprint than gasoline refined from oil (Grunwald 2008). India and China, currently enjoying rapid economic development with little regard for its side effects, will undoubtedly increase their carbon dioxide outputs significantly over the next decade. Without dramatic curtailments of carbon emissions in the next ten years, the earth may pass a tipping point beyond which catastrophic consequences are inevitable.

Other Environmental Problems

There are major environmental issues beyond global warming. In many parts of the world, forests, which help to absorb extra carbon dioxide, are disappearing fast. In two decades, the Amazon rainforest has decreased by 20 percent as a result of gratuitous clearing of land for ranching or farming. Another 20 percent has been weakened by logging and road building, allowing enough sun to reach the forest floor to set the stage for widespread fires (Brown 2008). In recent years air pollution has become a serious health hazard in many Asian cities, from New Delhi to Shanghai, while in the United States a haze from air pollution blankets the entire region east of the Mississippi River much of the time. Finally, the destruction of animal habitats by industry, pollution, and global warming has substantially decreased the number of viable species. In immediate danger of extinction are 12 percent of birds, 20 percent of mammals, and 39 percent of fish. The rate of decline of species has been described as "the sixth great extinction" since animals initially appeared on earth about 500 million years ago (Brown 2008).

To sum up, human beings are making their home less habitable at a fast pace. Some climatologists believe we have already passed the point beyond which devastating consequences for the planet are inescapable.

Population Growth and Diminishing Resources

Unfortunately, environmental deterioration is far from the only problem the earth faces. Unchecked population growth also presents serious concerns. The population of the earth quadrupled from 1.5 billion to over 6 billion people in the twentieth century, and is expected to reach 9 billion by 2050. Almost all of this population growth is expected to occur in developing countries affected by severe poverty, disease, and diminished availability of food, water, and other basic resources. As of 2007, about 50 percent of these people were living in cities, up to half of these in slums that lack adequate housing, sanitation, transportation, clean water, or health care (Nierenberg 2006). The implications of such rapid population growth are especially grim in the light of diminishing resources; these include water, oil, and food (due to rising prices and climate destabilization).

At present, 80 percent of the earth's natural resources are used by the wealthiest 20 percent of the population, and the situation is expected to get even more lopsided. To give just one example, it is estimated that by 2015 as many as 3 billion people will be living in water-stressed areas, subject to limited availability of water for drinking, let alone agriculture (Renner 2005). At present, 20 percent of the world's population lacks clean drinking water. Hundreds of Chinese cities already face severe water shortages, with many households limited to a mere trickle of water a few hours each day. With the prospect of an increasingly radical division of the world between a wealthy minority and impoverished majority, the risk of unrest, conflict, war, and terrorism increases.

Impoverished people are subject to disease. The statistics are horrific. Approximately 15,000 Africans die each day of preventable diseases—mainly malaria, HIV/AIDS, or tuberculosis (Sachs 2005). The poor die in hospitals that lack basic drugs, in areas that lack antimalarial nets, and in towns that lack sanitary drinking water. In the past fifteen years, HIV/AIDS has killed 20 million people and sickened an additional 34 to 46 million. By 2010 the number sickened will reach 75 million worldwide. In parts of Africa the adult death rate is so high that there are not enough teachers for schools (Pirages 2005).

Looking at disease in general, up to 7 million people, mostly in poor countries, die each year of diseases that could easily be prevented by immunization. The situation has begun to turn around due to widespread humanitarian efforts, though eradication of disease and poverty in sub-Saharan Africa still has a long way to go.

Lastly, around the world, approximately a billion people are presently subject to malnutrition or semi-starvation. The combination of rapid population growth and environmental instability from global warming is likely to increase this number over the next decade.

All of these conditions—climate change, diminishing resources, population growth, poverty, disease, and hunger—interact to produce an increasingly dismal picture for a large proportion of the earth's population. The Worldwatch Institute sums up this situation as follows: "Nations around the world, but particularly the weakest countries and communities, confront a multitude of pressures. They face a debilitating combination of rising competition for resources, severe environmental breakdown, the resurgence of infectious diseases, poverty and growing wealth disparities, demographic pressures, and livelihood insecurity" (Renner 2005, 5).

In this brief chapter it's only possible to touch on some of the factors of the present global predicament. Twenty years after Willis Harman coined the term, our planet's macroproblem has worsened on a variety of fronts. If conditions continue along this trajectory, the quality of life for *everyone*—not just those in impoverished areas—is likely to decline.

Source of the Problem

What is the ultimate origin of this global crisis? Harman's answer still rings true today: having lost any consensus on ultimate meanings and values, the industrialized world steers itself primarily on the basis of economic values. Governments, in combination with all-powerful multinational corporations, base policy decisions on a misguided vision of unlimited future economic development. While problems such as climate change, poverty, and disease are becoming more salient to public awareness, it is still economic values that drive the most powerful corporate and political institutions on the planet. The primacy of economic considerations shows up in a multiplicity of ways, one of which is the commercializing of institutions not intended to be commercial. For example, science is justified and funded on the basis of the technology it can produce; education is justified on the basis of the jobs it can prepare youth for; and medicine—specifically managed care—is regulated more by economic constraints than patients' needs. Economic values also dominate humanity's relationship with the environment, which continues to be degraded in order to ensure the maintenance and continued expansion of industries dependent on fossil fuels.

On a positive note, there is some good news on the horizon. European governments such as those of Germany, Denmark, France, and Spain are taking climate change seriously, making far-reaching efforts to develop alternative sources of energy based on wind, solar power, and biofuels. Specific states and regions within the United States, such as California and New England, have established guidelines to cut carbon emissions substantially by 2020. Both at grassroots and governmental levels, many efforts are currently underway to mitigate both climate change and pressing social issues such as sub-Saharan poverty and disease. On the downside, developing countries such as China and India, which together include more than one-third of the world's population, are just beginning their phase of rapid economic growth. While acknowledging climate change and other environmental problems, they show less initiative to constrain the adverse environmental impacts of their growth than do many developed countries.

A future based on continuing economic expansion and growth is, of course, unsustainable. It is widely recognized that natural resources, particularly oil, will simply run out at current rates of utilization long before this century ends. Even by optimistic projections, worldwide oil demand is already exceeding production, with the global oil supply likely to top out in the near future. Without rapid, widespread conversion to cleaner forms of energy that do not rely on fossil fuels, global warming will accelerate, and the continuation of petroleum-based transportation, power generation, and industry as we know it will grow increasingly tenuous. As the demand-to-supply ratio for oil increases, the rising cost of oil and everything dependent on it, is likely to lead to serious economic consequences in many places.

If the prospect for economically developed countries is not favorable, the situation for third world countries is likely to be far worse. The continued economic expansion of multinational corporations owned by the wealthiest countries can only lead to increased misery and conflict in less-developed areas. Industrial growth has multiple impacts, including increased carbon emissions (that can cause flooding and droughts in the third world), widespread air and water pollution, increased disparity between rich and poor, increased pushing of peasants off the land into urban slums, and increased unemployment because of the breakdown of local agriculture in a global economy. In general, the prognosis for a global society based primarily on economic and materialistic values is poor.

Toward a New Vision for the Earth

A growing number of concerned people voice a common sentiment: the world needs nothing less than a new vision for the future, based on a new set of values. This new vision needs to include a worldwide respect for the earth and a reliance on sustainable resources. Such a vision also needs to consider the plight of billions of people suffering from poverty, disease, and dislocation in underdeveloped countries. The new values need to be more inner-directed than outer-directed. Responsibility for the planet and its people needs to take precedence over economic advantage and unlimited expansion.

Such a vision exists. This book could not have been written unless a broad new vision and plan for rescuing the earth were in the process of developing. In fact, the development of a new global outlook and set of values can be traced back forty years. It began with the social movements of the 1960s, including the peace movement, the women's movement, the environmental movement, and the civil rights movement. All four of these movements sought to overcome social institutions perceived as unjust and dehumanizing. They all placed humanitarian values—respect for the earth and all of its peoples, regardless of their differences—above materialistic values. In addition to these broad social movements, a wave of interest in Eastern religions and spirituality emerged in the 1970s, leading many to question Western religious institutions based on dogmatic views of original sin and a punitive deity. Transcendence of ego conditioning and compassion toward all humanity—indeed toward all forms of life—became important aspirations for many people, influencing mainstream thinking through books, workshops, yoga and meditation classes, and spiritual teachers. This spiritual renaissance continued for the rest of the twentieth century, with a new theme emphasizing mind-body wholeness and holistic health emerging in the late 1970s. The idea of integrating body, mind, and spirit in the healing of both physical and emotional distress has had an enormous impact on Western society. Industries embraced by millions—such as the health food, supplement, and fitness industries—grew out of this holistic vision, which continues to the present day.

The 1990s saw the emergence of holistic medicine, with alternative physicians such as Deepak Chopra and Andrew Weil having widespread impact. By 1997, 85 percent of Americans had utilized one of twenty-three kinds of alternative health care, and visits to alternative health care providers by 87 million Americans had actually exceeded the total number of visits by all Americans to conventional physicians. Meditation and yoga, popular mainly among New Agers in the seventies and eighties, went mainstream during the nineties. Meditation groups became common in hospitals and assisted-living centers. By the turn of the century, a huge segment of the American population—20 million adults—were practicing some form of yoga.

In the 1990s, the ideal of the whole person became complementary to the vision of a "whole planet": a place where humanity is perceived as an integral, interdependent part of nature (rather than separate from and exploitative of nature), and where all people can live together in cooperation and peace, regardless of racial, ethnic, and religious boundaries. Nonviolent communication groups based on the book *Nonviolent Communication* (2003) and related programs sprang up in cities all over the world.

Even more telling has been the impact of the environmental movement on big business. In *Natural Capitalism* (2000), authors Paul Hawken, Amory Lovins, and Hunter Lovins convincingly argue that the world economy is shifting from an emphasis on human productivity to resource productivity, which amounts to using natural resources from ten to a hundred times more efficiently. The authors present a wide array of practical inventions that already do this. They discuss using hydrogen fuel cells for cars and plug-in generators for electricity in the home; utilizing fibers more efficiently to produce cloth; and ways to improve food production; among other things. According to the authors, businesses that avoid dealing with environmental problems or increasing their energy efficiency will jeopardize their own viability. So in the coming decades, it may happen that big businesses shift to more environmentally conscious and sustainable technologies because it is the only way in the long run for them to survive.

An increasing number of large companies, including General Electric, DuPont, Wal-Mart, Toyota, Mitsubishi, Electrolux, and BP Amoco, are currently in the process of adopting more sustainable practices. The Worldwatch Institute's *State of the World 2008* reports an emerging trend of private-sector investment in eco-friendly projects: "More than $100 billion in venture capital, private equity, corporate research and development funding, and government support for technology development was invested in environmental start-up ventures over the past year" (Esty 2008, xvi). In both the United States and China, clean technology is now the third largest sector for venture capital investment. If companies large and small begin moving toward environmental preservation and resource sustainability, perhaps we may yet avert the environmental disasters currently in the making. At the present time it appears that private corporations are moving faster toward this goal, largely because of perceived economic advantage, than national governments.

By the end of 1990s, a paradigm shift—a shift in the predominant worldview—was under way on many fronts. Chapter 3 summarizes ten major trends that point to such a shift. Some of the best known of these trends include:

- The environmental movement, with its concern for protecting the environment and promoting reliance on sustainable resources

- A large holistic health movement and the emergence of holistic medicine

- The feminist movement and feminist spirituality

- Widespread interest in Eastern spirituality

- Renewed interest in ancient cultural perspectives (such as Native American or Celtic philosophies)

- A much wider acceptance of paranormal phenomena, including a more widespread belief in telepathy, remote viewing, and the survival of the soul after death (based on accounts of near-death experiences as well as communications with the deceased)

- The "new physics" and its radical implication that what we can know about phenomena at a quantum level is dependent upon human consciousness

- A widespread popularity of metaphysical topics ranging from reincarnation to channeling

- The Gaia hypothesis and its view of the biosphere as an intelligent, self-organizing whole system

- Development of more than one hundred thousand grassroots-based nonprofit organizations devoted to a wide range of causes relating to environmental preservation and social justice

All of these trends imply a fundamental change in perception—a variety of new ways of viewing the world and humanity's relationship with it. This book explores some of these new perceptions of the world in considerable detail. In particular, seven global shifts are described:

- *Understanding the universe to be conscious* (defined in terms of self-organization and intentionality) at all levels, from subatomic particles to galaxies

- *Recognition of the universe as multidimensional*, containing subtle dimensions that form a matrix for the material universe that we see

- *Acceptance of intuitive and visionary forms of knowledge* as equal in value to empirical, sensory-based forms of knowledge

- A greater *integration of science and religion/spirituality* as complementary ways of comprehending a single Cosmos

- *Recognizing the unity of consciousness*—the reality that all discrete minds are joined in one seamless unity

- *Embracing a global consciousness*, where cultural and national boundaries are transcended and human beings identify themselves as part of a planetary civilization

- *A natural ethics* where ought reduces to is (ethical behavior follows from acting out of authenticity to one's innermost nature); where love and compassion are seen as innate human potentials

As mentioned earlier, changes in how we see the world are generally accompanied by core value shifts. People who are open to spiritual growth, holistic health, environmental preservation, feminist philosophy, or the existence of paranormal phenomena tend to share some or all of the core values associated with the emerging worldview. Some of these values overlap with the perceptual shifts just mentioned. These values include:

Regard for the importance of individual self-actualization: Personal and spiritual growth are seen as equal to or more important than economic status and material achievement.

Preservation of the natural environment: Living in a cooperative, harmonious relationship with the earth is more important than exploiting it for economic gain. This relates to the perception, held by many indigenous peoples, that all levels of nature are inherently conscious, and thus sacred and deserving of reverence.

An appreciation of the unity of all human beings in mind and spirit: This is expressed by the popular phrase "we are all one" and conveyed in such popular songs as "Imagine" and "We Are the World." Such a concept envisions a world where human beings strive to be compassionate and cooperative toward one another regardless of gender, racial, ethnic, national, and religious differences.

Valuing intuitive, right-brain understanding as well as rational, left-brain knowledge: Intuitive knowledge and empirical, sensory-based knowledge are equally valued. One's deeper intuitions or hunches are considered good guides for making decisions.

Valuing spirituality relative to materialism: Shifting away from an emphasis on personal material gain and consumption toward a focus on a deep personal connection with a higher order. This can be defined either abstractly as a cosmic intelligence (or consciousness) or in more traditional theistic terms as God, Allah, Brahma, and so forth.

Cultivating a simpler life: Living simply and leaving a lighter footprint on the earth is chosen over supporting global corporate expansion through conspicuous consumption.

What percentage of the population embraces part or all of these shifts in perceptions and values? According to Paul Ray and Sherry Ruth Anderson in their 2000 book *The Cultural Creatives*, about 25 million Americans (or 12 percent of adults) strongly endorse most or all of the above values, while another 25 million are concerned about the ecology and well-being of the planet without necessarily embracing spirituality or personal spiritual growth. As this book goes to print, Ray is completing a new survey that estimates 30 percent of Americans to be cultural creatives. In western Europe, he has found the number to be slightly higher—about 35 percent of adults. Although sixty million Americans is a large group, Ray and Anderson suggest that up to now these individuals have not become sufficiently aware of each other to form a unified political force that could promote change at the governmental level.

Certainly the group these authors describe exists, but its influence may have been slow to gain political traction until the recent widespread concern with the environment and climate change while the cultural creatives have not yet gained significant political leverage at the national level, their strength is clearly increasing at the grassroots level and in local communities. With the Internet available today to over a billion users, these concerned citizens are now better able to both communicate with each other and become a unified force in developed countries.

Seven years after the appearance of *The Cultural Creatives*, environmentalist Paul Hawken explored a similar theme in his book *Blessed Unrest* (2007). The earth's best chance, he believes, resides in a vast network of nonprofits and community organizations dedicated to both environmental protection and social justice. Like the cultural creatives, many of these grassroots organizations are not aware of each other. Yet collectively they are making a significant difference in the world on a wide array of fronts, such as climate change, species loss, poverty, disease, indigenous peoples' rights, conservation, and the development of alternative energy technologies, to mention just a few. Hawken suggests this vast humanitarian movement can be seen as humanity's "immune system"—a pervasive response to the "disease" perpetrated on the planet by corporate values of unlimited economic growth and exploitation of natural resources. Though this diverse movement has no single ideology, Hawken believes that its basic values—respect for the earth and the dignity of all human beings—will gradually infiltrate the culture at large, including, ultimately, the very corporate and governmental institutions that the movement presently confronts. This will happen from the ground up and offers the basis for some optimism in a time when so many are sounding pessimistic warnings about the earth's future.

Ways a Global Shift Can Occur

A broad-based global shift has been going on for some time now. How can such a shift continue to grow and broaden further? In hundreds of different ways, at both the individual and collective level. Change must begin in each individual's consciousness; like-minded individuals may then come together to promote larger transformations. Such shifts are likely to occur first at a local level, but ultimately, with the help of the Internet and other global forms of communication, at much broader levels. When large numbers of the populace demand change, governments are compelled to respond.

Individuals can participate in the global shift in many different ways. At a purely individual level, a person might choose to:

- Live more simply, reducing consumption and energy use

- Overcome a health problem through holistic or alternative approaches

- Engage in a spiritual practice that leads to a basic change in priorities

- Discover joy in nature and take up the cause of helping the environment

- Make a microcredit loan to help someone start a small business in a developing country

- Purchase energy-efficient products to save money as well as help the earth

- Join a community-based support group, such as a women's group, to overcome feelings of isolation

- Invest in environmentally screened mutual funds

- Cultivate more peaceful interpersonal relationships, for instance by studying the principles outlined in Marshall Rosenberg's book *Nonviolent Communication*

- Buy a hybrid car and install a solar-based water heating system to reduce one's carbon footprint

- Join a study group centered around spiritual-growth titles such as *A Course in Miracles* or *The Power of Now*

Think of each individual consciousness as a cell in the body of collective human experience. As each person raises their consciousness, one by one, the entire collective consciousness of humanity is subtly affected.

At a collective level, this shift can come about in similarly numerous ways. For example:

- A corporation can switch to a more energy-efficient technology that will ultimately also save money.

- A medical school can develop an integrative curriculum that includes complementary health approaches.

- A higher-education institution can develop a program in consciousness studies.

- Progressive high schools can offer a course in environmental studies.

- A nonprofit organization can set up local clinics to provide quality health care in impoverished areas such as Rwanda and Haiti, as Partners in Health has done.

- Youth can attend megaconcerts intended to raise aid for impoverished regions of the world, such as sub-Saharan Africa.

- A major retail chain can introduce a labeling program to encourage consumers to buy products that promote energy conservation, clean water, and sustainable forestry, as Home Depot has done with its Eco Options.

- States can pass legislation to reduce industrial and energy-sector carbon emissions, as well as encourage development of hydrogen-based fuel technologies, as California has.

- A group of scientists can endorse a plan to maintain biodiversity (reduce species extinction) in a variety of places around the world.

- Alternative energy technologies, from cheaper photovoltaic cells to biofuels from algae, are rapidly developed in Europe and America. When the United States finally establishes a cap on carbon emissions, these emerging technologies become competitive and eventually cheaper than coal, oil, and natural gas.

- Youth from Israel and Arab countries can meet and jointly develop their own Middle East Peace plan, as they do through Seeds of Peace.

- A mayor can sign on to the Mayors Climate Protection agreement, pledging to meet the carbon emissions reductions designated by the Kyoto protocol in their own communities.

- The United States Congress can finally pass a cap-and-trade system for reducing industrial carbon emissions, following the example of the one already in place in Europe.

For many people, the immensity of global-scale challenges—and their seeming remoteness from everyday life—makes it difficult to imagine how a single individual could possibly make any difference. The good news is that there are virtually thousands of organizations, all with websites, that make it easier than ever to get involved and make a difference. Numerous nongovernmental organizations are working on issues regarding climate change, loss of biodiversity, overpopulation, development of sustainable energy alternatives, reduction of poverty and disease, and the encouragement of responsible patterns of consumption in developed countries. Their collective efforts are leading to positive changes in social, economic, and environmental conditions throughout the world. Significant change is underway—the world is beginning to wake up. The critical question is, will it do so in time?

Breakdown versus Breakthrough

Visions of apocalyptic disaster in the twenty-first century have come from many quarters, including Nostradamus, Hopi Indian prophecies, the Mayan calendar with its end in 2012, premonitions of the future by people who have had near-death experiences, and famous psychics such as Edgar Cayce, to name just a few. The question is, how literally should we take these prophecies of doom? Do these visions refer to literal cataclysms, or are they largely symbolic? Are most of the probable futures for our planet *literally* filled with global disaster, or are these visions, like dream symbols, metaphors for huge shifts in consciousness that are inevitable, sooner or later, for humankind?

Without a doubt, global society is headed for increasing disruption and disturbance. Climate change alone would predict that. The number of natural disasters worldwide per year has increased from around 100 in the early eighties to over 500 per year recently (Gilbert 2008). Humanity's depletion of vital resources such as oil, water, and arable land is on a collision course with population and economic growth in developing countries, particularly China and India. The question of how severe and prolonged this future disruption is likely to be is still open; at this time it's too early to offer a definitive answer. The best we can do is examine a few educated opinions and then draw our own conclusions.

The famous Harvard sociologist Pitirim Sorokin argued that materialistic eras alternate with more religious and spiritual ones (1941). For example, almost two thousand years ago, the secular, materialistic Roman Empire disintegrated and a long era dominated by medieval Christianity followed. That era was replaced 1,400 years later by the modern era, which emphasized science and more secular, materialistic values. Sorokin believed that the pendulum would again swing the other way and our modern, materialistic culture would begin to unravel by the end of the twentieth century. He correctly foresaw that scientific materialism would gradually begin to lose its hold on humanity's view of reality, which has already begun, at least for some of us. The dramatic socioeconomic falling apart Sorokin predicted has not happened—yet. However, he was correct in anticipating the increased moral decadence of modern culture and a decline of the arts, similar to what happened at the end of the Roman Empire. Whether his most pessimistic predictions will come true in our time—the collapse of materialistic society followed by the emergence of a dominant worldview based on spiritual values—remains to be seen.

One View of the Future

In *The Cultural Creatives* (2000), Ray and Anderson outline a kind of middle course for the future, something between outright global collapse and a smooth transition to environmental stability and economic sustainability. As discussed earlier, 20 to 25 percent of Americans are cultural creatives, people who currently hold some or all of the progressive beliefs and values (such as spirituality, holism, protecting the environment, and promoting sustainability) needed for a global shift. A paraphrase of their vision for the future, entitled "Muddling Our Way to Transformation," goes something like this:

Suppose the cultural creatives come together as a united political force and put enough pressure on society to foster significant movement toward a new way of life. Yet at the same time, across the developed world institutions of modern finance and multinational corporations aligned with governments continue to emphasize economic values and resist a less materialistic worldview.

In some sectors of society, the new values of the cultural creatives are welcome and lead the way to positive cultural change. Industries that see environmental sustainability and the information revolution as sources of profit decide that the cultural creatives are their natural markets and become aligned with them.

In these sectors, real change occurs. However, other sectors of society remain opposed to major cultural and political change—not only out of self-interest but because most people and institutions resist new worldviews, even if it's not in their long-range interest to do so.

Meanwhile, environmental destruction continues: global warming increasingly takes a toll on climate, overpopulation and diminishing resources create massive suffering, and conflicts heat up between haves and have-nots. The world becomes increasingly unstable. Collectively it may "fall into a hole," such as another Great Depression, a worldwide ecological disaster, and/or a debilitating series of wars triggered by great inequities and competition for resources. Whatever form this "hole" takes, suffering and death worldwide could be devastating for a period of decades. (This, though bad enough, falls short of total societal collapse and reversion to something like the Dark Ages.)

Whatever happens next could be the most surprising aspect of this scenario. In general, when a society gets itself into a bad place, a creative minority develops very different beliefs and ways of life, and then a wide spectrum of society starts to listen to them because they appear to offer a way out. (The historian Arnold Toynbee calls such a state of affairs *challenge and response* (1947).) In this scenario, the world draws upon an increasingly large proportion of the population that knows how to reframe events and develop new cultural solutions and institutions. At the same time, a number of old political and economic authorities are discredited, and some of the rich and powerful lose their status and position. Under the pressure of considerable global suffering, the world might be able to bounce back or spring into a new place within the span of a few decades (Ray and Anderson 2000, 239-240).

Ray and Anderson give this bounce-back scenario about a 50-50 chance of happening. The implication is that human society may collectively fall down, but that we can get back up again in relatively short order. It assumes that a creative minority—the cultural creatives—are numerous and powerful enough that the world has a reasonable chance of being able to respond positively to the growing crisis that will unfold over the next few decades.

Evolutionary Crash versus Bounce

In his well-received book *Promise Ahead*, Duane Elgin takes a similar position (both his book and that of Ray and Anderson came out in 2000). After describing a series of "adversity trends" (such as global warming, loss of biodiversity, overpopulation, poverty, and diminishing resources) that are pushing humanity toward an "evolutionary crash," he raises the possibility of the world coming together to achieve an "evolutionary bounce"—a new global consciousness that leads a majority of people worldwide to learn to live sustainably, honor the environment, and honor each other regardless of racial, national, ethnic, and economic differences.

Elgin describes four "opportunity trends" that could help turn a potential global crash into a bounce:

A Living Universe

The first is a perceptual shift similar to that described in this book: coming to see the planet—in fact, the entire universe—as conscious and alive, and therefore deserving of our respect (instead of manipulation and exploitation). Seeing a meaningless, mechanistic universe transition into one that is conscious and alive at all levels is a profound change. The key question is whether such a perceptual shift will occur *before* or *after* the enormous rite of passage that the earth and society are bound to go through in the next fifty years. While the view of a conscious universe is now shared by a number of progressive people, it is far from the prevailing view in a world still dominated by materialistic perceptions, values, and behaviors.

Voluntary Simplicity

The second opportunity trend is voluntarily shifting toward more sustainable and satisfying ways of living. Drawing from his first book, *Voluntary Simplicity* (1993), Elgin outlines ways we can all downsize and simplify our lives, thereby minimizing the harm we cause to our vulnerable planet. For example, each of us can:

- Buy products that are durable, easy to repair, environmentally friendly in their manufacture and use, energy-efficient, and not tested on animals

- Choose smaller and more fuel-efficient cars or use public transit, carpooling, or riding a bicycle

- Recycle metal, glass, plastic, and paper as well as cut back on things that waste nonrenewable resources

- Reduce undue clutter and complexity in our lives by giving away or selling things seldom used, such as clothing, books, furniture, and tools

- Buy less clothing, jewelry, and cosmetics; focusing on what is functional, durable, and esthetic rather than on passing fads and fashions

- Pursue a livelihood that benefits others and enables us to use our creative capacities in ways that are fulfilling (32-35)

Certainly a number of people in developed countries are presently pursuing lives of voluntary simplicity. Such a lifestyle represents a profound shift in priorities from external-based values of consumption and material acquisition to inner-based values of a fulfilling family life, gratifying friendships, and spiritual growth. Many of these people are likely also doing what they can to help the environment, promote social justice, and live sustainably on the earth. The question is whether these people, as a group, can have a significant impact on the global economic and political institutions that are driving Elgin's adversity trends. How important are values of voluntary simplicity in developing countries such as India and China, which together contain a third of the world's population? Many people in these countries want to emulate the lifestyles of wealth and success they see on television. One Amazon.com reviewer of Elgin's book *Promise Ahead* (2000) suggested that consumption-oriented societies would have to be *forced* into a "necessary simplicity" before they would begin to embrace values associated with environmental preservation and sustainability.

Global Consciousness via the Internet

Elgin's third opportunity trend lies in global communications technologies. He writes that "the Internet is collapsing the world into an electronic village where we are all neighbors, while television is providing a common world-language through its visual images" (2000, 97). Given these developments, it seems likely that "within ten to twenty years, we will have in place the communications infrastructure that could support a quantum increase in collective communication—and the collective consciousness—of our species" (103). Although Elgin is certainly correct in observing that humanity is creating the tools to increase global dialogue, how we will collectively use these tools remains an open question.

At present, TV isn't used much to raise collective consciousness about the plight of the planet. The Internet, with its many socially and environmentally conscious websites, looks more promising. The next ten years will tell whether these globalizing technologies will be used—and how much so—to empower people to respond effectively to the mounting challenges the planet faces.

Compassion

Finally, Elgin speaks of compassion. Eliminating world poverty is a requirement for an evolutionary bounce to occur. He notes that the cost of universal health care, nutrition, sanitation, clean water, and education could easily be paid by the developed countries of the world. Europeans spend more on cigarettes per year than the annual cost of providing basic services to the poor around the world (126-127). The question is whether the developed countries of the world can embrace compassion fully enough to help overcome poverty in the third world. While developing countries such as China and India are making significant strides in overcoming poverty, sub-Saharan Africa, with over 800 million people, is sliding deeper into poverty, most recently because of steep increases in food prices. Aid to these countries continues to fall short of developmental goals established by the United Nations. Low levels of international aid are compounded by unfair trade practices that restrict developing countries from trading with the markets of rich nations. Many of these countries pay more to service their debts than they receive in aid. The problem of world poverty is complex and requires a multifaceted solution.

Conclusion

What conclusions are possible regarding our planet's future? Without a doubt, both the earth and human civilization are at a crossroads. Scientific evidence is unambiguous: the earth's environment is in danger and rapidly approaching a tipping point beyond which destructive trends will not easily be reversed. A certain level of tension is needed to motivate widespread change. It may well take a great deal of global disruption, perhaps even chaos—environmentally, economically, politically, and socially—

to jar large numbers of people out of the materialistic and consumption-oriented mindset that still prevails in many sectors of society.

Yet a global shift is definitely underway. Sooner or later, a critical level of consciousness will be reached that provides a profound and far-reaching basis for the emergence of a new culture—following whatever destruction of the existing socioeconomic order is necessary to clear a space for such an emergence.

To close this chapter, consider the following two quotations, both from *Healing Our Planet, Healing Our Selves* (2004), edited by Dawson Church and Geralyn Gendreau. The first is somewhat ominous; the second offers distant hope:

> *"We are, as a race, going into the eye of an apocalyptic hurricane that will decide the future of the race and the planet. This storm of destruction will demand everything of all serious seekers who long to see the future transfigured. As the hurricane deepens and darkens, it is critical to know in the deepest part of ourselves that what will look and feel like destruction is actually the necessary stripping away of illusions we do not need anymore, the smashing of fantasies we have outgrown, and the necessary, unavoidable waking up to our true divine power."*
>
> —Andrew Harvey (99)

> *"The enormous changes we are seeing in the outer world are part of an evolutionary leap our species is in the process of making. Part of this evolutionary leap involves a change in the way our brains work and in what we can perceive. We are a very young species—so new we are not finished yet."*
>
> —Patricia Sun (296)

2

The Rise and Fall of the Scientific-Materialist Worldview (But Not Science)

Beliefs shape reality. The world we see is deeply influenced by the prevailing assumptions of the society and historical epoch into which we are born. In the past five hundred years, the dominant worldview in the West has gone through three stages. Prior to the Renaissance, the world was a sacred but rigid hierarchy with God at the top. Divinity commanded unquestioned power and authority in the unfolding of world events. This power was mediated to the people through God's appointed representatives on earth, primarily popes and kings. The Renaissance and Scientific Revolution changed all that. The church was divested of its authority to dictate the nature of the world, and the world became a neutral object for scientific investigation and ultimately technological control. What was deemed sacred retreated from the outer world and into the subjective minds of human beings, while the universe (nature) was assumed to be devoid of spiritual meaning and significance.

In the final decades of the twentieth century, this story of the world told by science began to break down, heralding a tentative but definite return to a more spiritual view of the world. The Cosmos is once again coming to be understood as sacred. This restoration of spirituality to the world, however, is very different from what existed in the Middle Ages. Rather than a rigid hierarchy governed by a transcendent Christian god, this new worldview regards the universe as a conscious, evolving, and intelligent process. Something akin to a conscious intelligence is thought to order the natural world into self-sustaining systems from atoms all the way to galaxies.

In the twenty-first century, it is becoming more widely accepted that the Cosmos has two faces, both equally real. The universe has an *objective* face—the proper object of scientific inquiry. But there is also greater recognition of its *subjective* face, which can be understood not only through the social sciences but also through intuitive forms of inquiry. Such inquiries (as in transpersonal psychology, for example) involve consensual insights and revelations that cut across the boundaries of traditional metaphysical systems or culture-based religions. Both inner and outer faces belong to the same Cosmos, and both will eventually be regarded as equally credible and worthy of understanding.

This chapter traces the evolution of worldview in the West—from the Middle Ages through the Scientific Revolution all the way down to the ultimate breakdown of the scientific-materialist worldview (though not science itself) in the late twentieth century. It begins with an historical account of how the scientific worldview replaced the medieval one, then concludes with an appraisal of the limitations of the scientific worldview. Subsequent chapters will explore a variety of dimensions of the new, emerging worldview.

The Medieval Worldview

Throughout the Middle Ages, the Western view of the world and humanity's place in it was dominated and dictated by the Roman Catholic Church. The most comprehensive philosophical account of this view can be found in the writings of the thirteenth-century theologian Thomas Aquinas.

For more than a thousand years—up until the early seventeenth century—Earth was widely perceived as the center of the universe, surrounded by a series of concentric spheres that comprised Heaven. The sun, moon, planets, and fixed stars each belonged to a particular sphere with defined motion around the Earth. The motion of these spheres was fixed, eternal, and governed by God. In fact, everything that happened in the world was understood to be created and sustained by God or divine providence.

Humanity had a unique and central importance in this scheme. Not only did human beings inhabit a world that was at the center of the universe, they also occupied a fulcrum point in the vast hierarchy of reality. This hierarchy began with God—its apex—and extended down to the lowliest creatures and plants. Humanity was assigned dominion over the animal and plant kingdoms, and, in turn, God and various legions of angels and archangels governed and had dominion over man. In this hierarchy, ordinary humans were subject to the authority of the church (vested in the pope and bishops), and women and children were subordinate to men. Few questioned the relative order of authority in this hierarchy because it was believed to be the revealed will of God. Everything had its precisely arranged place in the total plan, and obedience to God required not questioning the reality of this cosmic order. Indeed, the church maintained the authority to prosecute and persecute those who publicly raised questions about the nature of the world that it legislated.

In this world, neither natural sciences nor psychology would have made sense. Natural events were understood to be the manifestation of divine will. While natural processes like the weather could be understood to have some relative independence of God, their continued functioning depended on God's sustaining activity (mediated both directly and via angels). Human behavior was understood in strictly moral terms, as resulting from obedience to God or being swayed and perverted by the devil and his legions. The meaning of human behavior thus lay in its moral and religious implications, not in its possible psychological causes or motivations.

Such a vision of the world was fundamentally static; all the diverse levels of reality existed in their final and fixed form. There was little room for novelty or evolution except through God's direct acts on the world. This vision of the world was modeled after a kingdom, with humanity at the center of the kingdom's divine drama. Human history was a divine play in three acts: the fall, redemption, and salvation. The fall of man introduced sin into the world, while the life of Jesus Christ allowed for the possibility of redemption. Through aligning one's behavior with Christ's teachings and God's will, one might find salvation in the life to come.

In brief, the medieval world was fundamentally understood and interpreted in religious terms. The entire universe was a fixed and sacred order with man at its center. What happened in that universe was sanctioned and maintained by God. Humans alone were given free will, and the meaning of human action was to be found in its moral rectitude—its accordance with divine will—rather than physiological, psychological, or sociological causes.

The Scientific Revolution and Its Radical New Image of the World

With the Scientific Revolution of the seventeenth and eighteenth centuries, a radical change in humanity's perception of the world came about. As a result, we look out today at a very different universe than did our medieval forebears.

Prior to the Scientific Revolution, the universe was perceived as *alive*—inspirited with divine forces (angels in Christian theology, various deities in other spiritual traditions, whether Celtic, Hindu, or Native American). The universe was also construed as *purposive*: in every detail it revealed the unfolding of God's divine plan. Events were explained in terms of divine purpose. Humans existed in a sacred relationship with all events, which could potentially be altered through religious acts such as prayer, animal sacrifice, and ritual dance. While many indigenous cultures maintained this sacred relationship into the twentieth century, in Western Europe—and all cultures that subsequently adopted the materialistic and technological outlook—it disappeared with the advent of the scientific worldview.

For science to develop, it had to separate itself from the authority and dogma of the medieval church. The major thrust of the Scientific Revolution was to provide an entirely new way of seeking and validating knowledge. Understanding the world was no longer the privilege of the priesthood; knowledge was sought through free and open inquiry, validated through public, agreed-upon means. Observation of the senses was given priority over armchair reasoning by church scholastics in understanding the natural world. Direct empirical observation rather than the authority of the church became the basis for accepted knowledge.

Divested of its former spiritual significance, the outer world was cast as a neutral object to be explored and explained in mechanistic terms. Divine providence and purpose were replaced by physical forces that followed mathematically precise laws, such as gravity and electromagnetism. Purpose was removed from the universe through a series of steps:

- Newton's mechanics cast nature as a vast clockwork following strictly mechanistic laws. According to the contemporaneous Deist theology (popular among the founding fathers of America), although God started the clockwork, after this initial impetus, the universe followed a strictly mechanistic course that could be entirely explained by mathematical laws.

- Darwin's theory of evolution explained the origin of species in terms of a mechanistic process of random mutations. Those mutations that were most adaptive to changing conditions in the environment survived. The specific forms of animals in the evolutionary record represent these survivors and their offspring. There could be no divine order or purpose in the gradual appearance of progressively more complex types of animals over the ages.

- Finally, Freud reduced all human endeavors to various displaced or sublimated expressions of blind sexual and aggressive instincts seeking expression. Art, ethics, and religion could all be explained in terms of healthy or unhealthy dynamics involving blind, unconscious drives.

While divesting nature of purpose, the Scientific Revolution brought far-reaching technological advances to the world. The inventions that form the foundation of modern life—the electric light, the telephone, radio and television, the combustion engine, and flight—all arose from a scientific understanding and explanation of nature. So have the cure and elimination of various infectious diseases, nearly doubling the average human lifespan over the last three centuries. However, along with the technological revolution that brought such convenience and ease to human life came a materialistic worldview that divested nature and the outer world of spiritual significance.

To understand the Scientific Revolution more thoroughly, it's worth looking at each of its major founders and contributors in greater detail.

Copernicus

More than anything else, it was Copernicus's insight in the first half of the sixteenth century that led to a fundamental break from the medieval worldview. Until Copernicus, humanity inhabited a *geocentric* universe, in which the planets and stars revolved around Earth. For over a thousand years the explanation of the movement of the planets, fashioned by Ptolemy and his successors, had become increasingly complex, relying on an array of arcane mathematical devices such as major and minor epicycles, deferents, equants, and eccentrics. Describing this unwieldy explanation as a "monster," Copernicus claimed the universe was explainable in terms of simple and harmonious mathematical principles. The Creator, in his mind, would not have it otherwise. Turning the geocentric worldview on its head, Copernicus developed a *heliocentric* model, which explained the daily movement of the sun, planets, and stars in terms of Earth's rotation on its axis and annual revolution about the sun. This theory explains all of the apparent motion of the stars and planets in a much simpler, more elegant fashion.

For a hundred years religious authorities—first Protestants (especially Martin Luther) and later the Catholic Church—condemned the Copernican paradigm as sacrilege. His view demoted Earth from its longstanding central position. No longer was Earth—and man—the center of God's creation and God's plan for salvation. To take Earth out of the center of the divine drama, to view it as just one among many planets, was seen as a form of atheism. Yet over the next two hundred years, the Copernican worldview would be vindicated, and thus began our modern view of the earth as a very small part of a universe vast in scope.

Galileo

In 1609 Galileo turned his just-constructed telescope toward the heavens. What he saw were craters and mountains on the Moon, four moons revolving around Jupiter, phases of the planet Venus, and an unbelievably large number of stars in the Milky Way. Craters and mountains on the Moon meant that celestial objects were not the perfect, immutable entities that the older view of the heavens, inherited from Aristotle and Ptolemy, required. The moons revolving around Jupiter and the phases of Venus strongly confirmed Copernicus's heliocentric understanding of Earth's relationship to the heavens. Further, the multitude of stars in the Milky Way suggested a much larger universe than had previously been conceived. With one simple act of observation, Galileo radically and fundamentally challenged the medieval worldview.

Perhaps even more critical was the fact that Galileo's view of the universe was based on simple observation, not what church authority legislated. This was the fundamental thrust of the Scientific Revolution—to understand nature on its own terms rather than by the metaphysical dictates of the church. From Galileo forward, the investigation of nature through direct sensory observation would take increasing precedence over the medieval propensity to deduce the nature of reality through armchair reasoning. It has remained that way during the dominance of the scientific worldview over the past four hundred years.

Descartes

Galileo initiated the process of divesting nature of conscious attributes, such as purpose and goals, by seeking to understand natural phenomena in terms of material causes and mathematical laws. Descartes then completed this process with his conception of a radical dualism between matter and mind. The external world was conceived as lifeless, unconscious matter that extended in space. It had no purpose. Mind, on the other hand, was radically separate from the outer world—a thinking substance with no extension in space.

For Descartes, reason was the ultimate arbiter of human knowledge. Only human reason, aided by direct empirical observation, could provide an infallible understanding of the workings of nature. Gone was the infallibility of the holy scripture and the pope. God still existed for Descartes, but only as an inscrutable abstraction whose existence must be assumed for the universe to be possible. Rational intelligence could be the only basis for understanding the world.

Perhaps the most profound implication of Cartesian thinking for the modern scientific worldview was its radical separation of subjective mind from objective nature. No longer did humanity inhabit an enchanted world; nature was a strictly material phenomenon without purpose or intention. The only place where purpose existed was in the human mind, set radically apart from nature. Thus Descartes placed the human mind—and reason—in opposition not only to traditional religious authority but to the world and universe itself. Such a view would dominate science and have far-reaching implications over the next three hundred years. In the words of Richard Tarnas, "The fruit of the dualism between rational subject and material world was science, including science's capacity for rendering certain knowledge of the world and for making man master and possessor of nature" (1991, 280).

Newton

Isaac Newton formulated a series of mathematical laws that seemed to explain all natural phenomena, from the smallest object in the laboratory to the farthest planet. Through his three laws of motion and his law of universal gravitation, he was able to describe the motion of the tides, the orbits of the planets, the motion of projectiles, and a host of other natural phenomena. Newton's discoveries suggested a world that behaved like an intricate machine, a world following mathematical laws that allowed every detail of motion to be predicted. His theories reinforced the emerging materialism and determinism that would become the central working assumptions of science for centuries to follow.

Newton affirmed Descartes' view of the world as a material phenomenon, explainable in terms of rationally derived laws, without intention. God may have started the great clockwork going, but God was not actively involved in its continuing operation. A single set of mathematical laws governed both the celestial and terrestrial realms. Gone was the medieval distinction between transcendent (heavenly) and earthly orders of reality. Everything, except the human mind, was composed of material particles moving in an infinite, neutral space. It could all be explained mathematically, in terms of a few basic principles, such as inertia, mass, and gravity.

Kant

Immanuel Kant developed the view that the mind does not simply receive sensory data passively; rather, it actively organizes such data in accordance with innate ordering principles. The information we receive through our senses is not perceived at face value but organized in terms of the categories of space, time, and causality. These categories, in turn, do not come from experience but are a part of the mind's intrinsic makeup *prior* to experience. So we can never perceive and understand the world as it truly is—we cannot know "things in themselves," Kant would say—but instead we interpret our experience in terms of preexisting categories. In short, Kant was the first to anticipate our twentieth-century view that all knowledge is interpretive. The human mind cannot understand the world directly, for its experiences are structured according to the mind's own internal organization.

Modern disciplines from sociology to quantum physics have embraced Kant's basic viewpoint. The world is in essence a construct. Our knowledge of the world is fundamentally interpretive. Gone is the assumption, held from the Greeks all the way through Descartes, that our knowledge of the cosmos directly reflects the reality of what actually exists. With his dualism of subjective mind and objective matter, Descartes separated man from nature ontologically. Kant widened the gap by separating man from nature in an epistemological sense. We cannot know nature as it is on its own terms; we can only know it from a certain distance, through our own perceptual categories for ordering our experience. (*Ontology* refers to theories about the nature of reality, while *epistemology* refers to theories about how we come to have valid knowledge of reality.)

Darwin

Darwin's theory of evolution undermined two assumptions that had been fundamental to humanity's worldview prior to the Scientific Revolution: that the evolution of species, from microbes to man, had been divinely ordered, and that man had a special and unique position relative to God that set him apart from the animal kingdom. In brief, Darwin's theory of natural selection posited a strictly mechanistic model of evolution. The appearance of new species was the result of natural selection of random variations that were adaptive to the environment. When a variation confers a slight advantage to certain organisms in the intense competition for survival—both among members of a species and among different species—those individuals having such an advantage on average live longer, have more offspring, and reproduce more rapidly. In short, the most adaptive variations survive and the least adaptive ones do not. Over long periods of time, the combination of random variation, survival of the fittest variations, and natural selection explains the origin of new species without recourse to any notions of divine intervention.

This process explains the appearance of humans as no different from the appearance of other species. Human mental capacities differ in *degree* rather than *kind* from the capacities of animals and, in fact, evolved naturally from primate predecessors. Man is no longer the sacrosanct being, the special creation of God that the medieval mind assumed. He is only the most complex animal in a long evolutionary sequence governed strictly by mechanistic natural laws. Gone is the notion that man is a unique and central creation, made in the image of God. Human character and mind have come from the progressive adaptation of apes over eons of time, not from some type of divine design.

Freud

Freud cast man even further out of the privileged cosmic status he had been given by the Greeks and the medieval mind. Humanity's moral strivings, values, artistic efforts, and cultural creations were understood by Freud to be either defenses against or sublimations of basic instinctual urges for sexual gratification and aggression. As with Darwin, Freud saw human beings as comparatively sophisticated animals motivated at base by primitive aggressive and erotic impulses. Civilization was a veneer developed out of repression of these impulses, with no inherent meaning other than to provide human consciousness with a defense against the "unacceptable" urges that were freely expressed by infants and animals. To Freud, God was an infantile projection of the father image designed to reduce insecurities over the unpredictability of mature life.

To sum up a journey of three hundred years: Copernicus undermined humanity's privileged position at the center of the cosmos by demonstrating that Earth was just one planet among many revolving around the sun. Descartes then helped separate humanity from nature by proposing an absolute schism between the subjective mind and a purposeless, mechanistic world. Galileo and Newton confirmed Descartes' schism with their mathematical schema of the universe, revealing the universe to operate like a great clockwork or machine. Darwin further diminished man's status in the cosmos by showing how human beings were only the most complicated animal in a long evolutionary progression governed by random mechanistic processes. Finally, Freud extended the idea of man's fundamentally animal nature by proposing that all of humanity's moral, creative, and spiritual aspirations could be explained as sublimations or projections designed to keep unacceptable instincts out of conscious awareness.

The Breakdown of the Scientific Worldview in the 20th Century

Although the materialism and empiricism of the scientific worldview continue to strongly influence contemporary society, it was during the twentieth century that this worldview—but not science itself—began to break down. This happened in a number of ways and on several different fronts (a more detailed discussion of each point follows):

- Modern physics failed to provide a rational and intelligible foundation for understanding the universe. The implications of twentieth-century quantum and relativity theories led to paradoxes and conundrums impenetrable to the rational mind.

- Philosophical limitations of science and its approach to understanding the world were convincingly pointed out by philosophers such as Thomas Kuhn in his well-known book *The Structure of Scientific Revolutions* (1970).

- Fundamental metaphysical assumptions of the scientific worldview were called into question. Specifically, materialism, mechanism, reductionism, and strict empiricism were convincingly critiqued.

- Science and technology, for all of their benefits, resulted in serious sociological fallout: the dehumanization and alienation of humanity, widely recognized by social critics ranging from Erich Fromm to George Orwell.

- The earth suffered severe environmental fallout: the pollution of air, water, and soil; accumulation of toxic waste; global warming; deforestation; loss of biodiversity; and a profound disruption of the entire planetary ecosystem. All of these have been unintended but increasingly dangerous consequences of the relentless pursuit of a strictly materialistic and technological approach to nature.

Breakdown of an Intelligible Basis for Understanding the Universe

Relativity theory and quantum mechanics, elaborated in the first three decades of the twentieth century, radically undermined the long-established certainties of the Newtonian model of reality. Nearly every postulate of the old mechanistic, atomistic view of the world was set aside. Instead of solid, indestructible atoms, the world's smallest level was comprised of randomly fluctuating "probability waves." Space and time were no longer independent absolutes, rather they could shift relative to matter. Time and space could expand or contract, depending on an observer's velocity relative to the speed of light. Mechanistic causality, a major assumption for the prior three centuries, was contradicted by *nonlocal* connections between seemingly distinct objects (when two separate particles change in the exact same way simultaneously— without any intervening transmission or causality).

Perhaps most important, objective observation itself was called into question. Observation of subatomic particles could not proceed without affecting the very nature of what was seen. The more closely an observer tries to monitor a particle's velocity, the less it is possible to know where that particle is located. It has only a certain probability of being located at any particular position. Uncertainty appears to be built into the process of observation. If human observation of a quantum event is responsible for "collapsing" a distribution of quantum probabilities into an actual event, then strict objectivity is profoundly compromised. Confronted with the ambiguities of quantum physics, Einstein was reported to have said, "All my attempts to adapt the theoretical foundation of physics to these concepts failed completely. It was as if the ground had been pulled out from under one, with no firm foundation to be seen anywhere upon which one could have built" (Tarnas 1991, 356).

In short, as a result of relativity theory and quantum mechanics, the once rational and orderly world of Newton and Descartes became increasingly unintelligible and enigmatic. The ability of science to rationally comprehend the fundamental structures and nature of reality became increasingly questionable in light of the conceptions proposed by the new theories: a space curved by gravity; objects that were not really objects but rather patterns of wave fluctuations; elementary particles that did not take shape until actually observed; and particles that affected each other at a distance without any known causal connection. It was looking more and more as if reality were not structured in a way the human mind could fully comprehend. The goal of the Scientific Revolution to give a comprehensive, rational account of the universe had failed. The world looked not only strange but stranger than ever.

Philosophical Limitations

The ability of science to provide a true and unquestionable view of reality was further undercut by the work of Thomas Kuhn in the 1960s. In *The Structure of Scientific Revolutions* (1970), Kuhn makes a persuasive case that all scientific knowledge is undergirded, or embedded, in sets of prevailing assumptions or conceptual models he calls *paradigms*. Scientists conduct experiments, collect data, and test and confirm hypotheses all within an overarching model that goes untested and unchallenged. Instead of subjecting the paradigm itself to test, normal science proceeds by either ignoring or reinterpreting conflicting data in a way that supports the paradigm. Though scientific experiments and observations are guided by empirical data, the data itself is filtered through the lens of the prevailing paradigm. Conflicting data is ignored or adapted to the paradigm until it becomes so overwhelming that a radical revision of the paradigm is required. This happened, for example, in the case where Einstein's special and general theories of relativity finally overtook Newtonian mechanics, which had dominated physics for more than two hundred years.

Kuhn's critique has had far-reaching implications. If scientific knowledge is fundamentally historical—embedded in prevailing paradigms that can be overthrown—then it loses its claim to be absolute. Our scientific understanding of the world is fundamentally bound to our historical period and thus essentially tentative. Science can no longer give us a final, unimpeachable understanding of the nature of reality.

With Kuhn's critique of scientific knowledge and the loss of a fully rational, intelligible world in physics, a more tentative view of science emerged in the latter half of the twentieth century. Science was still powerfully applicable to many areas of human life, but scientific knowledge came to be regarded as increasingly relative: relative to the observer, relative to scientists' prevailing paradigm, even relative—according to some critiques—to Western society, a patriarchal mentality, and scientists' social and psychological predispositions.

By the latter half of the twentieth century, the old Cartesian-Newtonian view of the world with its mechanistic certainty was gone. The new, post-Newtonian, postmodern worldview that replaced it has left us with a world order that is much more tentative and much less easily explained. While science has provided us with enormous and diverse technical advances, its long-cherished goal of penetrating and fully comprehending nature—giving us a true, accurate explanation of the world—seems to have receded into the distance.

Metaphysical Assumptions of Science Called into Question

The dominant scientific worldview, still widely accepted in the contemporary world, rests on five basic assumptions about the nature of reality. These assumptions are not usually acknowledged by scientists. They are in fact metaphysical and cannot be proven. However, they deeply pervade our present-day consciousness and perception of the world. In the past fifty years, all five of these assumptions have been seriously called into question, further undermining not science as a method or scientific knowledge, but the *implicit worldview* science has led to. What are these metaphysical assumptions?

Dualism: A Sharp Demarcation Between the Objective World and Subjective Experience

This assumption, dating back to Descartes and Galileo, cannot be maintained in the light of modern quantum physics. In quantum physics, no sharp line can be drawn between the process of observation and what is observed. Phenomena are both constituted and dependent upon experimental observation—a quantum particle comes into existence only as a result of observing it. The old model of electrons as discrete particles orbiting around an atomic nucleus does not fit the actual phenomena. Quantum physicists view electrons as waves whose locations are characterized by probability distributions. It isn't possible to talk about an atomic system in isolation, only as a response to a particular experimental arrangement. In short, quantum phenomena can't be understood "in themselves" but only in interaction with an observer.

Materialism: The Material Universe Is the Only and Ultimate Reality

Fundamental to materialism is the assumption that what we call "consciousness" is a derivative phenomenon that arises entirely from neurophysiological and biochemical processes in the brain. As a metaphysical assertion, however, materialism is unable to account adequately for consciousness. To explain consciousness within the framework of materialism we have to assume that mental states—sensations, perceptions, emotions, motives, desires, purposes, intentions, logical thinking, creativity, and inspiration—are ultimately reducible to physiological and neuroendocrine processes in the anatomical brain.

On close examination, this is impossible for two reasons: First, there is no logically conceivable way to deduce mental phenomena from purely physical phenomena. They are *radically* different categories of events. Observation of brain processes will never reveal a color sensation, the experience of love, or the inspiration behind a poem. Second, brain processes and mental processes do not correspond in duration. The former take place over nanoseconds, while thoughts and feelings require whole seconds to occur. Whatever thoughts and feelings are, they are superordinate to the microprocesses of the physical brain.

Furthermore, consciousness, as experienced subjectively, appears to be coherent and continuous. Discrete thoughts and feelings are embedded in a "stream" of consciousness, whereas observed physiological brain events are very rapid and discontinuous. What is going on in subjective consciousness cannot be mapped onto brain physiology in any direct or obvious way, though correlations between specific mental states (fear, for example) and anatomical parts of the brain can be made. Consciousness in general appears to be a *global* phenomenon, one that doesn't easily equate with a specific part of the brain or with the millions of discrete electrochemical brain processes that occur from moment to moment.

Reductionism: The Component Parts of a System Define Its Fundamental Reality

Reductionism implies that all phenomena can ultimately be explained in terms of microscopic elements and processes at the material level (presumably atomic interactions). While analysis of a complex entity like a cell in terms of atomic or biochemical processes may be useful, to assume that a cell is *nothing more* than complex sequences of biochemical processes ignores the emergence of new patterns of behavior at higher levels of complexity. This is the basis of modern *systems theory*—that wholes have unique, irreducible properties that can't be fully explained in terms of their constituent parts. Most contemporary scientists do not dispute the validity of systems theory.

Mechanism: All Natural Phenomena, Including Those Which Appear to Be Self-organizing, Can Be Explained in Terms of Mechanistic, Causal Processes

There are numerous things that strictly mechanistic explanations are unable to adequately explain. For example, classical Darwinian theory tries to explain the emergence of new species solely in terms of random mutations and a process of natural selection. Those mutations that are most adaptive to environmental changes are the ones that survive. Random mutations accompanied by natural selection account for all evolutionary change.

Although few biologists would deny that genetic mutation and natural selection play important roles in the development of new forms and species, it is difficult to explain the sudden emergence of entirely new subsystems—such as the eye—or whole new species through these two processes alone. The sudden appearance of winged reptiles, for example, involves much more than a realignment of several genes through a process of mutation. It requires a large number of coordinated realignments of the entire organism (for example, different visual and sensory organs and different volume-to-weight ratios, not just wings). Many changes occur in an integrated, coherent way that cannot easily be explained mechanistically.

A purely mechanistic paradigm is also hard put to explain *morphogenesis*, the development of the characteristic form of an animal from the initial fertilized egg. In early embryological development, human beings, chimps, and pigs look pretty much alike. In fact, their genetic codes are about 99 percent identical. How is it, then, that they go on to develop into such different forms? Molecular biologists claim that all of the processes of morphogenesis can ultimately be explained in terms of specific genes turning on and off; however, in over forty years, they have not succeeded in demonstrating this. To be sure, gene functions explain quite a bit. They determine what type of material is needed for a specific tissue or organ, how much will be needed, when it should be delivered, and even the order in which specific elements of a system will be turned on or off. However, gene function does not fully explain how the final form of an entire organ is reached, let alone an entire organism. Molecular biology has yet to fully explain the formation of organs, organ systems, or entire organisms through purely mechanistic processes. Whether it will do so in the future is an open question.

Purpose Does Not Exist in Nature

According to the traditional scientific worldview, teleological explanations—explanations in terms of purpose—are unscientific and illusory. All phenomena can be explained in terms of a causal analysis based on mechanistic, homeostatic processes. Yet human behavior cannot be adequately explained without recourse to purpose or intention. (B. F. Skinner's radical behaviorism attempted to do so but failed.) So if human beings are to be included as a part of the universe or nature, then we need to resort to teleological explanations, at least to adequately account for *their* behavior. Otherwise we're left with a radical dualism that separates human behavior from the rest of nature.

The *anthropic principle* (at least in its strong form) proposes that we—and life in general—could not have arisen in the first place unless a large number of parameters in the development of the physical universe, from the Big Bang on, were finely tuned to within an extremely narrow tolerance. For example, if the rate of expansion of the universe one second after the Big Bang had been smaller by one part in a quadrillion, the universe would have recollapsed. If the strong nuclear force were weaker than it actually is to a miniscule degree, we would have only hydrogen in the universe, while if it were even slightly stronger, the universe would consist only of helium. So the entire universe appears to have been "designed" to produce stars, galaxies, and ultimately life—an evolution toward increasing complexity. The standard response to this is that our universe is but one among many universes, and the only one that by chance happened to produce life. While theoretically possible, the idea of multiple universes (with only one accidentally leading to life) is difficult to prove empirically, and thus still only speculative.

Sociological Fallout

The scientific worldview might have continued to grow in pre-eminence had it not been for problems resulting not only from its theory but its application. That is, from technology. By the middle of the twentieth century, many social critics decried technology as dehumanizing man, placing him in a context of artificial substances and gadgets, increasingly remote from nature. Today, much of the human living environment has become ugly, increasingly standardized, mechanized, and paved over. Many aspects of modern life, such as mass production, mass media, and pervasive urbanization, seem to alienate humanity from its basic connection with the earth. With an unending and increasingly sophisticated progression of technological innovations—in one century we went from the combustion engine to the Internet—humanity is becoming increasingly disconnected from nature.

Turmoil, noise, speed, and complexity are now inherent to the human environment. Lifestyles in modern as well as third world societies are increasingly fragmented and impersonal. The pervasive standardization, anonymity, and materialism of modern life can be deeply alienating, estranging humans from nature, from each other, from God, and from themselves. At the beginning of the twenty-first century, we have moved far away from the late-nineteenth-century view that technological inventions could lead us to a utopian society where we have mastered nature.

Environmental Fallout

The fallout from rapid technological development has not only uprooted humanity's fundamental connection with nature, it has begun to decimate and disturb the natural rhythms and cycles of nature itself, placing the future of the planet in serious jeopardy. As we enter the twenty-first century, the earth faces a number of serious ecological crises that, if unchecked, will inevitably lead to pervasive disruption of modern society as we know it within a few decades. These crises include:

- Widespread pollution of the earth's air and water

- Accumulation of toxic waste (including radioactive waste)

- Depletion of much of the earth's topsoil through erosion due to excessive agricultural development

- Elimination of more than one-third of the earth's biological species

- Rapid deforestation, further reducing the proportion of oxygen to carbon dioxide in the atmosphere

- Breakdown of the atmosphere's ozone layer, making the earth increasingly vulnerable to ultraviolet radiation

- Global warming, leading to serious destabilization of climate, an increase in weather-related disasters, and polar melting that could ultimately inundate all coastal cities

If you add to these crises rapid population growth (the global population is predicted to reach 9 billion by 2050), huge increases in carbon emissions from developing countries such as, China, combined with an accelerating depletion of irreplaceable natural resources such as oil, water, food supplies, and forests, the consequences are harsh. There is no scenario that does not foresee widespread societal disorganization and potential collapse within the next fifty years (if all of these trends continue unchecked). Notwithstanding all of its comforts and conveniences, the shadow side of technology's unbridled growth leaves us in a very serious predicament—one that is unlikely to be solved by further technological advancements alone. (For a more detailed discussion of the current global crisis, see chapter 1.)

Conclusion

The demise of the scientific-materialist worldview in the twentieth century has been marked by the following developments:

- A very enigmatic, post-Newtonian world revealed by quantum mechanics and relativity theory

- The realization that scientific knowledge is not absolute but relative to prevailing paradigms—assumptive frameworks typically taken for granted by scientific investigators

- A thorough critique of metaphysical assumptions underlying the traditional scientific worldview

- The increasing alienation of humanity from nature, resulting from industrial and urban developments fostered by technology

- The radical threat to the planet's environment engendered by a global corporate-industrial society that creates, sustains, and utilizes modern scientific technology

Of course, technology also has its positive side. Our standard of living is profoundly dependent upon modern technology. Furthermore, the technological innovation of the Internet allows people all over the world to join together to discuss and ultimately make an impact on global issues such as climate change, poverty, and disease. Science, upon which technology is based, continues to be a powerful and effective method for understanding the natural world in its objective aspect. Many important discoveries in fields such as astronomy, biology, genetics, and physics will be made in the present decade, and even more in the coming century.

While science as an empirical method of investigation will certainly continue, the scientific-materialist worldview inherited from the eighteenth-century Enlightenment has been seriously called into question. A new paradigm is beginning to emerge that reframes the cosmos in ways outside the bounds of traditional science. Aspects of this new paradigm are explored in chapters 4-16.

3

Signs of an Emerging Worldview

Humanity finds itself in the midst of a major shift in worldview. Such a shift involves a fundamentally new way of perceiving the world, the environment, each other, and ourselves. Accompanying this perceptual shift are fundamental changes in values and priorities, in what is deemed important. Stated most briefly, the shift involves a movement away from a material view of the universe and our place in it to a more spiritual view. Instead of the ultimate "stuff" of reality being material, with consciousness secondary and derivative, consciousness is coming to be understood as the underlying foundation of reality, out of which the entire cosmos arises. Nature is no longer merely a neutral object for scientific investigation or a resource for industrial exploitation. It is a sacred order infused with intelligence and purpose—one with which humanity needs to cooperate. The emerging worldview restores a profound sacredness to the world, but one that is entirely different from the medieval sacredness that existed prior to the Renaissance and Scientific Revolution.

The shift will affect our collective perceptions, beliefs, and actions concerning many areas of life: the environment, economics, religion, interpersonal relations, personal identity, health and healing, and even the scope and limits of science. It is a global shift—both in the sense that it is happening all over the world, and in the sense that it will impact all aspects of society: the way we live, share, and understand ourselves and the world.

Before exploring facets of this emerging global shift, it's worth examining a number of important societal trends that signal such a change is actually taking place. The following ten trends are just a few among many. Collectively they point to the emergence of a new worldview that both perceives the universe as fundamentally conscious rather than material, and places an increasing emphasis on spiritual values.

Popularity of Eastern Philosophies and Spiritual Practices

Interest in Eastern philosophy and religion in the United States and Europe can be traced all the way back to the teachings of Paramahansa Yogananda in the 1930s and 1940s. This fascination with the East gained traction with the introduction of transcendental meditation by Maharishi Mahesh Yogi in the 1960s and the widespread interest in the 1970s in going to India to study with saints and gurus. In the 1980s numerous American students of Buddhism and Hinduism, such as Ram Dass, Joseph Goldstein, and Jack Kornfield, helped disseminate teachings about meditation and yoga. Chinese and Ayurvedic medicine became more widely accepted, and transpersonal psychology emerged as a significant field of study. Finally, in the 1990s, the teachings of the Far East went mainstream. Traditional Western medicine incorporated mindfulness meditation, largely through the efforts of Jon Kabat-Zinn, and research on Chinese and Indian medical systems received government support. The National Institute of Health established a program on complementary and alternative medicine to study the efficacy of acupuncture, yoga, meditation, and contemplative practices. Presently, mindfulness meditation is being used by psychologists to treat depression and anxiety disorders.

The Environmental Movement

Over the past forty years, a group of diverse citizens—professionals, scientists, indigenous people, religious devotees, and others—have contributed to humanity's growing awareness of its essential interconnection with the earth. Though diverse, the environmental movement can be defined by certain common values: an emphasis on sustainable management of natural resources and stewardship (rather than exploitation) of the earth.

Historically, environmentalism can be traced back more than a hundred years, to American conservationists such as John Muir and George Perkins Marsh. However its emergence as a significant movement dates back to 1972 with the United Nations Conference on the Human Environment, the first time a large group of countries engaged in a discussion of the global environment's status. Significant environmental legislation, such as the Endangered Species Act and the Clean Water Act, was passed in the United States following the conference.

Since the seventies, the movement has grown on both scientific and popular fronts. The science of ecology—one of several scientific disciplines that emerged at that time—studies how the abundance and distribution of organisms is affected by interactions with their environment. Similarly, environmental medicine investigates, among many topics, the impact of environmental toxins on the epidemiology of diseases.

The current acute environmental crisis has catapulted the movement from a small group of people and organizations to a widespread concern of the public at large all around the globe. Movies such as *An Inconvenient Truth* and *The Eleventh Hour* have helped to sound the alarm about global environmental problems— particularly climate change—to wide segments of the population. Promoted in countless magazines, books, and TV programs, the current environmental movement offers many guidelines on how individuals can live more sustainably, embracing new products and technologies that reduce carbon emissions and preserve resources. (Some of these guidelines are described in chapters 19 and 24.)

The gravity of the environmental crisis is motivating many individuals, organizations, and corporate groups to make an effort to repair the significant damage caused by 150 years of industrial and commercial development. Thousands of citizen-based groups throughout the world are working on problems such as climate change, loss of biodiversity, deforestation, exploitation of animals, destruction of habitats, soil erosion, water depletion, and many other environmental issues. At the government level, states such as California and countries such as Denmark and Germany, are making major changes in their economic infrastructure, pursuing goals of increased energy efficiency and reduced carbon emissions. Last but not least, a few progressive corporations such as BP-Amaco, Dupont, Wal-Mart, and Toyota are demonstrating greater environmental awareness. A new respect for the earth is emerging. Venture capital investments in eco-friendly technologies have increased dramatically in recent years.

The New Physics

Authors such as Fritjof Capra (1975) and Gary Zukav (1979) have described numerous parallels between the findings of early-twentieth-century quantum mechanics and ancient Hindu and Buddhist conceptions of the universe. Physical reality is not what it appears to be. It is not solid but almost entirely space. At bottom it does not consist of substantial particles but highly interconnected fluctuations of energy. An actual particle of "stuff" only comes into existence as a result of somebody's *observing* these fluctuations or waves. In short, substance turns out to be a construct resulting from the observation of something fundamentally insubstantial. Time and space lose the absolute character proposed by Newton; rather, they can shrink or expand depending on the speed at which one travels. At light speed they vanish altogether. Empty space is not really empty; it is a sea of virtual particles constantly arising from and returning to nowhere. The energy contained in empty space exceeds that in all matter by a factor of ten followed by forty zeros. All of these findings suggest a correspondence, at least at the quantum level, with ancient Hindu and Buddhist notions that the entire visible world is *maya*—a transient illusion. Matter, space, and time have no absolute status; they are, as Immanuel Kant suggested long ago, constructs of our mind. The ultimate nature of reality is beyond our comprehension.

In the 1970s and 1980s it was empirically demonstrated that two particles separated by a great distance could affect each other simultaneously without any intervening signal (Radin 2006, 226-227). For any possible causal relationship to exist, an intervening signal would have to exceed the speed of light, something prohibited by Einstein's theory of relativity. Einstein himself referred to the potential for this sort of phenomenon as "spooky action at a distance" and never accepted the idea. The fact that it has repeatedly been demonstrated has led to the notions of quantum entanglement and nonlocal interactions in physics, phenomena that have not been adequately explained by quantum theory to this day. Physicist David Bohm has proposed a radically interconnected universe—interconnected through what he calls an *implicate order*, whereby the two ostensibly separate particles that simultaneously affect each other are ultimately one and the same event (1980). This, too, parallels ancient Hindu and Platonic philosophy. What appear to us to be separate events turn out to be merely different permutations of one seamless, underlying reality.

One of the great remaining challenges in physics is to integrate quantum theory with the theory of gravity implicit in Einstein's general theory of relativity. The two don't mesh, and physicists are looking for a grand theory that could explain everything in a single framework. A major development of new physics is string theory, as discussed in such popular books as Brian Greene's *The Elegant Universe* (1999). In string theory, fundamental particles observed in particle accelerators are replaced by tiny strings shorter in length than even the smallest subatomic particles. Different types of particles are understood as different vibrational frequencies of these exceedingly tiny strings.

To date there are many different string theories, none of which has yet been empirically verified. However, with the opening of the Large Hadron collider in France in 2008, preliminary evidence for string theory may become available. One intriguing aspect of string theory is that it requires additional dimensions beyond the usual four associated with space-time, anywhere from ten to twenty-six dimensions. The strings vibrate in these multiple dimensions. One can only speculate whether these additional dimensions correspond to the subtle dimensions proposed by various cosmologies and metaphysical systems throughout history (notions of astral and causal planes, heaven, or bardos). At the very least, these extra dimensions offer one way of explaining the seemingly mysterious connections that occur in nonlocal events. Thus string theory, though not yet verified, may turn out to support a basic tenet of the emerging worldview: all phenomena are fundamentally interconnected. Quantum entanglement—which has been empirically demonstrated—does so as well.

The Gaia Hypothesis

Thirty years ago, James Lovelock, a noted British biologist and environmentalist, proposed an interesting hypothesis in his 1979 book, *Gaia: A New Look at Life On Earth*. He claimed that Earth's biosphere consists of so many interrelated and delicately balanced processes that it behaves more like an intelligently organized system—an organism—than the complex machine exhaustively described by physics, chemistry, biology, geology and meteorology. The implication was that Earth could be viewed as a living being, capable of regulating environmental variables to suit its own needs. Borrowing from Greek mythology, Lovelock named this living system "Gaia."

During the 1980s the Gaia hypothesis was widely criticized by mainstream scientists as being mystical and untestable. Lovelock and his colleague Lynn Margulis subsequently modified their position, proposing that Gaia was sustained by a complex array of interconnected, self-regulating processes. While the biosphere still functioned as a coherent, organized whole, the long-term constancy of certain parameters such as atmospheric composition or ocean salinity was governed by self-correcting homeostatic mechanisms, not purposive or teleological "manipulation" by Gaia. In short, homeostasis does not necessarily imply conscious control.

In more recent times, the Gaia hypothesis has contributed to the development of *earth system science*, sometimes called geophysiology, which views the earth in its entirety as the ultimate object of ecological study. Perhaps most important, the Gaia hypothesis has influenced ecological science to study the *biosphere*—including biomass, oceans, and atmosphere—as a complex, organized whole system.

If the biosphere is a complexly organized system, humanity is clearly introducing imbalance into this system through global warming, air and water pollution, deforestation, and extensive destruction of biological species and habitats. Earth system scientists, including Lovelock, are currently examining the possibility that earth system dynamics can reach critical thresholds and then undergo rapid change. It appears that the earth system has made sudden state changes in the past, with some dramatic transitions occurring in periods of a decade or less. Thus global warming, for example, may have the potential to shift the biosphere into a different mode of operation, one that is less habitable for humans, within a relatively short time. In his most recent book, *The Revenge of Gaia* (2006), Lovelock offers a pessimistic outlook for Earth's future, proposing that widespread loss of forests and the ocean's phytoplankton—the two main ways our planet reduces atmospheric CO_2—is likely to create positive feedback loops that will make the earth uninhabitable within a hundred years.

While few scientists take such an extreme view, Lovelock and the Gaia hypothesis have influenced many scientists to focus on the earth as a whole system—and to recognize that the impacts of human energy consumption are far from negligible. A major challenge for all of us in the twenty-first century is to find ways to live in greater harmony with the matrix of life to which we are inextricably linked.

Appreciation of Indigenous Cultural Perspectives

The past few decades have seen interest in Native American spirituality and practices become widespread. Many people have been influenced by the Native American worldview described in popular books by Carlos Castaneda, Lynn Andrews, Mary Summerain, Black Elk, and Rolling Thunder. Traditional Native American beliefs closely parallel dominant themes of the emerging paradigm: the earth is seen as fundamentally sacred; all beings, animate and inanimate (from rocks to organisms to stars), are fundamentally interrelated; and a conscious intelligence underlies everything, including weather, crop cycles, the healing of disease, and the journey of the soul after death. Many people now engage in traditional Native American spiritual practices, such as sweat lodges, vision quests, and praying to the four directions of the medicine wheel. Underlying all of these practices is an affirmation of humanity's essential connection with the earth and the radical interrelationship of all elements of nature. Both are profoundly needed counterpoints to the fragmentation and alienation endemic to our materialistic, technology-based society.

Increasing Acceptance of Paranormal Events

Paranormal phenomena such as telepathy (perceiving another's thoughts), clairvoyance (also known as remote viewing—"seeing" an object that is hidden or at a distance), precognition (foreseeing the future), and psychokinesis (moving or affecting an object without any causal interaction with it) cannot be explained in terms of the known laws of physics. On the basis of the materialist worldview of conventional science, they should not even be possible. Yet such events are part of the experience of many, if not most, people. As long ago as 1978, a poll found that two-thirds of college professors accepted extrasensory forms of perception, and more than 25 percent of "elite scientists" believed in them. Given the growth of public interest in the subject in the last thirty years, one would expect these percentages to be even higher today.

An abundance of carefully conducted experimental studies has verified the existence of the best-known forms of psychic phenomena (telepathy, clairvoyance, precognition, and psychokinesis). These experiments—first conducted by Joseph Banks Rhine at Duke University in the fifties—have been replicated by investigators at many different universities, and bear statistical results that are far beyond what would be expected by chance. In the words of respected British psychologist Hans Eysenck, "Unless there is a gigantic conspiracy involving thirty university departments all over the world and several hundred highly respected scientists in various fields, many of them originally hostile to the claims of the psychic researchers, the only conclusion the unbiased observer can come to must be that there are people who obtain knowledge existing in other people's minds, or in the [remote] outer world, by means yet unknown to science" (Radin 1997, 96-97).

An indication of the increasing acceptability of paranormal research to mainstream scientists is the appearance of favorable reviews in respected academic journals. One on telepathy research appeared in a 1994 issue of *Psychological Bulletin*, a prominent journal published by the American Psychological Association. Another article, presenting a theoretical model of precognition, appeared in a 1994 issue of *Physical Review*, a mainstream physics journal.

Perhaps more than any other individual, Dean Radin, a senior scientist affiliated with the Institute of Noetic Sciences, has done much to increase the credibility of research on paranormal phenomena through his books, *The Conscious Universe* (1997) and *Entangled Minds* (2006). In *The Conscious Universe*, Radin provides a detailed review of the history of paranormal research, showing how improvements in experimental and statistical methodology have gradually led to results that are difficult to contest on methodological grounds. One of the most intriguing areas of research described in that book is the study of *field consciousness*, or the ability of the mental capacities of small or large groups of people to have an impact on the physical world, as measured by random number generators. For example, during events in which a large numbers of people are focusing on the same thing, such as televised coverage of the World Olympics or the Academy Awards Ceremony, random number generators positioned at multiple sites display significant departures from randomness. At other times, both preceding and following these key events, they exhibit randomness. This phenomenon has been replicated in multiple locales and suggests the possibility of a group—or even global—collective consciousness functioning as a unified field.

In *Entangled Minds*, Radin develops a coherent theoretical model for paranormal phenomena, for example, by demonstrating that telepathy can be understood as a form of entanglement of minds compatible with quantum-entangled particles in quantum physics. Radin describes brain-wave correlation studies that demonstrate that shifts in one individual's brain activity can be instantaneously correlated with identical shifts in another's brain activity, even when the two persons are separated by considerable distance and unaware of each other consciously (2006, 136).

The radical implication is that our minds are, at their foundation, connected with other minds, and that we can affect each other in subtle ways that remain largely unconscious. A subtle shift in mood or emotional tone that we experience may be intimately connected to a friend or loved one residing hundreds or thousands of miles away. Even more radical is the fact that such interactions don't appear to be constrained by time. We may experience anxiety, or even physical pain, *before* rather than after a loved one at a distance has an accident or injury. Such nonlocal connections seem to occur more frequently among close relatives or friends. To the extent that the data reported by Radin are replicated by further studies, we have evidence for the paradigm-breaking possibility that our individual minds are all deeply embedded in an interconnected, seamless whole. "Entangled minds" thus becomes a metaphor for the deep structure of human consciousness—a unitary, collective consciousness of which we are all a part. What happens in our private experience may not be entirely self-generated; rather, it may be influenced from afar.

Holding onto the mainstream materialist worldview, many scientists continue to reject paranormal phenomena on the grounds that no plausible mechanism yet explains what is going on. There has been an increasing trend, though, to question the old paradigm and preserve the phenomena. Telepathy, clairvoyance, precognition, and psychokinesis are increasingly viewed as anomalies that radically challenge the prevailing paradigm. They imply a universe where events can be connected without (known) energy transmission—without even causality.

Popular Interest and Belief in Areas Once Considered Esoteric

In the first half of the twentieth century it was rare to find books on metaphysical topics. Fear of being ostracized or ridiculed kept the few individuals who explored esoteric areas from being very vocal. Those who studied theosophy or Rudolph Steiner were in a small minority.

Today, every major bookstore contains multiple books on topics such as communication with the dead, portrayals of the afterlife, reincarnation, past-life regression, angels and spirit guides, astrology and tarot, psychic healing, channeling, or ghosts and poltergeists. In any major metropolitan area in North America, classes and workshops on these topics are not hard to find. While these phenomena have not been experimentally demonstrated in the lab (as telepathy, clairvoyance, and psychokinesis have) they have all been experienced by thousands of people throughout the world. The assumption that *virtually all reports* of such phenomena are based on imagination, wishful thinking, random coincidence, or outright fraud is itself a conclusion that requires a great stretch of the imagination and contains an implicit bias. A careful, unbiased review of the extant literature on phenomena such as the afterlife, reincarnation, ghosts, or communication with the dead reveals highly suggestive evidence for the existence of all of these things. Their purported existence also implies a universe much larger than the physical, space-time universe known to mainstream science.

The Emergence of Complementary Medicine

Physician authors such as Deepak Chopra and Andrew Weil have ushered in a whole new view of medicine: one that not only recognizes the importance of mind in the genesis and cure of disease but also acknowledges the profound role spirituality can play in health and healing. The terms "holistic medicine," "alternative medicine," "complementary medicine," and "integrative medicine" suggest a new paradigm that recognizes the importance of all levels of the human being—body, emotions, mental attitudes, and soul—in understanding and treating disease.

Conventional medicine is underwritten by a metaphysics of materialism and mechanism: disease is defined in terms of symptoms and underlying pathology. The body is an anatomical-physiological system curable through mechanical and biochemical manipulation—primarily surgery and drugs. The patient is assumed to be ignorant and passive relative to the doctor, either compliant or noncompliant with "doctor's orders."

Holistic medicine turns most of this on its head. Disease is not just a breakdown of bodily functions but an indication of imbalance in an individual's attitudes, values, and spiritual outlook, as well as important lifestyle factors such as nutrition, interpersonal relationships, and physical environment. Treatment is multimodal and may include conventional allopathic approaches such as medication as well as alternative approaches such as chiropractic, acupuncture, herbs, massage, yoga and meditation, counseling, or homeopathy. Patients are held responsible for their own health; doctors are collaborators—rather than authorities—who assist patients in determining what combination of interventions may best support optimal well-being. The new paradigm behind holistic medicine goes far beyond a materialistic universe, stressing fields, subtle energies, and the importance of consciousness in both disease and health.

There are many indications that complementary approaches to health care are entering mainstream medicine. Integrative medical clinics have appeared throughout the United States, and many medical schools now offer courses—if not entire programs—in complementary medicine. The National Institutes of Health program on complementary and alternative medicine has grown from an office with a $2 million budget to a national center with a budget of $123 million in 2006. Medical institutions are even beginning to take a look at the role of prayer and contemplative practices. A decade ago only a couple of medical schools offered courses on the role of spirituality in medicine; today, more than a hundred such courses exist. Many medical centers currently offer courses in meditation and yoga to their patients. The mindfulness-based approach to stress and disease developed by Jon Kabat-Zinn in the early nineties is now available at hospitals and clinics throughout the country. Research on the efficacy of meditation for controlling pain and reducing stress, anxiety, and depression is now accepted and reviewed by mainstream professional journals. Both theoretical conceptions and research pertinent to the new paradigm in medicine are explored in depth in *Consciousness and Healing: Integral Approaches to Mind-Body Medicine* (2004), co-edited by Marilyn Schlitz and Tina Amorok and sponsored by the Institute of Noetic Sciences.

The Rise of Feminism and Feminist Spirituality

The emergence of the feminine archetype socially, politically, and in reconceiving our relationship to the earth's environment is a vital—some would argue central—force in the global shift to a new paradigm. Since the advent of feminism in the 1960s, values of cooperation, inclusiveness, interrelationship, receptivity, and intuition have increasingly permeated areas as diverse as medicine, education, corporate management, environmental politics, and economics—not to mention personal relationships and daily interactions. The ascendance of the feminine is evident in the widespread interest in—and enormous amount of literature about—women's rights, feminist spirituality, and the ecofeminist movement. Initially many women wanted to replace three thousand years of male dominance and patriarchy with a society based on feminist values, where women would hold dominant positions of political power. As time has passed, for many feminists the challenge has shifted to finding the right balance and integration between male and female values. Both are seen as necessary to guide and preserve our world in these difficult times.

The Global Rise of Citizen-Based Organizations

One of the clearest indications of a shift in consciousness is the almost explosive growth of charitable and nonprofit organizations worldwide. Environmentalist and social entrepreneur Paul Hawkin describes this as a global movement without ideological boundaries or leaders, one that is both self-organizing and dedicated to making the world a better place (2007). He also describes it as humanity's "immune response" that has assumed the task of saving and protecting itself from "toxins" such as political corruption, social injustice, and environmental degradation. Thousands of organizations and millions of people appear to be ready to actively contribute time, money, or skills to make a difference, either in their local communities or by contributing to causes with a global reach. If the movement toward taking responsibility for the planet and humanity's condition continues to grow, there is some hope for our collective future. There are many who believe, like Hawkin, that we are in the midst of one of the largest social transformations in human history. The recent movie, *The Shift*, directed by Rochelle Marmorstein, vividly documents this rise of humanitarian activism.

Conclusion

These nine trends, among many others, point to the emergence of a far-reaching shift in humanity's perception of the world and of itself. Together they represent a movement away from ideas and institutions that embrace material values, reductionism, hierarchical control, and the supremacy of the personal ego toward a new paradigm that embraces spiritual values, wholeness, integration, cooperation, and the interrelationship of all human beings, regardless of their differences—indeed the interrelationship of all elements of the universe itself.

Global Shift: A Preview

Chapters 4 to 16 outline a new way of seeing the world, ourselves, and the relationship between the two. For a significant portion of the population, this new perspective is beginning to replace the mainstream scientific-materialist worldview. As previously described, its dominant themes include:

A conscious universe: Perceiving the Cosmos as a conscious, creative, and evolving process rather than a purely static, mechanistic object. Every whole system in the universe, from atoms to galaxies, exhibits attributes of consciousness such as self-organization, coherence, and intentionality.

Multidimensional reality: Reality, the sum of all that is, exceeds the bounds of the physical universe. It contains subtle, transcendent dimensions not well understood by present-day science These more subtle dimensions form the matrix of the physical universe that we see.

Interconnection of all minds: Though our minds appear to be separated by our individual bodies, they are, at depth, unified in a common, collective consciousness. This consciousness is not only shared by all humans, it is part of a larger matrix that includes the consciousness of the universe as a whole.

A synthesis of science and spirituality: Though their methods and ultimate concerns differ, both science and religion seek to reveal the "truth" about the Cosmos. Science, relying on sensory experience, examines the objective, spatial universe. Spirituality, utilizing intuition and revelation, plumbs the depths of the cosmos's interior, symbolic face.

Radical empiricism: Both sensory observation and intuitive modes of knowing have equal validity in humanity's quest to understand the universe, though the sensory forms lend themselves more easily to replication and consensus.

Consciousness has a causal influence: Consciousness has inherent properties—such as a capacity for self-organization, intentionality, and meaning—that cannot be explained in terms of the material laws and processes of the natural sciences. Yet it has a causal influence on physical processes.

Natural ethics: Ought reduces to is. Ethical behavior—what we ought to do—arises naturally from acting out of personal authenticity and integrity, rather than from conforming to culturally imposed norms.

The sketch presented in these chapters is provisional. Fifty years from now it will likely be viewed as a rather primitive version of the new worldview. It's better to view it as an approximation rather than as a finished picture.

For some readers, the ideas presented in the following chapters may appear unscientific. Yet to dismiss them as such is to miss this book's basic point: a full account of the cosmos requires ways of knowing and knowledge that lie outside of the empirical methods of science. (This does not in any way diminish the power of science to disclose the objective, physical universe.) In its meaningful, symbolic, and creative aspects, reality has grander scope than can be fully disclosed by present-day science. This realization leads to a deeply revised way of seeing the universe and our relationship with it.

An alternative point of view is possible: science may someday revamp its basic working assumptions to embrace what William James described as *radical empiricism*—an acceptance of all modes of knowing, including intuition and revelation, as providing valuable evidence for understanding the world. Such a revised science might use systematic methods to investigate the inner, subjective domain of experience, a domain that has historically been the province of religion and the humanities. Science would thus enlarge its scope beyond what is revealed by sensory experience alone. We could have a science of consciousness alongside the conventional empirical sciences. As Ken Wilber has proposed, such a science would still rely on replicable observations and interobserver consensus, much as the empirical sciences do now (1998). Of course, the interpretive quality of inner experience is likely to make consensus about the universal features of the inner world more difficult to obtain across observers and cultures, though not necessarily impossible. Perhaps a consensual map of the inner domain of consciousness, revealed in its many levels, might eventually be drawn.

It seems likely that for the foreseeable future science will continue to restrict itself to the sensory domain of objective reality, as its methods lend themselves well to this domain. Although paranormal phenomena such as telepathy, clairvoyance, and precognition may be studied experimentally with increasing rigor, intuitive or "psychic" knowing itself is unlikely to be used as a basis for constructing scientific theories of nature any time soon. Nonetheless, a broader science utilizing the full range of human experience is a long-term possibility that cannot be ruled out.

Even so, such a future science would not supplant the humanities, arts, or spirituality. Wisdom, beauty, and goodness cannot be reduced to strictly scientific terms. A future science of consciousness would not seek to answer—nor would it be interested in answering—questions of meaning. The intent of science is to understand the how of things, not the why. Nor can any science, even one of consciousness, provide us with satisfactory ethical standards. Although reality is both phenomenal and normative in its different aspects, science is only about the former.

The new worldview sketched in chapters 4-16 also transcends the boundaries of traditional world religions: Christianity, Judaism, Hinduism, Buddhism, and Islam. It employs terms like "universal consciousness," "conscious universe," and "cosmic intelligence" to refer to the idea that the Cosmos—the sum of all that exists (within and beyond space)—is, at the very least, conscious and meaningfully ordered, if not actually purposive. To speak of the Cosmos as conscious, intelligently ordered, creative, and potentially purposive is a radical departure from the scientific-materialist worldview that regards it as a neutral object for empirical investigation. Such attributes place the Cosmos in a context similar to that of traditional religion. Many readers, in fact, may prefer to use traditional terms such as God, Allah, Brahma, or Yahweh in thinking about an intelligently ordered cosmos.

There is no conflict here. If ultimate reality (the ground or source of everything) is indeed conscious and intelligent, it's possible to use either impersonal language (universal consciousness, cosmic order) or personal language (God, Allah) to refer to it. Ultimate reality is ineffable; it is large enough to transcend human distinctions between personal and impersonal. It is both something we can think of abstractly and something with which we can have a deeply personal relationship. It also transcends, the distinction between "in space" and "beyond space" (traditionally, immanent versus transcendent). By its very nature, ultimate reality is all-inclusive, ineffable, unimaginable, and certainly beyond all dualities and distinctions that the human mind can invent. In speaking of a conscious, intelligent universe—something of enormous beauty, intricacy, and creativity for us—we may only be describing a single, minute expression of the Ultimate Mystery.

Thus the emerging worldview moves beyond both the perspective of conventional science, as well as the multiple perspectives of traditional religions. It suggests a new perspective, in which scientific and spiritual approaches to understanding the world are synthesized. The same cosmos is both explicable by science and sacred, conscious, and creative.

4

The Re-enchantment of Nature

For most of the history of humanity, the natural world has been perceived to be enchanted. Ancient Greeks and Romans saw the activity of a pantheon of gods behind the unfolding of world events. Most ancient indigenous societies viewed the material world as "ensouled," or replete with spiritual forces. Natural processes were directed or influenced by invisible forces. These could be either idealized and abstract (such as Platonic forms) or quite concrete (such as nature spirits, devas, fairies, and elementals). As a result, the course of natural events could potentially be influenced by human prayer, ritual, or even sacrifice.

Over the past three thousand years in the West, the physical world has been gradually divested of spirit. This can be traced to three major historical developments:

- *The spread of Christianity (100 AD to present):* God came to be seen as transcendent, existing above and beyond the natural world. Attributing spiritual forces to nature was considered a serious heresy by the Catholic Church.

- *The Scientific Revolution (1600 AD to present):* The outer world came to be seen as totally objective, devoid of meaning and purpose. Meaning and purpose were understood to reside solely in the human mind, which was seen as a detached witness set apart from nature.

- *The technological revolution (1800 AD to present):* The material world came to be viewed as a resource to be exploited. Human fulfillment was to be found through adaptation to and mastery over nature and the material world.

The disenchantment of the outer world paralleled the emergence of the modern self—in particular, the individual's self-concept as autonomous and independent, free to determine and shape his or her own destiny. Ever since the Enlightenment and revolutionary period at the end of the eighteenth century, this awareness of the human self as independent and self-determining has been fundamental to humanity's concept of itself. A desacralized outer world and an autonomous, empowered individual became complementary to each other. All spirit, purpose, intentionality, and interiority were confined to human consciousness. Nature became a neutral object for scientific analysis and explanation. For the modern, scientific mind, to attribute purpose or intention to outer events is to regress to primitive, prescientific thinking. This is commonly viewed as a projection of human mental attributes onto a fundamentally neutral, meaningless cosmos.

On the positive side, this progressive separation of the human self from its matrix in nature has resulted in enormous scientific and technological advances. In the past two hundred years, we've achieved mastery in a wide array of scientific disciplines, ranging from physics and chemistry to geology and biology. Detailed scientific knowledge of the world has likely increased by a factor of one hundred in the twentieth century alone. Technologically, humanity has progressed from a predominantly survival-oriented existence to a postindustrial civilization, in which the average person enjoys many more conveniences and comforts than royalty did in previous times. Witness the development in the last 125 years of electric lighting, the automobile, flight, refrigeration, electric stoves, the telephone, radio, television, and, more recently, the personal computer, the Internet, cell phones, and digital forms of information storage and transfer. Life today doesn't even remotely resemble life just a hundred years ago.

But the shadow side of humanity's differentiation from and domination over nature has been as profound as the technological progress achieved. As documented by sociologists and cultural historians from Weber to Reisman, Fromm, and Sorokin, humanity has progressively alienated itself from its source. In his recent book, *Cosmos and Psyche* (2006), Richard Tarnas explains that humanity's achievement of autonomy has been paid for by a widespread experience of alienation. In a cosmos devoid of meaning or purpose, in which all meaning and purpose reside only in the human mind, humanity is left fundamentally alone. According to physicist Steven Weinberg, "The more the universe seems comprehensible, the more it also seems pointless" (Tarnas 2006, 28). The disenchantment of the outer world leaves us without a foundation for our deepest spiritual and psychological aspirations. What is left is a world vulnerable to being turned into a commodity and exploited for purely materialistic ends. Richard Tarnas eloquently sums up humanity's current predicament:

> Since the encompassing cosmological context in which all human activity takes place has eliminated any enduring ground of transcendent values—spiritual, moral, aesthetic—the resulting vacuum has empowered the reductive values of the market and the mass media to colonize the collective human imagination and drain it of all depth. If the cosmology is disenchanted, the world is logically seen in predominantly utilitarian ways, and the utilitarian mind-set begins to shape all human motivation at the collective level. What might be considered means to larger ends ineluctably become ends in themselves. The drive to achieve ever-greater financial profit, political power, and technological prowess becomes the dominant impulse moving individuals and societies, until these values, despite ritual claims to the contrary, supersede all other aspirations.
>
> The disenchanted cosmos impoverishes the collective psyche in the most global way. Nothing is immune. Majestic vistas of nature, great works of art, revered music, eloquent language, the beauty of the human body, distant lands and cultures, extraordinary moments of history, the arousal of deep human emotion: all become advertising tools to manipulate consumer response. For quite literally, in a disenchanted cosmos, nothing is sacred. The soul of the world has been extinguished: ancient trees and forests can then be seen as nothing but potential lumber; mountains nothing but mineral deposits; seashores and deserts are oil reserves; lakes and rivers, engineering tools. Animals are perceived as harvestable commodities, indigenous tribes as obstructing relics of an outmoded past, children's minds as marketing targets. At the all-important cosmological level, the spiritual dimension of the

empirical universe has been entirely negated, and with it, any publicly affirmable encompassing ground for moral wisdom and restraint. The short term and the bottom line rule all. Whether in politics, business, or the media, the lowest common denominator of the culture increasingly governs discourse and prescribes the values of the whole (2006, 32-33).

It is this crisis in humanity's conception of itself and the earth that has brought forth responses on many fronts, as described in chapter 3. A new worldview is emerging, the essence of which points to a re-enchantment of the outer world, but a re-enchantment on an entirely different level from the mythologies that existed in prescientific and indigenous societies. What has been retained is a conception of the Cosmos as fundamentally conscious.

In recent years, several trends and developments have pointed to a re-enchanting of the Cosmos.

Sheldrake's Morphic Fields and Critique of Evolutionary Theory

Rupert Sheldrake's ideas, presented originally in *A New Science of Life: The Hypothesis of Formative Causation* (1981), introduced the notion that all living systems are able to oppose entropy and maintain themselves as organized wholes as a result of invisible, intelligent fields he calls *morphic fields*. He offers considerable evidence for why a theory of morphic fields is necessary. According to Sheldrake, evolutionary theory, with its mechanistic operation of random mutations and natural selection, does not sufficiently explain the emergence of new species. In the fossil record, new species appear suddenly, requiring the coordination of a great number of changes over a short period of time (for example, the appearance of the eye). According to Sheldrake, the biochemistry of DNA is not up to this task. Nor could such biochemistry explain morphogenesis, the development of an entire organism from a fertilized egg. DNA can provide instructions for different types of cells—and even the timing of when they are to be produced—but it cannot organize them in three-dimensional space to produce a finished organism. Thus, Sheldrake believes that DNA sequences have to be supplemented by invisible fields that act as structural blueprints for molecules and cells as they grow in number and complexity to become organs.

Sheldrake's ideas have influenced many scientists who critique Darwinian evolutionary theory. His theories are one of the more sophisticated attempts to explain what we informally refer to as the "life force." Although one critic proposed that all of Sheldrake's books be burned (Maddox 1981), his ideas point to a universe that is teleological and purposive, rather than purely mechanistic. It is a universe where consciousness must be included as a causal reality in the explanation of biological events.

Anthropic Principle in Cosmology

The strong version of the *anthropic principle* in cosmology states that many different parameters had to be finely tuned at the time of the Big Bang for the development of galaxies, stars, and ultimately life to be possible. Even a minute change in any one of a large number of physical constants would have led to an uninhabitable universe—or even no physical universe at all. For example, according to Stephen Hawking, if the rate of expansion one second after the Big Bang had been smaller by $(1/10)^{16}$ the universe would have recollapsed before reaching its present size (1988). If the strong nuclear force within the nucleus of the atom had been only very slightly weaker, we would have had only hydrogen atoms in the universe. An increasing number of scientists believe that these fine-tunings imply that some kind of purposive intelligence guided the formation and evolution of the universe. Others argue that our universe is just one among many universes—one in which all of the parameters just randomly *happened* to fall in such a way that life could develop. Though there is no way to disprove this hypothesis, it's also very difficult to confirm, since it would be quite difficult to observe or communicate with other universes. We are also left with the basic metaphysical question: why have any universe that is capable of evolving to the point where it becomes aware of itself?

Restoration of Consciousness to the Cosmos in Philosophy

Theologians such as Charles Hartshorne (1991) and philosophers such as Christian de Quincey (2002) have helped to advance the thinking of early-twentieth-century philosopher Alfred North Whitehead (1933). Contrary to the prevailing scientism of his time, Whitehead developed a model of the universe as an organic, self-creating process. The universe is understood as analogous to an organism rather than a machine, involving a dynamic interplay of interdependent events. Every part of the universe, from atoms to organisms to galaxies, contributes to and is modified by the unified activity of the whole. Events are not mechanistic: each event reacts to and takes account of interrelating events. In fact, every particular event is a center of spontaneity and self-creation contributing its unique role to the whole.

This is a profoundly different view of the world from that of materialistic science, and it anticipated the current shift in worldview by about eighty years. De Quincey elaborated on this idea of nature as conscious at all levels in his well-received book, *Radical Nature* (2002). For de Quincey, consciousness exists not just in the minds of humans and animals but in every organized whole system, all the way down to atoms and quarks. This is not a new idea. For more than two thousand years, the philosophical model of *panpsychism* has proposed that the entire universe is conscious. De Quincey's defense and development of the panpsychism thesis is one of the most compelling models of the nature of reality found in philosophy today.

The Concept of Synchronicity

Formulated by Carl Jung toward the end of his life, the concept of *synchronicity* refers to a meaningful correspondence between the human psyche and outer, natural events which occur in the world. The connection is not causal but symbolic. For example, when we are driving in a car concerned about a relationship issue, a song might come on the radio that not only provides insight into our concern, but also mentions the name of the person we've been thinking about. We are left with the impression of uncanny coincidence—or the feeling that whatever happened was more th.... just coincidence. Prior to Jung, such events were thought of as signs originating from heaven or a particular deity. Sometimes during major life transitions, many synchronicities occur in sequence, as illustrated by the 1981 movie *My Dinner with Andre*.

Synchronicities point to a conscious universe: one that operates not just causally but symbolically. Events are juxtaposed according to their symbolic relationship instead of causally. (Such connections don't replace causal sequences, they simply coexist with them.) According to Carl Jung, synchronicities reflect the activities of universal *archetypes*. Archetypes are meaningful patterns within the collective unconscious psyche of humanity. They are neither purely subjective nor purely objective but transcend the boundaries of subject and object, inner psyche and outer cosmos. They constitute meaningful patterns within the collective psyche or "world mind" in which our individual lives and psyches participate. This idea is summarized in the ancient Hermetic axiom "As above, so below."

The existence of synchronistic connections provides a basis for supposing that divinatory arts such as the I Ching or Tarot might have some type of validity, as many who have worked with these arts can attest. Luminaries no less than Johannes Kepler and Carl Jung regarded astrology and planetary astronomy as providing alternate explanations of the same phenomena, one from an "inner," meaning-oriented perspective, the other from an "outer," causal-oriented one. Astronomy provides a detailed description of each planet and its motion around the sun. Astrology, relying on more intuitive/interpretive forms of knowing, reveals meaningful correspondences—synchronicities—between planetary positions at the moment of an individual's birth and the unique constellation of archetypal influences that shape an individual's personality. In the current worldview, however, astrology and other divinatory practices are regarded as invalid pseudosciences. (Synchronicity and the relevance of divinatory arts will be discussed further in chapter 16.)

Paranormal Events

Telepathy, clairvoyance, precognition, and psychokinesis—all of which have been experimentally verified—imply that consciousness not only *informs* the physical world, it can *transcend* it altogether. If my dream or waking self foresees detailed events that turn out to happen three months later, some process appears to be involved that operates independently of both space and time—that is, the future is witnessed in the present. (As mentioned earlier, such processes are often described as "nonlocal.") The implication is that there are aspects of reality that transcend the physical universe (as we presently understand it) and operate beyond space and time. Unfortunately, as Kant demonstrated long ago, we can't conceive of the world apart from constructs of space and time; thus we are hard put to conceptualize how nonlocal or paranormal phenomena actually occur.

Paranormal phenomena radically undermine the Cartesian isolation of consciousness from the rest of the world. Consciousness not only participates in ordering the world into meaningful relations and sequences, it connects events separated in space and/or time in an instantaneous, acausal fashion. This makes it tempting to adopt an idealistic philosophical stance in which space, time, and matter are viewed as derivatives of consciousness.

These are a few among several trends that suggest a new worldview is emerging. It is one that perceives a universe that is somehow guided and orchestrated by consciousness (or a conscious intelligence) at all levels, from the quantum to the galactic.

In some respects, there is nothing new about such a perception. A tremendous amount of lore about such a conscious intelligence exists within various religious, philosophical, and metaphysical views of the world. Native Americans, Polynesians, and Celtic people, for example, each have had their respective pantheons of nature spirits or deities. The Hindu religion sees the activity of its respective deities (such as Vishnu and Shiva) immanent within the world. Indeed, religions commonly regard deity as immanent. (The wholly transcendent view of God sustained by the Catholic Church throughout the Middle Ages is actually an exception.) In a more abstract way, most idealist philosophy, from Plato down to

Spinoza and Hegel, has argued for the primacy of consciousness or mind in the ordering—and even the origination—of the Cosmos.

All of these theologies, metaphysics, and philosophies view the world as imbued with intelligence and purpose. Today, the modern resurgence of interest in Native American and other indigenous worldviews, the Gaia movement with its premise that the earth is sacred, and the revival of ecofeminism and paganism by women visionaries such as Starhawk, all presage the emergence of a worldview that similarly perceives nature as conscious, even enchanted.

Despite dismissal by hard science, these "prescientific" or "unscientific" theologies, mythologies, and philosophies are not based on sheer fantasy. They have arisen out of the collective experience of those who created and believed in them. They can be seen as experience-based interpretations of the world, drawn from a variety of strands of experience, not just sensory. Contemplation, intuition, revelation, and existential life experience all contributed to the construction of these models of the world. There is an implicit epistemology—theory of knowledge—that underlies these interpretations of the world, but it's of a different kind than the one utilized in the natural sciences. (More will be said about this in chapter 7.)

If consciousness is understood as being somehow embedded in the "outer world," then the sharp distinction between "subjective" mind and "objective" nature fostered by the Scientific Revolution (and particularly Descartes and Newton) appears to diminish. The boundary has already been blurred in quantum physics, where the very existence of a particle is dependent upon the process of observing it. It has also been blurred by the modern view that scientific paradigms set limits on the way scientists can perceive and think about the world. Yet the most profound sense in which the sharp distinction between psyche and cosmos breaks down is in the realization that human consciousness and the "consciousness" of the larger world or universe are interdependent. Synchronicities reveal a correspondence between our minds and outer events. Paranormal processes such as telepathy and precognition reveal instantaneous events transcending boundaries of space and time. Mystical experiences disclose the ultimate connection of our personal awareness with a universal field of awareness that is unbounded in scope.

For the new worldview, the vision of a meaningfully ordered cosmos is not, as conventional science would have it, an anthropomorphic projection of human fantasy. The human mind is not the sole domain of consciousness. Instead, individual, human consciousness is just a single locale (perhaps a localization of an inherently nonlocal phenomenon) in an unbounded field of consciousness that informs all things at all levels. In fact, it seems extremely anthropocentric to imagine that human beings (along with other animals) are the only points in the entire universe in which consciousness resides. This may be one of the last anthropocentric perspectives humanity will have to relinquish, having already let go of the idea that the earth and the human drama are fulcrum points of the cosmos. The human mind is no more likely to be the center and source of consciousness than the earth is the center of the universe.

Self-Maintaining Whole Systems

At what points might we find consciousness in nature? Mechanistic causation, as in the case of one billiard ball hitting another or the movement of a piston in a combustion engine, is clearly not a conscious or intelligent process. Indeed, much of what is described by empirical science appears unequivocally mechanistic. Although the old materialistic, machine model of the universe that prevailed during the Scientific Revolution is relevant to explaining much of what goes on in nature, it does not provide a complete account. Quite simply, it cannot fully account for the self-creating and self-maintaining properties of organized systems—emergent wholes that are more than the sum of their constituent parts.

The activity of consciousness is most conspicuous at the level of these *self-maintaining wholes*. The emergence of self-sustaining whole systems at all levels of existence—atoms, molecules, cells, organs, organ systems, organisms, communities, nations, the earth, the solar system, galaxies, the cosmos as a whole—suggests the activity of consciousness. The universe can be understood as an organic *holarchy*, a term adapted from Arthur Koestler's *holons* (1967). A holarchy is a coherent hierarchy of self-organizing, self-maintaining wholes, from the subatomic level to the galactic.

In brief, a new vision of reality is emerging in which we, as humans, no longer perceive ourselves as split off from a meaningless, objective world. We are not alone and cut off in a remote solar system in a remote galaxy amid a vast sea of empty space. Instead, we are simply one interdependent part of a much greater, possibly infinite conscious order. As will be seen, this new vision of reality can lead us away from an exploitive attitude toward nature and toward a deep reverence for all of creation, including ourselves.

Implications of a Re-enchanted World

Perceiving the outer world as "enchanted," or imbued with consciousness at every level, has profound implications. Whether phrased in traditional theistic terms of God or more abstract terms of a cosmic consciousness, the emerging worldview regards the universe as ordered by an intelligence that far surpasses our own.

A conscious universe calls us to reverence. We stand in awe of such a universe and come to appreciate that our planet is much more than merely a material entity to be subdued and exploited for our own ends. The earth comes to be seen as a sacred matrix in which we are embedded and upon which we profoundly depend. One hundred and fifty years of unrestricted exploitation has led to very serious consequences that will require all of humanity to move away from materialistic values toward a deep respect, if not reverence, for the environment.

When we perceive nature as fundamentally sacred, such respect comes more naturally. Our actions and attitudes toward every aspect of nature change. Forests are valued as an essential part of the earth's ecosystem, necessary to absorb excess carbon dioxide and replenish oxygen. Rivers, lakes, oceans, and the air itself are seen as precious resources vital to the sustenance of life rather than acceptable dumping grounds for industrial pollution. Animals, whether wild or raised for food, are respected as living beings, with the same rights to comfort and humane treatment as ourselves. Finally, we come to view ourselves as sacred partners in the evolution and destiny of the earth, rather than unlimited consumers of the planet's finite resources. By coming to perceive the earth as a conscious, organized whole worthy of our honor and respect, we become empowered to save it—and ultimately ourselves—from serious destruction.

Perceiving the universe as conscious also leads to a fundamental shift in the way we perceive ourselves. Over the past 2,500 years, most of us, particularly in the West, have come to regard human beings as highly autonomous, individual egos who fully determine their own destinies. Although we live in relationship with our families and communities, we still see ourselves as autonomous beings, more or less completely independent of the outer world. The emerging worldview holds a very different vision, one in which all of us are highly interconnected in a unitary field of consciousness. Our conscious experience of ourselves as having a discrete ego obscures an underlying reality: even though born into an illusion of individuality, we are ultimately one and the same consciousness. Not only are we joined in consciousness to all other humans, we are joined to all other elements of nature—animals, trees, rocks, and stars—in ways more intimate than we can fathom. The consciousness that we claim as our own is in fact merely a node in a network of many different points of consciousness, including those of our loved ones, the collective groups to which we belong, perhaps even our so-called spirit guides and angels, and, possibly, many other inputs of which we are not aware. Our very feelings, moods, and inspirations may be only in part our own and in part joined with other streams of consciousness.

Such a view involves a radical shift away from the notion of a totally autonomous ego. It calls for a deep humility. If each of us is an interdependent part of a larger whole, then each of us has a special part to play for the benefit of the whole. No longer is it all about "you and me against the world." Instead, each of us is called to live in harmony with the more universal consciousness that underlies our conditioned mind—what the Buddhists refer to as Dharma. As we attune ourselves increasingly to our innermost being—our soul—we come to live increasingly in harmony with ourselves and with others. We come to find greater peace and contentment in our daily life. Also we come to find a deeper sense of purpose in what we do with our lives. As each of us finds our own inner peace, we contribute to the cause of world peace. (Practical guidelines for cultivating greater peace and harmony in your life can be found in chapters 19-23.)

Assuming that there is a universal consciousness of which we are an interdependent part, we can, in each moment, choose to go with it or to resist it. When we let go, allowing ourselves to move in harmony with the universal consciousness, we may find ourselves in attunement—synchrony—with the wisdom of our inner being and nature itself. We can only control and micromanage our lives to a certain degree before we become out of touch with ourselves and everything else. There is a right balance between controlling—indeed creating—the events of our lives and letting go and trusting our life's process. The popular expression for this balance is "going with the flow." The traditional religious metaphor is "following the will of God."

There are probably many degrees of such attunement. At the highest level we may experience synchronicities, intuitive insights, revelations, or even visions. At a more intermediate level we simply experience our day as going well—things seeming to work out as we go along. At the lowest level, when we are out of sync, we experience conflict, resistance, stress, suffering, and ultimately disease. We may be thrown off-course by either our own choices or unforeseen circumstances. Yet we can always choose to put ourselves back on course. As will be seen in the chapter on natural ethics, it generally feels good to do so. Feeling at peace is one indication that we are in alignment or "flow" with the larger order in which we're connected.

Conclusion

The Scientific Revolution and Enlightenment left humanity with a world disenchanted, a world devoid of purpose, meaning, or spiritual significance. Over the past few centuries, this has led to the ascendance of materialistic values. This disenchantment of our world underlies our present emphasis on unlimited (and thus unsustainable) economic growth and on placing the needs of multinational corporations over the needs of the environment and impoverished peoples.

However, a new worldview is emerging, in which the Cosmos is understood as inherently conscious, and thus re-enchanted. Several different trends and developments suggest a conscious universe, including Sheldrake's notion of morphic fields, the anthropic principle, paranormal events, and the phenomenon of synchronicity. The points at which consciousness appears in nature are self-organizing wholes, ranging from atoms to galaxies. While a cell or a solar system may not be conscious in exactly the same way a human mind is, it still has properties associated with consciousness, such as self-organization, self-maintenance, intelligence, and even intentionality.

Perceiving the cosmos, and, in particular, our planet as conscious or enchanted calls us to treat our natural environment with awe and respect. Rather than being apart from us, we come to see it as a sacred matrix of which we are a part.

5

Return of the Feminine

For nearly four thousand years, the Western mindset and world-view have been largely "masculine" in character. Autonomy, separateness, and control have been the root metaphors influencing religion, science, and humanity's very conception of itself in Western Europe and America. The ascendance of the male archetype over the feminine can be traced back to nomadic conquests of ancient matrifocal cultures, such as the Minoan culture in Crete around 1500 BC. It continued from ancient times up through the Middle Ages in the Judeo-Christian repression of women and earth-based spirituality, and was evident in the Enlightenment's exaltation of the rational intellect, separate and in control of a disenchanted, objective world. Nineteenth- and twentieth-century science represented the culmination of this masculine project.

The traditional masculine archetype affirms not only qualities of autonomy and freedom but also control and manipulation. Science, from its inception, has cast nature as a neutral object devoid of meaning or purpose, subject only to mechanistic and causal explanation. A desacralized nature can readily be controlled and exploited for humanity's ends. There is, of course, nothing wrong with such an approach up to a point—certainly it is the basis of enormous technical advancement of civilization over the past few hundred years. Through technical mastery and control of nature, we have been better able to adapt to our environment. However, the excesses of industrial and technological development in the last two centuries—the unrestricted exploitation of nature without regard to ecological cycles and sustainability of resources—has led to our current global environmental crisis. Pursuing the masculine archetype without regard to the complex interrelations and balances in nature—interrelations which have evolved over hundreds of millions of years—has left us in a serious predicament. After a period of only two hundred years or so, we are facing a potentially major breakdown in the environment that sustains us. It's more somber than humorous to describe humanity's "marriage" to the earth as, at best, "on the rocks" and possibly headed for a divorce.

It is not an overstatement to say that our current world crisis can be viewed as a primarily *masculine crisis*. Old paradigms based on masculine values of autonomy, authority, hierarchy, and top-down control are in trouble, not just as they relate to the environment but across the board, in fields as diverse as medicine, education, politics, business, and—most critically—science and technology. Our very way of life is in trouble, as evidenced by the widespread disconnection, alienation, and social fragmentation many of us currently experience. Large numbers of us feel fundamentally disconnected—from nature, from community, from our families, from spirit, and from ourselves. Addictions, to everything from drugs to overwork to unbridled consumerism, are grasped at in an attempt to fill the existential gap, but a basic emptiness remains. We are well-connected electronically, but often disconnected from our own hearts and souls.

Obviously, our cultural institutions and ways of life cannot continue indefinitely in their present form. The old world order is on a collision course with and increasingly disrupted environment, and no one really knows how hard or soft the impact is going to be. Old paradigms based on traditional masculine values of separateness, hierarchy, and control are gradually giving way to worldviews embracing traditionally feminine values of interrelationship, integration, balance, holism, cooperation, and love. It's not that a feminine-oriented worldview is replacing the masculine one—rather, that feminine archetypal forms and energies are gradually being integrated into the current worldview. The emerging world order reflects a *marriage* of masculine and feminine principles and values.

The past thirty years have seen widespread indications of such a shift. It is a shift that goes well beyond the ascendance of the feminist movement. We've seen a growing worldwide concern for the environment and a reaction against political and corporate policies promoting domination and exploitation of natural resources. Longstanding political and ideological barriers are steadily collapsing, such as in the breakdown of the Soviet Union and the formation of the European Union. Such a shift is evident in the human potential movement's interest in reconnecting with the body, emotions, unconscious, and intuition. It's also evident in the emergence of holistic medicine, which regards disease as an imbalance in the whole person rather than an isolated entity to be fixed by surgery or drugs. It's evident in the popularity of the Gaia movement, which restores consciousness to nature by viewing the entire earth as an intelligent being. The ascendence of the feminine is also apparent in a host of other places, ranging from appreciation of indigenous, nature-centered cultures (such as traditional Native American and Celtic cultures) to the recent popular interest in the role and influence of Mary Magdalene. A common theme running through all of these developments—and many others—is an attempt to heal the excesses of masculine-based paradigms emphasizing domination, hierarchy, and control by introducing feminine-based values of inclusiveness, interrelationship, holism, and cooperation.

The Ascending Feminine

What are the implications of this shift for science and our conventional scientific way of understanding the world? For the past two hundred years, Western societies have embraced not only science as a method of investigation, but also a scientific worldview that makes certain basic assumptions about reality:

- The physical universe is all that exists; thus consciousness, and qualities of consciousness—such as meanings and purposes—are purely subjective and in principle reducible to the brain.

- The only way we can know the world is through sensory observations replicated by multiple independent observers; other forms of knowing, via empathy, intuition, or revelation, are unreliable and, again, purely subjective.

- Finally, the physical world (which is all that exists) can be explained entirely in terms of mechanistic causes; that is, the world operates something like a vast machine.

These three assumptions are themselves unscientific because they cannot be subject to empirical tests; they are in fact *metaphysical assumptions* about the nature of the world, a perspective inherited from the great scientists and philosophers of the seventeenth and eighteenth centuries: Descartes, Locke, Hume, Galileo, and Newton.

Dubbed *scientific materialism*, this position has been the dominant worldview in the West for three centuries, influencing human life in numerous ways, many of them positive. Scientific materialism underlies the tremendous technological progress that has provided countless conveniences and made life far less laborious than previously. In the future, technology will continue to make life easier for most of us. However, as described in chapter 2, a strictly scientific-materialist approach to the world creates serious problems, both for the environment and for humanity's connection with the earth, each other, and its spiritual foundation. The scientific-materialist worldview has also consistently failed to adequately answer such age-old questions as the meaning and ultimate purpose of life, the survival of consciousness following death, and the existence of a higher intelligence in the universe.

Sooner or later, the return of the feminine archetype is likely to modify the West's prevailing scientific worldview. In the next fifty to one hundred years, the current scientific-materialist paradigm may be superceded by a much broader and far-reaching view of the universe—one that embraces a more participatory view of consciousness, both in terms of our ways of knowing as well as our knowledge about reality. The traditional scientific-materialist worldview has been based on a radical split, the detachment of consciousness from the outer world. The emerging worldview reintegrates consciousness with outer reality in two ways:

- More participatory ways of knowing, such as empathy and intuition, are accepted and legitimized alongside purely sensory forms of knowledge. Radical empiricism—the acceptance of all forms of experience as valid bases for knowledge—is already beginning to supplant the strictly sensory empiricism of the eighteenth through twentieth centuries. (More will be said about this in chapter 7.) In philosophical terms, this might be called the "epistemological" reintegration of consciousness.

- Consciousness is being reintegrated into the physical universe itself. The absolute separation of subjective consciousness from an abstract objective nature is breaking down. This has been developing since the time of Kant with the notion that our very perception of the outer world is framed in terms of mental constructs such as space, time, and causality. More recently, it has been reinforced by Thomas Kuhn's insight that scientific paradigms render all observations of nature interpretive or "theory-laden." In the next few decades, it's quite possible we will take a more radical step. Nature itself may be conceived (or reconceived) as suffused and ordered by consciousness. The emergence of organized wholes at all levels of nature, from atoms to organisms to galaxies, may be viewed as an expression of an intelligent, ordering principle associated with consciousness. In philosophical terms, this would be the "ontological" reintegration of consciousness.

Radical Empiricism: The Acceptance of Participatory Ways of Knowing

From a conventional scientific standpoint, only knowledge based on evidence of the senses is valid. This masculine approach to the world requires a detached observer to check his observations against those of other independent and detached observers. The knowledge that results from this process is thought to be free of the subjective biases of any one observer.

While it is true that conventional scientific knowledge is relatively free of the bias of any one observer or investigator, it is not free of the collective bias of a society or culture of scientific observers. Thomas Kuhn's study of scientific paradigms in *The Structure of Scientific Revolutions* (1970) demonstrates that scientific theories of nature contain implicit assumptions associated with the prevailing paradigm of a given generation of scientists. Over long periods of time, scientific paradigms are challenged and eventually replaced. Thus the ideal of purely objective knowledge of the world, entirely free of human bias, is unattainable.

The emerging worldview—one that integrates masculine and feminine archetypes—will deeply revise Western humanity's view of what constitutes valid knowledge. There are two ways in which this is likely to happen:

- All types of experience, not just sensory experience, will count as evidence of our knowledge of the world. Intuitive and empathic experiences, as well as visionary experiences of "subtle" realms (emotional, mental, and spiritual) apart from the strictly physical world, will contribute to our construction of *consensus reality* (the accepted worldview) in addition to science. As more people become conversant with intuitive forms of knowing, the scope of consensus reality is likely to expand beyond the bounds of the universe as presently understood.

- Participatory forms of knowing—whereby the knower's awareness participates in the phenomenon being known—will gain equal status with sensory knowledge. Participatory knowledge is already honored in the social sciences—for example, in cultural anthropology, sociology, and clinical psychology. Knowledge of both culture and the inner workings of the human psyche depend on empathic perceptions that go well beyond purely sensory observation. Modern social sciences study the interiors of individual, group, and cultural behavior. Ecobiologists study the interiors of individual and group animal behavior, such as power hierarchies and the "meaning" of grooming behaviors among primates. Though we can directly observe the exterior behavior of an individual or culture, we cannot fully understand the inner experience of that person or culture without relying on more communal forms of knowing, in which the "observer's" consciousness in some way enters into (communes with) the consciousness of the object—or rather, subject—of observation.

In the future, we may come to understand the "interiors" or consciousness of even *inanimate* systems such as molecules or clouds. We may also understand interior phenomena that have no apparent external counterparts available to sense observation, such as subtle energy fields within the human biofield (see chapter 10) and even what are presently referred to as spiritual beings (for example, discarnate souls, angels, spirit guides, devas, and elementals). Furthermore, we may gain an understanding of how these more subtle phenomena interface with physical phenomena, which may give us some clues to solving philosophy's ancient mind-body and free-will-versus-determinism problems. All of these future inquiries will rely on intuitive forms of knowing, forms of knowing that go beyond mere sensory experience of physical events. For example, clairvoyant perceptions of disease processes in an individual's biofield, or of angelic presences in an alternate dimension, require an intuitive "feeling into" the phenomena that goes beyond mere sense perception.

Participatory forms of knowing reflect traditional feminine values of interrelationship and connection. Rather than detached observation, there is a more communal relationship between knower and what is known. To be sure, such forms of knowledge are more subjective or interpretive than those based strictly on sensory experience. Intuitive forms of knowing are more subject to individual interpretation and thus harder to cross-substantiate over independent observers than sensory knowledge. A group of psychics is less likely to agree in their perceptions of a disease process (viewed in an individual's "aura") than a group of expert physicians conducting standard medical diagnostic tests. However, empathy and intuition are not totally unamenable to interobserver agreement. The cross-cultural convergence of knowledge regarding near-death experiences, the nature of the afterlife, and intermediary spirit beings (common to most religions, though the names for these beings differ) suggests that a certain degree of consensus is possible. The fact that there already is some cross-cultural consensus lends credibility to these phenomena. In the future, the reliability of our methods for investigating such phenomena are likely to improve, leading to increasingly credible, accepted models of the subtle aspects of reality.

The Reintegration of Consciousness with Nature

Along with the legitimization of more participatory forms of knowledge, the emerging worldview surmounts the Cartesian split between subjective mind and objective nature. As discussed previously, consciousness is not restricted to the human mind but is also an inherent, inner aspect of the cosmos at all levels, from the atomic to the galactic. Once again, this breakdown of rigid dualism reflects traditional feminine values of interrelationship and reciprocity, in this case between inner subjective awareness and the outer world. No longer is there an absolute separation of mind and nature.

From the time of Descartes through the late twentieth century, the universe revealed by science has been an abstract object, devoid of purpose, ruled by chance and necessity, and without intrinsic meaning. The emerging worldview is not a return to the pre-Renaissance, medieval view of a world overseen by an authoritarian male god and legions of angels. Rather, it embraces a view of the Cosmos as both infused with consciousness at all levels of order as well as transcended by that same consciousness. Events across space and time are conceived as radically interdependent. Such a view is sometimes referred to as *panentheism*—consciousness both informs and at the same time transcends nature—as opposed to *pantheism*, which equates the natural order with a cosmic consciousness or deity.

The foregoing discussion is by no means an attempt to disparage science itself; science and technology hold solutions for many of the earth's current environmental problems. Nature will continue to be investigated by scientific analysis of causes and mechanisms at all levels of phenomena. There is obviously still much to be learned from scientific inquiry. Scientific fields such as cosmology, astronomy, physics, genetics, and nanotechnology are on the cusp of crucial new discoveries at the present time. However science, in its current form, cannot give us the full story about how the universe operates. New forms of explanation will be introduced at junctures where strictly causal, mechanistic, or even probabilistic explanations do not suffice. Consciousness will be understood to play a causal role in the explanation of processes that cannot be fully understood mechanistically (or probabilistically). If science wants to provide a complete account of nature, it will have to expand to include consciousness in its theories.

Conclusion

To sum up, the emerging feminine archetype is coming to be associated with both an acceptance of more participatory ways of knowing and a new model of the world where consciousness is not radically separated from nature.

No longer a meaningless, neutral object running on blind mechanistic or probabilistic laws, nature is becoming re-enchanted. Natural phenomena are coming to be understood both in terms of exterior causal sequences as well as interior, intentional processes— and not just for living organisms but for all levels of phenomena, from subatomic to the evolution of the entire cosmos. The emerging worldview embraces subtle phenomena and consciousness as no less parts of "reality" than material events. Something like what Arthur Lovejoy (1960) spoke of as the "Great Chain of Being"— which has been a part of so many spiritual and philosophical traditions since antiquity—may become the dominant paradigm. Reality is coming to be understood as a multileveled phenomenon, with the physical world described by present-day science at the most basic level, and the subtle, archetypal, and formless levels as invisible, progressively less form-dependent levels beyond (but inclusive of) the physical. These "higher" levels interpenetrate and interact with the physical level. This spectrum model of reality has been proposed in detail by contemporary philosophers such as Ken Wilber and Huston Smith in anticipation of its likely return as the dominant worldview in the West. However, its roots stretch all the way back to ancient Hindu conceptions of reality as well as those of Plato.

Finally, integrating the feminine archetype will entail a shift in the status of science, from ultimate authority in arbitrating humanity's understanding of the cosmos. Science as a *method* of explaining, predicting, and controlling the natural world, will continue to be an important, if not dominant, method for understanding reality. However, scientism as a metaphysical view of the world will diminish. Science will come to be viewed as one way of approaching reality alongside other equally credible ways that rely on more "feminine" intuitive ways of knowing. However, just as presently occurs in science, replicable observational procedures and interobserver consensus will be required to ensure credibility of these more participatory forms of knowledge.

6

Toward a Larger Universe: Reality Outgrows the Bounds of Physics

In the twentieth century, the scope of the physical universe has turned out to surpass our wildest expectations, containing over 100 billion galaxies spread out over an area that is at least 30 billion light-years across. Yet conventional science holds fast to the view that the known universe is *all there is*. The assumption underlying modern science is that what's real is only what can be discovered by science (both natural and social sciences). Everything else is either subjective or sheer fantasy. In brief, the physical world in space and time must be all there is.

This contradicts thousands of years of human experience. Virtually all of the world's religions subscribe to the idea that consciousness or the soul survives physical death and continues on in a heavenly realm existing apart from space and time. For the past thirty years, an extensive literature on near-death experiences has provided compelling (though not indubitable) evidence that this may be true. A strong case can be made for the ability of consciousness to separate from the body; many individuals near death report being in a remote position relative to their bodies and give detailed descriptions of objects and events they cannot have possibly seen with their physical eyes. They also report meeting already deceased relatives that they didn't know about (but whose existence is independently confirmed by other relatives). This evidence alone suggests a cosmos larger than the physical, space-time universe familiar to conventional science.

Paranormal Events

Beyond the evidence for life after death, a variety of paranormal phenomena point to a universe larger in scope than is presently understood. The evidence for basic processes of telepathy, clairvoyance, and precognition is strong, based on a number of controlled double-blind experiments done at universities around the world. These studies are nicely summarized in Dean Radin's book *The Conscious Universe* (1997). Many conventional scientists remain skeptical, but this is often because they have not seriously reviewed the experimental evidence or are requiring a standard of proof considerably higher than that held for the physical sciences. Their usual argument is that because psi researchers (researchers who study paranormal phenomena) have not provided a satisfactory theoretical explanation for the data, the data must be wrong. Yet, the experimental methodology of many of these experiments has been of high quality. If even one experiment demonstrating the existence of telepathy or clairvoyance is valid, then we have a universe where nonlocal, acausal events happen.

In physics itself the existence of nonlocal connections is well established for particle phenomena: two particles change their spin in exactly the same way at exactly the same time, without any intervening causal connection. The connection occurs instantaneously, without any intervening signal traveling at the speed of light or slower. Although it isn't clear how the nonlocality in quantum physics relates to the nonlocality of consciousness implied by telepathy and clairvoyance, the parallel is intriguing. At the very least, the existence of telepathy and clairvoyance requires a universe where acausal, nonlocal processes occur. It also requires explanation in terms of forces other than the four known to operate causally in the universe of conventional physics: gravity, electromagnetic forces, and the strong and weak nuclear forces. In brief, paranormal evidence requires a larger universe than what is presently understood. Whether physics can eventually expand to accommodate paranormal processes remains to be seen.

While experimental evidence for telepathy, clairvoyance, and precognition is the strongest, hundreds of independent reports from cultures around the world support numerous other paranormal phenomena. These accounts include experiences of ghosts, poltergeists, channeling, the existence of spirit guides, materialization and dematerialization (the appearance or disappearance of material forms out of nowhere), levitation, thought photography (a process in which a mental state produces an image on photographic film), and psychic healing (healing that occurs without the intervention of any known physical forces), to name a few. Though such phenomena are difficult to study experimentally in the lab, they have been repeatedly described, both throughout history and across many cultures—not to mention in hundreds of reports from impartial observers in both the British and American Societies of Psychical Research. This again points to a cosmos broader than what is understood by conventional physics. At the most basic level, it suggests the possibility of a dimension or dimensions beyond physical space-time as we understand it.

There is an interesting parallel between modern physics and the multidimensional universe implied by paranormal events. Current paradigms in physics that attempt to unify the four known physical forces mathematically require the assumption of multiple dimensions—dimensions beyond the four known dimensions comprising space-time. Whether this mathematical requirement of contemporary models of the universe (such as superstring theory, discussed in physicist Brian Greene's *The Elegant Universe* (1999)) has anything to do with the multidimensional universe implied by survival and paranormal phenomena is an open question.

Human Consciousness

The most obvious, close-to-home example of a "subtle" or invisible nonphysical phenomenon is the human mind. No matter how hard you look inside the physical brain or body, you will never find the mind: thoughts, feelings, desires, memories, or sensations *as you experience them*. Do thoughts and feelings really arise out of the millions of neuronal signals and synaptic transmissions that occur every moment in the brain? We can certainly observe the activities of the brain through functional magnetic resonance or positron emission scans, but where would we ever "see" a restless mood or a feeling of mirth?

Consciousness does not easily fit into a materialist definition of reality; as a result, from a scientific standpoint, consciousness is often reduced to physical processes. The conscious mind is assumed to be either identical to brain processes or a product of brain processes. This kind of materialist model of the mind is still prevalent among scientists.

But can feelings, sentiments, motivations, personal meanings, and creativity really be reduced to the neurophysiological and neuroendocrine processes of brain cells? The two seem categorically and fundamentally different. Saying the mind is identical with the brain merely evades two fundamental questions. What is the mind (or consciousness)? How does this mind/consciousness interact with the physical brain?

This brings up philosophy's long-standing mind-body problem. There is no obvious way of reducing mental events to brain events. We cannot eke sympathy or joy out of neurons and neurotransmitters. For one thing, mental events appear to be of a more global (inclusive) order than neural brain events. A single thought, however rapid, takes place over a longer period of time than each of the thousands of neurophysiological events that co-occur with it. Thus, in the hierarchy of systems that make up a human being, the thought is likely to be of a "higher" order than neural brain events. It's likely that a particular thought process organizes or subsumes hundreds or thousands of neurophysiological processes, much like a command in a computer program orchestrates many electrical processes in the computer's hardware.

The Mind-Body Interaction

But what is a thought? If, like Descartes, we argue it's an altogether different category of stuff from matter, then we have to invoke metaphysical explanations for how mental and physical stuff interact. Viewing mind and brain as simply interior and exterior aspects of some common underlying reality is probably closer to the truth, yet still doesn't explain how the two interact. To be sure, mind is an *interior* phenomenon—it is the inner, subjective aspect of something experienced "from the inside out." We are not going to find the stream of consciousness *as we experience it* to be an object of our senses. There is no way we can view our own consciousness as an object, because *we are it*. Nor can we see another person's stream of consciousness as an object. However, we can perhaps *experience* the other's consciousness empathically.

If we could actually "see" another person's mind, we might possibly witness some kind of subtle energy phenomenon. Psychics have been known to see shifting fields (in multiple colors) around people; this is commonly referred to as the human aura or auric field. If such fields exist, they may be as close as we're going to get to an objective, exterior aspect of what we subjectively experience as mind/consciousness. These subtle fields are not physical fields as we understand them; they do not appear to involve any of the four known physical forces. Otherwise, we could measure them or perhaps correlate them to electrical nerve impulses or brain waves. The fact that we cannot measure them or observe them with instruments suggests that they are dynamic but not spatial. If they comprise some type of "energy," it's not an energy we can observe scientifically at this point in time.

The Nature of Thought

The fundamental question here is: If we could view mental processes *objectively* (not as we experience them from the inside out), what would they actually be? Are they field fluctuations within the brain that can be explained in terms of known energies—perhaps the global electromagnetic activity of the brain, or possibly quantum fluctuations of photons generated at a very microscopic level? From the outside, is consciousness simply a global type of electrical or quantum energetic phenomena? Certain considerations would argue against this. If there is any survival of consciousness following the death of the body, then consciousness (again, in its objective aspect) cannot be reduced to any type of electrical or even quantum field activity of the brain, both of which would end at death. While it may depend on such activity while an individual is alive, the fact that it persists after the individual's death implies a nonphysical type of process independent of known forces understood by physics. Further, if telepathy, clairvoyance, and precognition occur—and again, the evidence that they do is very ong—then consciousness can behave in a nonlocal, acausal way. The remote viewing of clairvoyance implies the mind can easily cross spatial boundaries; precognition (knowledge of the future) implies the mind can operate beyond linear time as well. Such behavior defies the known forces and laws of conventional physics, suggesting again that consciousness is fundamentally nonphysical and capable of operating independently of the physical world as we presently understand it.

So we are still left with the question, "What is consciousness?" More will be said about this in chapter 11, but let's discuss two basic approaches to the answer now. One approach, called *energy monism* by philosopher Mark Woodhouse (1996), views consciousness in its objective aspect as a subtle, nonphysical form of energy. Energy monism assumes that *everything* that exists is a form of energy, whether part of the space-time universe of physics or more subtle, transcendent dimensions beyond the physical. This has been a popular view throughout the history of philosophy.

In his classic study, *The Great Chain of Being* (1960), Arthur Lovejoy states, "The conception of the universe as ranging in hierarchical order from the meagerest kinds of existents through every possible grade up to perfection has, in one form or other, been the dominant official philosophy of the larger part of civilized mankind through most of history" (Woodhouse 1996, 98). While modern science focuses on only the lower part of the chain (matter, physical energy, and the four forces of nature), virtually all religions and many other metaphysical models of the cosmos speak of subtle domains (heavens, bardos, astral and causal planes, nirvana) where activities still go on, presumably involving various subtle forms of energy. The main difference between the physical universe and the subtle realms is not that the latter are non-energetic but that they simply exist at *higher frequencies or are faster-vibrating forms of energy*. Presumably they would have to travel faster than the speed of light, the cosmic speed limit for anything existing in physical space-time. From this metaphysical point of view, thoughts are still considered energies, they're just higher-frequency or higher vibrational energies. Though energy monism has its roots in ancient Hindu philosophy, two modern offshoots of it are *theosophy* (which proposes astral, causal, and spiritual planes of reality beyond the physical) and the popular late-twentieth-century philosophy of Ken Wilber. As touched on earlier, Wilber proposes a spectrum model of the universe with a hierarchy of eight progressively subtler levels, physical matter as the "lowest" and a transcendent formless realm as the "highest" (1998).

Energy monism is an elegant theory. It claims that everything is made of the same ultimate "stuff." The main difference between what exists in the physical universe of space-time and what exists in transcendent, nonphysical dimensions (the abode of ghosts, angels, devas, and other spirits) is not qualitative but quantitative. Energy that travels slower than light speed is in the physical universe; energies that travel faster are in the subtle realms.

Most physicists reject this model on the grounds that it conflicts with Einstein's general theory of relativity, which maintains that nothing can exceed the speed of light. Proponents of energy monism reply that Einstein's theory is simply one paradigm that will someday be replaced by a new physics that allows events to exceed light speed. Even if such a paradigm emerges, however, we are left with the paradox of how events can take place apart from space or time. The notion of angels or ghosts interacting with the physical world from outside of space is hard enough to grasp; the idea of subtle events taking place outside of time is truly paradoxical. This paradox of nontemporal processes and events is energy monism's greatest difficulty, unless the theory can be modified to allow for some different kind of "time"—perhaps time in an alternate form, something like the time experienced in dreams—in a different dimension that is parallel to the physical universe.

The alternative to energy monism is the proposal that what happens beyond space-time is not energy or a field phenomena at all, but something else that we cannot fully conceptualize or understand. Perhaps only information exists outside of space-time—but if so, how does anything get done in the transcendent realms? Information by itself is totally static; it doesn't do anything. Yet religions propose that souls continue to go about their lives in heaven (or hell) and angels or guides are constantly assisting us from some dimension beyond the world. The very existence of subtle or transcendent phenomena seems to imply some type of energy, or energy-like aspect, by virtue of the fact that they *act*—indeed, they *interact*—with the physical world. How they do this, or how any process could occur apart from linear time as we understand it, remains paradoxical. It is difficult to even conceive of events without time.

Some Mysteries Remain

While the evidence for a cosmos larger than the physical universe is quite compelling—perhaps beyond serious dispute—most of us are hard put to conceptualize exactly how it works. Perhaps there is a form of time in the transcendent realms, just not the kind of clock time we measure here on earth. Perhaps "time" in other dimensions is more like the "dream time" we experience while sleeping. This may be the closest we can get to understanding the nature of processes and events in so-called subtle dimensions.

Let's assume, for now, that the objective aspect of consciousness is some type of invisible or subtle "energy." As yet we don't have a very clear idea of what a nonphysical energy might be like. It would seem that for the mind (as subtle energy or fields) and brain to interact, some kind of energy must be exchanged between them. That means that energy could somehow be transferred between the observable physical world to dimensions beyond, and vice versa. (This brings us back to energy monism or a spectrum model of the cosmos.) Such energy transactions appear able to cross dimensional lines. When I decide to raise my hand, some form of energy moves from subtle to physical levels—between the mental process involved in my decision and the motor cortex of my brain that initiates the movement of raising my arm. So "energy," as it is defined broadly here, is whatever gets something done. We're assuming that if something gets done (as when mental intention actually moves my hand), then some kind of energy had to be involved in getting it done.

If this understanding of energy and consciousness is even partially correct, then the Cosmos must be larger than the physical universe. It must include other, nonmaterial dimensions in which mental and spiritual phenomena/processes occur. These processes are non-spatial—and perhaps nonlocal—in origin, but they can and do interact with the physical world. Perhaps the brain is a device for "localizing" the nonlocal, mental-spiritual aspect of identity so that we can negotiate the physical world. After the body dies, consciousness remains, either embedded in a nonmaterial subtle vehicle such as the soul or not. Perhaps we will have enough evidence someday to get a clear idea of what actually survives death.

Reality Includes Matter and Consciousness

The model of reality suggested here is neither strictly materialistic nor idealistic. The world isn't fundamentally only matter or fundamentally only mind; it is both. Both matter and consciousness are equally real. If we allow nature to expand to encompass all phenomena that exist, not just those observed in physical space-time, both matter and consciousness should be considered part of nature. The two interact with each other constantly and can influence each other by transfer of energy/information. Consciousness is nonlocal and not visible in space; the activity of the brain orchestrated by consciousness is both visible and measurable. (It's worth repeating that we are talking about the *objective* aspect of consciousness here, not its *interior, subjective* aspect.)

In short, while consciousness certainly involves information, it also involves a certain type of dynamic energy phenomenon. Consciousness is intelligent information that *acts*. We are left, then, with some form of energy monism: consciousness (in its objective aspect or substrate) and material reality may be viewed as different points along a continuum. The underlying fabric from which both matter and consciousness arise is the same.

Conclusion

The main point of this chapter has been to suggest that reality—the Cosmos in the broadest sense of the word—exceeds the bounds of the physical, material universe studied by science. Paranormal events such as clairvoyance and precognition imply the existence of processes independent of space and time. Much closer to home, the subjective contents of consciousness itself—the *qualities* of a person's feelings, sensations, desires, and inspirations—cannot be found anywhere in the physical brain or body. They can be experienced directly in the present moment but only become objects to awareness in memory.

Two hypotheses about the relationship of subjective mind to the brain (or material events) were suggested. One proposes that subjective mind is purely informational and doesn't require any form of energy as its substrate. A problem for this model is explaining the interaction of consciousness with the physical brain.

Energy monism, the other hypothesis described, proposes that subjective consciousness is based in a subtle form of energy that is not electromagnetic but interacts with electromagnetic fields in the brain. Energy monism implies a spectrum of energies of varying frequencies, with slower frequencies appearing as matter in the physical world and higher frequencies operating beyond space-time in other dimensions. It is compatible with the great chain of being proposed by many philosophical traditions as well as Ken Wilber's developmental model of consciousness. The difficulty with this hypothesis is explaining how subtle energy can "operate" beyond space and time.

In sum, the jury is still out on exactly what consciousness is and how it interacts with the physical world. Although reality currently exceeds the bounds of contemporary physics, a future physics may possibly provide us with a better comprehension.

7

Expanding the Scope of Valid Knowledge: Sensory vs. Intuitive Ways of Knowing

For the last three hundred years, what has been considered valid knowledge in the West has been largely restricted to scientific knowledge—that is, knowledge derived from scientific methods of inquiry. Only knowledge verified by the replicable sensory experience of multiple observers has been accepted. This excludes other types of knowledge that:

- Appear to correspond, at least in part, with events or phenomena other than what can be directly observed via the senses

- Are experiential but not solely based on sensory experience

- Have the characteristic of being considered "true" or "false"

The following are examples of types of knowledge that do not rely solely on sensory experience yet still involve statements we would hold to be either true or false.

Empathic Knowledge

This is a feeling-based type of knowledge that we gain about another person through direct interaction. For example, we might describe Sally as dependent, or Paul as authoritative. Our knowledge of another individual's personality characteristics is based both on sensory observation of the individual's behavior as well as a feeling-based capacity to understand—or share and participate in—that person's internal feelings, motives, and desires. We would have no basis for understanding personal traits like dependence, shyness, dominance, or compliance without interior knowledge of what these personal qualities are like—knowledge based on our personal experience of what it is like to be dependent, shy, dominant, or compliant. Sensory observation from the outside gives us only so much to go on; we further construct our knowledge of another's personality based on empathic knowing of their personal qualities from the inside out.

Psychology—particularly the subfields of personality, abnormal, and clinical psychology—expands the notion of empirical knowledge to include not only sensory but empathic knowledge as well. Clinical interpretations of personality are based both on sensory observations of behavior as well as empathic perceptions of a person's internal motives, impulses, feelings, defenses, projections, sense of self-worth, and other factors. Such perceptions are not possible on the basis of sensory observation of external behavior alone (though radical Skinnerian behaviorists once believed this was possible).

Practical "Life Experience" Knowledge

This is knowledge we gain about life through everyday experience. In philosophy it's often referred to as *existential knowledge*, or knowledge arising from the daily experience of living as a human being.

Existential knowledge is similar to what Aristotle calls "practical wisdom." Common examples are found in statements such as "sustaining an intimate relationship takes commitment and work," "forgiving someone else's mistakes frees the one who forgives," and "it is rewarding to be of service to others." Such knowledge is publicly acknowledged. We concur that there are certain truths or principles about life that are gained (sometimes hard-won) through life experience. Agreement varies depending on the statement involved. "Do unto others as you would have them do unto you" probably commands greater consensus across people and cultures than "one cannot live by bread alone." The greater the consensus such knowledge claims, the greater its universal acceptability.

Existential knowledge is not typically included in the domains of natural or social science (unless we are studying a particular culture's norms and moral prescriptions). The pure sciences are primarily concerned with theoretical and descriptive knowledge of overt phenomena—the "how things work" type of knowledge. Existential knowledge is practical; the most universal and widely applicable forms of it are usually spoken of as common sense or wisdom. Wisdom is a type of existential knowledge that has widespread applicability and has stood the test of time.

Existential knowledge has one thing in common with scientific knowledge: the more experiments that are done—that is, the more experiences gathered—the greater the trustworthiness of the knowledge. Scientific knowledge gains credibility with the replication of findings over time; similarly, we tend to grow wiser—have increasingly valid existential knowledge of life—through repeated experiences over the course of time.

Paranormal Knowledge

Paranormal knowledge is gained through processes of telepathy, clairvoyance, precognition, or retrocognition. In some ways, such forms of knowing are akin to sensory knowledge, even though they are often referred to as extrasensory. A concealed or distant object that is clairvoyantly "seen" can be empirically verified by an independent observer. Multiple independent clairvoyant observers may all see the same disease process occurring in an individual and come up with the same medical diagnosis. Someone who has experienced an out-of-body journey to a distant country can check the details of that journey against what is actually in the locale that was "visited."

Personal Insights and Intuitions

This is knowledge based on hunches or intuitive perceptions. Such knowledge is not publicly acknowledged and tends to be highly individual. If a hunch turns out to be confirmed by later experience, we feel it is valid or true. Others may or may not agree with us.

Intuitive knowledge may overlap with existential knowledge. When we have an intuitive sense about what is the "right" course of action in a situation, it's likely that we are drawing on our collective life experience. Other intuitive hunches may lead to new scientific or public knowledge. A classic example is the discovery of the benzene ring in chemistry through Friedrich Kekule's daydream of a snake chasing its own tail. This mode of knowing is not sensory. It is, however, *noninductive*: we immediately grasp something as a whole, without inferring it from a series of sensory experiences. Private insights and hunches are not part of a scientific inquiry's validation or verification of hypotheses. However, they play a role in the generation of hypotheses. They also contribute to our knowledge of others and can overlap with empathic knowledge.

Visionary-Mystical Knowledge

This is knowledge gained through meditation, contemplation, or direct revelation of a higher order or reality. Such knowledge is "perceived" in the mind's "inner eye" but does not involve an external, physical object revealed by sight, hearing, or touch. Examples include mystical experiences of the oneness or deep interconnection of all things; visionary experiences of angels, devas, and various spiritual beings; and near-death experiences of an afterlife or afterlife realm. (An entity such as a ghost or angel might appear like an ethereal or energetic "object," as if it were external, but it is not actually an external, physical object in the ordinary sense.)

All of these ways of knowing are experiential, yet in a broader way than experience based solely on seeing, hearing, touching, smelling, and tasting. They are all *participatory* ways of knowing, since they all involve a certain merging with or participation in the consciousness of what is known. Although sensory knowledge of material objects and processes involves an interaction with the object being observed, mediated by electromagnetic or mechanical vibrations, it does not involve participation—a merging of consciousness—between the knower and what is known. Participative forms of knowing are also, for the most part, intuitive. Knowledge tends to be grasped as an intuitive whole rather than built up from discrete sensory observations (though sensory knowledge may contribute to the finished result).

Sensory vs. Intuitive Knowledge

Throughout the past 2,500 years, there has been tension between sensory and intuitive/participative forms of knowledge. They tend to move in opposite directions. Sensory knowledge is usually atomistic. It begins by seeing things as parts and moves toward inferences about wholes. Intuitive knowledge, on the other hand, is global. It begins by grasping things as wholes, and may then break them down into parts.

The tension between the two forms of knowledge dates back to pre-Christian Greece, with Plato and the Pythagoreans coming down on the side of intuitive or direct, insight-based knowledge of ideal forms, and Aristotle, Democritus, and the sophists favoring sense-based knowledge. Plato held intuitive knowledge of the divine forms to be superior to sensory knowledge of outward appearances. In fact, he believed the entire visible world was a mere reflection of eternal, transcendent archetypes that could be grasped only through deep intuitive reflection. This view contrasted with more naturalistic explanations. Democritus and the atomists explained the world in terms of the random movements of an infinite number of neutral particles (anticipating in some ways modern atomic theory). Sophists such as Protagoras wanted to dispense with metaphysical explanations altogether, in favor of a skeptical pragmatism. In their view, the effort to understand the universe is misguided, and we can never really attain a true understanding. Thus knowledge should be practical and applicable to human life.

The problem with the sophist view is that it tends to degenerate into skeptical relativism and a purely utilitarian outlook ("whatever works for me or my culture must be true"). This left a spiritual vacuum in ancient Greece and leaves a void today in our current time when replayed as postmodernism. If human nature is the measure of all things, and there is no transcendent order, then how can there be any stable foundation for morals or knowledge other than what one particular society, culture, or individual happens to believe relative to another?

Socrates and his student Plato renewed the quest to find a solid foundation for morality and knowledge. Plato's concept of an archetypal "Good" and his belief in the ultimacy of pure mathematical/geometric forms provided the requisite foundation for moral, esthetic, and "scientific" judgments of his time. His view of the entire material universe as simply a reflection or outward manifestation of ultimate, nonmaterial, ideal forms subsequently came to be called *idealism*.

Aristotle developed a contrasting position. He believed that the quest for knowledge should begin not with intuitive knowledge of transcendent absolutes, but with sensory knowledge of concrete objects. Knowledge must be based on the evidence of our senses, and we must consider the concrete objects in our world as real. Qualities such as substance, shape, and movement are properties we abstract from concrete objects, not transcendent realities in and of themselves. Actually, Aristotle maintained that the abstract forms of objects such as trees or tables really did exist—and he referred to them as the "formal cause" of the object. However, form could not exist apart from an object, so its reality was fully embedded in the object and not independent. In fact, every object, according to Aristotle, had four different causes or explanatory principles associated with it: a formal, material, efficient, and final cause. So although, like Plato, Aristotle believed the patterning and ordering principles of the world were real, unlike Plato, he believed that reality was embedded in the objects themselves and neither transcendent nor self-existent. Aristotle's views—that sensory experience was the basis of knowledge and that we need to give primacy to the existence of material objects—were the beginning of the scientific approach to the world and its basic assumptions of *empiricism* and *materialism*.

Ever since the time of Plato and Aristotle, a tension has existed between these two fundamentally different approaches to understanding the world—the one based primarily on intuitive, participatory ways of knowing and the other relying primarily on sensory experience. Giving primacy to sensory experience leads us to a view of the world that is restricted to the natural, material universe we can observe, from atoms all the way up to galaxies. Giving primacy to the intuitive/participatory forms of knowledge leads to a view of the world that includes a more subtle, nonmaterial order—one that transcends or underlies what we can explicitly see. Throughout the ages this subtle realm has been described by mystics, visionaries, and sages, and forms the basis for the world's religions.

Jung's Functions of the Psyche

Twentieth-century psychology provided a new context for understanding these two approaches. Carl Jung differentiated four functions of the psyche: thinking, feeling, sensing, and intuiting (1976). Each individual tends to specialize in one or two functions, with the other two remaining less developed. The Myers-Briggs Type Indicator is a questionnaire that attempts to evaluate the relative primacy of these four functions in any particular individual. In Jung's theory, the goal of psychological development—what he called *individuation*—is to bring all of the functions into full, integrated expression. That is, if we tend to emphasize the sensory and thinking functions in our personality (what could be equated to the scientific approach to the world), then we need to develop and integrate the intuitive and feeling functions. Conversely, if we are well developed in the feeling and intuitive areas (what could be equated with a more participatory, inclusive way of knowing), we need to develop the rational and sensing functions. A fully actualized human being should be able to embrace all four functions. A fully functioning society should be able to do so as well.

Once again, looking at the history of Western thought over the past 2,500 years, we see that these two forms of knowing have frequently been in tension with each other. Different paradigms or worldviews have selectively emphasized one or the other.

Since the Renaissance, we've seen a renewed ascendance of sensory knowledge in the scientific approach to the world, beginning with Francis Bacon and continuing with scientists such as Galileo and Newton, as well as empiricist philosophers such as Locke and Hume. Intuitive/participatory ways of knowing—and the more subtle domains they reveal—were marginalized as subjective, irrational, or simply nonsensical by the Enlightenment as well as nineteenth- and twentieth-century science. Up until the late twentieth century, scientific empiricism continued to dominate humanity's conceptions of both valid knowledge and the nature of the world.

Over the past thirty years, there have been many signs that participatory/intuitive knowledge is starting to regain legitimacy after centuries of disregard. Several books have dealt with intuition as a basis for creative knowing. Humanistic psychology, which emphasizes empathic awareness, has played a large role in our modern understanding of human personality, motivation, and development. There has been a resurgence of interest in paranormal phenomena and knowledge gained through paranormal processes such as telepathy and clairvoyance. There has been a similar interest in visionary ways of knowing of indigenous societies. Contemporary philosopher Ken Wilber has called for recognizing all forms of knowing as equally valuable and appropriate to their particular spheres (1996).

It would seem apparent that both ways of knowing—intuitive/participatory and rational/sensing—are part of the full human capacity to comprehend the world. Ultimately we need to stop relegating one or the other and, instead, integrate them in our approach to understanding the world. Any epistemology (or ontology) that fails to do so is limited and cannot provide a complete picture of the cosmos.

What has given sensory knowledge a consistent advantage (in being accepted as valid) is that it lends itself more easily to consensual validation. Nearly everyone can agree, based on direct observation, that "the cat is on the mat," if indeed there is a cat sitting on a mat. There is a simple, direct correspondence between observation and what is observed. Because of the easy replicability and reliability of sensory observation, the hard sciences have restricted themselves to descriptions and explanations of the sensory domain. However, the "soft" sciences—such as clinical psychology and the more interpretive aspects of sociology and anthropology—have attempted to go beyond the sensory level to the empathic-participatory domain. Yet philosophy, literature, art, and religion still provide the primary modes of inquiry into the existential and intuitive-visionary domains of knowing.

The Question of Validity

For the past three hundred years, intuitive/participatory knowledge has stopped short of being considered valid because it commands less consensual agreement. Two people may have different empathic perceptions of the same individual, or different interpretations of the significance of some news event. Although some people see angels, not enough of us do (at least as yet) to give angels the same objective credibility as apples or apple trees. So all of the participatory forms of knowing are interpretative; however, the same can be said for scientific knowledge framed within the context of a ruling paradigm.

Participatory knowledge gains credibility as the level of its consensus increases across individuals or cultures. The greater the level of interpersonal and cross-cultural consensus, the more widely accepted a piece of intuitive knowledge tends to be. "Do unto others as you would have them do unto you" has a high level of acceptance—most people in most cultures agree on it. "A higher power exists who/which can answer prayers" has a slightly lower degree of consensus but is still widely accepted by many people worldwide. "Angels and spirit guides inspire us" has considerably lower public acceptance, as relatively fewer people (and cultures) have experiences that support such a proposition. Yet the general belief in a spirit world holds some credibility simply because it is part of so many religions throughout the world, even if different concepts and terms are used to describe it. Thus we can *begin* to evaluate the validity of participatory knowledge based on intuition or revelation according to how consensually accepted it is. The greater the degree of consensus across individuals and cultures, the greater the potential for the knowledge to acquire widespread credibility. On the other hand, intuitive/participatory knowledge that is not highly consensual is not necessarily false. It does, however, have less basis for being accepted into the body of established, public knowledge on a par with scientific knowledge.

Does a high degree of consensus across individuals and cultures guarantee that knowledge is "valid"? Not always. After all, for centuries people across the world believed that the earth was flat and the stars revolved around it, even though these beliefs turned out to be false. However, the same could be said for scientific knowledge based on sensory experience. Nineteenth-century atomic theory was overthrown by twentieth-century quantum mechanics. The Newtonian understanding of motion and gravity were overthrown (or rather enlarged) by Einstein's special and general theories of relativity. Ultimately, all knowledge of the world is interpretive and subject to revision, although this may be less the case for the most universal forms of existential knowledge, what is referred to as wisdom. Could the highest forms of wisdom be more universally and lastingly true than our best scientific theories of the universe based on sensory experience? Greek philosophers such as Plato would have argued that this is so.

The New Paradigm: Expanding the Concept of Valid Knowledge

A fundamental realization of the new paradigm emerging in our time is that the distinction between sensory and other-than-sensory forms of knowing is largely arbitrary. *It's equally arbitrary to reduce the universe or reality to only what is revealed through sensory knowledge.* Just because the sensory domain is more easily validated through consensual observation than the other, non-sensory domains does not make it more real, only more easily observed. The mistake of the past three hundred years has been to confuse the *reality (ontological status) of phenomena with their accessibility to consensual, sensory observation.* When we do so, we reduce the universe to what Ken Wilber has called "flatland"—a neutral material object devoid of purpose, spirit, or meaning (1996). As we reclaim all forms of knowing, with full awareness of the difficulties of validating the subtler (empathic, intuitive, and visionary) forms, we begin to reclaim a much more comprehensive and spiritually meaningful universe. We also begin to bridge the four-hundred-year-old split between science and religion. There is only one cosmos "out there" (and subjectively within all things). Although we tend to project our own dichotomies onto it, *the Cosmos is inherently undivided and whole.*

The evolution of consciousness over the next few hundred years may lead to greater acceptance of wider portions of intuitive/participatory knowledge. When the day arrives that many people are clairvoyant and telepathic, knowledge based on clairvoyant and telepathic perception may gain validity, much the way sensory knowledge has now. When most people, rather than very few, are able to "see" spirit guides and angels, the existence of such entities may be validated and knowledge about them may join the domain of public knowledge. In short, as consciousness evolves, so will the credibility of intuitive knowledge. (Granted, this process may take a few centuries to unfold in Western society.)

When intuitive/participatory knowledge gains equal footing with sensory knowledge in the public domain, a universe much grander in scope than the physical universe will be readily accepted, even in academia. A cosmos containing subtle, nonphysical dimensions along with the observable physical ones will be common knowledge for everyone.

At present, intuitive knowledge tends to be more interpretive and more culturally determined than sense-based, empirical knowledge (though a case can be made that the sensory knowledge of science is also highly interpretive and culture-based). Do we thus need a fundamentally different approach in evaluating the credibility of intuitive/participatory knowledge? Or can we use the same criteria for validity—that is, correspondence, consensus, and replicability—that are used with sensory knowledge, albeit with lower expectations regarding how well intuitive-based knowledge can meet such criteria? This question is left for the reader to ponder.

Conclusion

To conclude, for the past few hundred years, empirical knowledge mediated by the senses has been the sole arbiter of our understanding of the world. More participatory forms of knowing—including empathy, insight, paranormal knowledge through processes such as telepathy and clairvoyance, and spiritual revelation—have been deemed purely subjective. The emerging worldview broadens the scope of what constitutes valid knowledge. Equal credence is given to intuitive ways of knowing alongside those based strictly on the senses. One hundred years ago, William James spoke of this idea— that all forms of human experience might have evidential value in our knowledge of the world—with his proposal of a radical empiricism (1902).

It appears that the cosmos we inhabit has both an objective and a symbolic, meaningful face and can only be grasped fully through the entire range of human experience, both sensory and intuitive. These two forms of knowing draw upon different human faculties, though they are confirmed in a similar way. Repeated observations and consensual validation across observers and cultures enhance the credibility of intuitive knowledge, just as they do in the case of empirical knowledge of science.

8

Toward a Synthesis of Science and Religion

Science developed by separating itself from religion. It needed to distinguish itself from the medieval-scholastic view of the world about four hundred years ago to make any genuine progress. As Willis Harman points out, "This division of realms [between science and religion] gave the scientists a relatively free hand in physical discovery. It provided a respected barrier behind which they might conveniently pursue their research, untrammeled by the constraints of personal conscience and/or political and religious censorship"(1990, 21). It would have been confusing for scientists, attempting to deduce natural laws based on observation of natural phenomena, to have to contend with teleological or purposive processes like those which informed the Aristotelian worldview. Nor would it be easy for science to deal with consciousness, active minimally in organisms and, potentially, at other levels of the objective world as well. No wonder science has since the Renaissance completely divested itself from association with religion and theological explanations of nature.

Science and religion have a long history of conflict. They are two areas of human endeavor and experience that are fundamentally different in purpose, yet share an interest in understanding the world. Both seek to plumb the nature of reality, even if their methods and results are quite different. Both seek to fathom and uncover the "truth," albeit different kinds of truth. Science seeks *objective* truth about the laws and principles that govern natural phenomena. Religion seeks *existential* truth about the ultimate meaning of human life in the face of inevitable death. In theology, it seeks a metaphysical understanding of realities presumed to lie beyond the physical world. Giving equal credibility and legitimacy to these rather different types of truth is essential to resolving the long-standing conflict between science and religion. What is needed is a view of reality and the cosmos large enough to embrace both kinds of truth.

To be sure, there are some very significant differences between science and religion. Their fundamental goals differ. Science basically tries to account for natural phenomena in terms of mechanistic and statistical laws and principles. Religion is primarily concerned with providing a way of life that offers an overall worldview, ethical norms for human behavior, and institutions that serve a worshiping community. The generalizations of science are primarily descriptive; those of religion are both descriptive and *prescriptive*. The kinds of questions asked by science and religion also differ. Science asks how does something work or how can it be explained in terms of natural causes. Religion, on the other hand, often asks why is human life the way it is, or what is the meaning of life. In explaining why something happened, it may invoke cosmic or divine purposes or symbolic meanings. Finally, the basis of knowledge and understanding in the two domains differs. Scientific knowledge is based on replicable sensory experiences of independent observers. In religion, knowledge is often based on intuitive or revelatory personal experiences that are not easily replicated.

In short, science and religion differ in their fundamental goals, the kinds of questions they ask about events, and the types of experience on which their respective worldviews rest. Yet despite these significant differences, there is one respect in which they are quite similar: science and religion share a mutual interest in arriving at an understanding of the world and of human life, at "getting at the truth" of reality.

Historically, the different accounts they give about the world and life have tended to clash. Scientists claim that while religion is a matter of personal preference, there is no objective evidence for any religious claims about God or what lies in or beyond the physical world we see. From a strictly scientific perspective, although religious beliefs serve important psychological and sociological functions, they have no inherent validity because no scientific evidence supports them. Thus religion oversteps its bounds in claiming that religious beliefs are true statements about what actually exists in or beyond the world.

Religious authorities, on the other hand, claim that although science is a valid enterprise within its own sphere, it cannot answer fundamental questions about life and its ultimate meaning or purpose. Thus it has no business evaluating the legitimacy of theological or metaphysical beliefs. Scientists cannot *disprove* the existence of God or religious beliefs, such as those about redemption and grace, or karma and reincarnation. From the standpoint of religion, science oversteps its bounds when it makes metaphysical claims about what does or does not exist (for example, the materialist thesis that nothing but physical phenomena can exist, or the empiricist assumption that only what is observed by the senses can exist). According to religion, just because we can't systematically observe and measure angels or divine providence doesn't "prove" that such things don't exist.

How can science and religion be brought closer together? One way is to focus on the similarities—rather than the differences—in their respective attempts to understand reality. At least two points of similarity come to mind.

Both Science and Religion Rely on Paradigms to Interpret Reality

A *paradigm*, according to Thomas Kuhn, is a cluster of conceptual and methodological assumptions embedded in a particular tradition of scientific work (1970). Paradigms blur the sharp distinction between theory and observation science once claimed. New data are accommodated and understood within the frame of reference of a particular paradigm. An established paradigm tends to be resistant to falsification, since discrepancies between the paradigm and new data are—for a while—set aside. Anomalous data that do not fit the paradigm are often marginalized or neglected. For example, experiments on quantum entanglement have demonstrated nonlocal, "simultaneous influence" between separate particles that cannot be explained by conventional physics. This anomaly has not been adequately accounted for by mainstream theory in physics, and, in spite of its momentous implications, has been relatively neglected by adherents of the prevailing paradigm.

Religious paradigms or theologies are even less subject to falsification and more inclined to explain anomalous phenomena by ad hoc hypotheses than are scientific paradigms. For example, all kinds of ad hoc hypotheses have been proposed by Christian theology to explain the existence of evil in the world, which appears to be incompatible with the existence of a loving and omnipotent God. The point is that the difference between scientific and religious paradigms is one of *degree*—it's not an absolute, irreconcilable difference. In both cases, paradigms are not easily displaced by conflicting evidence.

In Both Science and Religion, Phenomena of Interest Are Shaped by the Subjective Characteristics of the Observer

Observed events can never be totally independent of the theories and assumptions of the observer. Thus interpretation enters into observation for both science and religion, though clearly more so for religion (the multiple interpretations of the Bible and other sacred texts attest to this).

In quantum physics, the influence of observation on the system observed is crucial. In relativity theory, the measurement of the mass, velocity, and length of a moving object depends on the frame of reference of the observer. In experimental biology and psychology, the outcome of an experiment is often skewed in the direction of the preferences or expectations of the experimenter, a phenomenon called experimenter bias. This is the basis for doing blind or double-blind experiments in research on human subjects.

In religion, the concepts of the believer shape what is seen to an even greater degree. Near-death experiencers who are Christian may see Jesus or angels, while those who are Hindu may see Hindu deities such as Krishna or devas. The concepts of each religion tend to influence their adherents' perceptions of numinous phenomena. However, again, the difference between the "observer" in science and in religion is one of degree, not kind. In both cases, the phenomena being observed are shaped by the categories and perceptual biases of the observer.

In brief, though religion and science differ in their primary functions and roles, they share a common interest in uncovering the truth about reality. Certainly, their approaches to understanding the world differ: scientific knowledge relies on direct, replicable sense-experience, while religious knowledge relies on intuition, revelation, and visionary experience. Science attempts to explain the world in terms of mechanistic or probabilistic factors, while religion is more concerned with symbolic meanings and purposes. However, despite these differences, their respective approaches to the world converge in three respects: both rely on creative insights in developing views of the world; both rely on paradigms that are relatively resistant to falsification; and in both domains observations are shaped by the assumptions of the observer.

Integrating Science and Religion

What would it take for scientific and religious conceptions of reality to be brought closer together—even married? The view of reality shared by most of humanity would certainly need to be enlarged beyond the materialistic and mechanistic view that presently prevails in mainstream science. *Materialistic* implies the assumption that only material phenomena have real existence, and that anything else—such as mind and consciousness—can be reduced to them. *Mechanistic* implies the assumption that everything in the universe can be accounted for in terms of mechanistic processes (or statistical probabilities in the quantum world), and that anything else—such as evolution and human intentions—can ultimately be explained in terms of such processes. What would such an enlarged view of reality look like? It would likely include at least the following three characteristics:

- A Way of Combining Mechanistic Explanations with Teleological Explanations (Explanations in Terms of Purposes) into a Single View of the World

Nature would be understood to be intrinsically purposive or intentional on all levels; purposes would not be reduced to causal mechanisms. For example, a biological cell has a purpose to maintain and replicate itself. Yet the constituent processes of the very same cell can also be understood causally—cellular metabolism can be understood in terms of numerous biochemical and biophysical processes. This would certainly be a radical change from the prevailing view, but it's not a new idea. Aristotle, Plotinus, and Aquinas all proposed this type of view in the past, while Whitehead (1933) and Sheldrake (1981) proposed models of the world along these lines in the twentieth century.

- ## A Way of Including Consciousness in Nature or the Universe Without Reducing Consciousness to Material Processes

Consciousness would be understood as a phenomenon in its own right, one that can both influence and be influenced by material events. In chapter 6, it was suggested that consciousness (in its outward aspect as an ordering intelligence, not as subjectively experienced) and matter may be understood as different levels within a common spectrum of energy phenomena. Consciousness and matter are viewed as different forms (some would say vibrational frequencies) of some ultimate energy, one material and observable, the other subtle and invisible to ordinary sense perception. It follows that interactions between consciousness and matter involve specific types of energy exchange. Someday, the details of this interaction may be understood scientifically. If they are, we will finally have a solution to the age-old mind-body problem. The idea that consciousness and matter are different levels of a common spectrum is not new. It's been around for a long time, from ancient Hinduism through modern theosophy and the writings of contemporary philosopher Ken Wilber.

- ## Ways of Relating Ego Consciousness (Ordinary, Everyday Awareness) to "Higher" Levels of Consciousness

Relating ego consciousness with higher levels of consciousness—for example, Jung's collective unconscious and the supraconscious described by transpersonal psychologists such as Ken Wilber and Stan Grof—would be a major expansion of the prevailing consciousness paradigm. Right now, psychology tends to marginalize

Jung and transpersonal psychology. (This larger view of consciousness is explored in detail in chapter 9.)

A Broader View of Valid Knowledge

These expansions of the consensus view of the world would need to be accompanied by a broader view of what constitutes valid knowledge. As suggested in chapter 7, in addition to ways of knowing based on sense perception, other, more participatory/intuitive ways—such as empathy, insight, revelation, and visionary experiences—would also come to be regarded as valid bases for knowledge. One hundred years ago, William James referred to this idea as *radical empiricism*: the notion that nothing within the full domain of human experience should be excluded as a potential basis for knowing reality.

If radical empiricism is adopted as the basis for the *consensus* view of reality, then ideas of what constitutes a satisfactory level of consensus may need to be modified as well. Current scientific standards of consensus may need to be relaxed somewhat. This is not because radical empiricism is methodologically sloppy, but because the phenomena of interest do not so easily lend themselves to replicable, consensual observation. Presently, the level of intersubjective consensus required for scientific knowledge is quite high. This is appropriate for sense-based knowledge of natural phenomena such as subatomic particles, cells, tectonic plates, stars, and galaxies. However, intuitive and revelatory experiences do not lend themselves as easily to such high levels of intersubjective consensus. The fact that they are more subject to individual and cultural interpretation should be taken into account when evaluating the validity of knowledge based on such forms of experience. Not as many people have experiences of synchronicities or spirit guides as have experiences of thunderstorms or solar eclipses—and yet, experiences of synchronicities and spiritual guidance are common enough to achieve a *relative* level of consensus. If radical empiricism is to become the basis for a much broader view of reality than allowed for by present-day science, then we must also accept that the more subtle, nonphysical aspects of such a reality are less amenable to the high levels of consensus possible with sense-based knowledge of physical phenomena.

A Radical Departure from the Scientific-Materialist Worldview

This shift toward radical empiricism may be the most significant departure of the emerging worldview from the current, prevailing scientific view of the world. Such a shift is necessary if science and religion are ever to be even partially integrated. Science has dictated that we can only reliably know what lends itself to a very high level of replicability and consensus among independent observers. The broader view suggested here includes a much wider range of experiences as legitimate. It does not exclude intuitive, paranormal, or revelatory experience just because they are more subject to interpretation and less amenable to interobserver consensus. Instead, it maintains that there may be a wide variety of phenomena that we can include in our view of reality, even if they are more difficult to experience and less easily agreed upon. Such a viewpoint may not be acceptable to many mainstream scientists, but for those who find it compelling, a bridge between science and religion becomes possible.

Conclusion

To conclude, it would seem that the distinction between scientific and religious approaches to understanding the world will ultimately turn out to be an artificial one. Why? *Because there is only one world or universe that should ultimately require only one explanation and understanding.* There cannot be two entirely separate realms—one explained in terms of physical, causal laws and the other in terms of spiritual forces, purposes, consciousness, or conscious intelligence. Although science and religion offer two very different kinds of explanations about the universe, these interpretations ultimately apply to the same universe. Apparently the Cosmos is so wonderfully rich and complex that it requires both types of understanding. The outer, spatial domain has its explanations in terms of natural, causal laws, and the interior, conscious domain has its explanations in terms of psychological, sociological, archetypal, and spiritual concepts. However, both the outer and inner domains map onto the same underlying "reality."

If there is only one reality that both science and religion are seeking to understand, it seems evident that the clash between their respective views of such a reality *is in our minds*, not inherent in the nature of things. It seems inevitable that eventually—perhaps even in the twenty-first century—humanity will arrive at (or actually rediscover) a more unified view of the world, in which scientific and religious accounts complement rather than clash with each other.

9

A New Map of the Psyche

Science has provided a detailed map of the objective world, from subatomic to galactic levels of phenomena. But what kind of map exists of the subjective domain of consciousness? At present, there is no single such map, but a variety of partial maps—maps that are incompletely sketched, sometimes conflicting, and not yet fully integrated with one another.

Levels of the Psyche

One way to conceptualize the inner world of consciousness is in terms of levels. The three most common levels distinguished since the advent of transpersonal psychology about thirty years ago are the conscious, subconscious, and supraconscious mind or awarenness. These three basic levels vary along a dimension metaphorically described in terms of both depth and height. The subconscious, for example, is said to be at a "deeper" level than the conscious mind. Similarly, the supraconscious is said to be at a still deeper level. Alternatively, the supraconscious is also said to be a "higher" state of consciousness than ordinary, everyday, wakeful consciousness. (The *supraconscious* transcends personal history and provides the spiritual foundation of awareness.)

But what do these metaphors of depth and height actually correspond to—if anything? Ancient Vedanta philosophy and modern theosophy would probably say "subtlety or frequency of vibration"—that is, spiritual or supraconscious levels of awareness are thought to be vibrating at a higher frequency than the more gross, ordinary states of consciousness. The question is, vibrations of what? Is there a "stuff" of consciousness that vibrates at variable frequencies? Is it some form of energy—perhaps, as some have suggested (for example, Laszlo 2004), the zero-point energy contained in empty space? Or if consciousness can survive and exist independent of the physical body, is it ultimately something beyond all physical measurement? (The question of what consciousness might actually be made of, if anything, is discussed in greater detail in chapter 6.)

Another characteristic of deeper, or higher, levels of consciousness is that they are usually thought to be more inclusive. The "lowest" level of consciousness—immediate conscious awareness—is associated only with an individual's own personal ego. If we follow Jung, collective or archetypal levels of consciousness exist beyond the individual person (even the personal unconscious described so well by Freud) and are connected with all of humanity. Finally, consciousness at its highest level—the supraconscious—may be associated with the entire universe or all that exists.

It's worth looking at these various levels a little more closely. Freud distinguished between the preconscious and unconscious mind. The former contains recent memories of which we are unaware at any given moment, while the latter contains repressed memories from the past associated with unpleasant or traumatic experiences. Unacceptable, repressed sexual and aggressive impulses also reside in Freud's unconscious. Freudian defense mechanisms such as repression, projection, and sublimation work at an unconscious level to protect immediate awareness from painful or unacceptable memories and impulses.

Jung's collective unconscious goes a step further. It is a repository of archetypes: universal patterns of experience common to humanity in general but highlighted in the lives of certain individuals. The hero archetype, for example, is played out in any life that overcomes enormous obstacles in order to achieve some social good, such as the life of "Superman" Christopher Reeve. The earth mother archetype is embodied in the life of a woman who gives herself over completely to caring for children, animals, or anyone in need.

Beyond the collective unconscious lies the supraconscious mind, a realm of visionary and mystical experiences that transcends the bounds of ordinary human experiences and concerns. The Jungian self emerges out of this supraconscious domain; it orchestrates the individuation or unfolding of a human life from a point of reference well beyond ego goals and projects. *Psychosynthesis*, developed by Roberto Assagioli (1975), speaks of a "higher self" along similar lines: a superordinate force in the psyche that serves to integrate all of the disparate subpersonalities that underlie an individual's inner conflicts. Beyond the higher self is the universal self or Atman spoken of in Hinduism, which is the point of contact and convergence between individual consciousness and the universal consciousness underlying all that exists. Mystical experiences of oneness—involving a complete disappearance of ego boundaries—can occur at this level.

Consciousness, as it progresses to deeper and more inclusive levels, forms a sort of enlarging cone. At the apex is individual ego consciousness, and at the base is the unbounded consciousness of all that is. Moving into deeper (or higher) levels of awareness through meditation or other means, we approach a level where there is no longer any boundary between individual awareness and the unlimited awareness behind everything. What is important is that all of these levels of consciousness are seamlessly connected. Distinctions among levels are ultimately conceptual, not real. Immediate awareness can open into collective and supraconscious levels of awareness as we move more deeply into our innermost being through meditation or perhaps drug-induced experiences. Individual consciousness is simply the fountainhead of a vast wellspring that ultimately has no bottom or boundary.

Various Hierarchies of Consciousness

According to transpersonal philosopher Ken Wilber (1977), the different levels of the inner domain of consciousness are not only increasingly inclusive but hierarchical. Each progressive level supersedes and contains all previous levels. Wilber's writings span thirty years, and his "spectrum" model of consciousness varies somewhat between his earlier and later writings. However in essence it contains the following stages:

- *Sensory*: physical body sensations

- *Emotional*: feelings and impulses

- *Mental*: thoughts, reasoning, the realm of rational mind (sometimes broken down into Piagetian stages of concrete and formal operations)

- *Centauric*: awareness of the integrated body-mind, capable of vision and creativity

- *Subtle*: awareness of the soul and intuitive perceptions of subtle dimensions (including the universal Jungian archetypes mentioned above; also the level of the "higher self"; in reincarnation models, it is the aspect of us that endures between lifetimes and carries the complete knowledge of all of our lifetimes)

- *Causal*: the inner spirit or spark around which the soul develops (the realm of deities, angels and archangels, creator-gods such as Shiva and Vishnu, and Platonic forms; the first point of manifestation of the unmanifest Godhead or Source; everything here exists in unified resonance with the Godhead)

- *Ultimate*: the formless ground of all that exists, totally beyond rational or even visionary comprehension (this level can only be experienced through complete dissolution of a personal sense of self and total unification with all that is; it is the "suchness" or "thatness" that both utterly transcends and yet interpenetrates everything)

In a similar vein, theosophy goes from mental to etheric, astral, causal, spiritual, and finally nirvanic levels, with various "subtle bodies" (for each individual) corresponding to each level. In his book *Forgotten Truth* (1992), Huston Smith also differentiates between subtle, causal, and spiritual levels of consciousness.

Quite a bit of lore from the world's various spiritual traditions describes different phenomena that can be experienced at each of these levels. The subtle or astral level is said to be the abode of psychic phenomena, Jungian-type archetypes, and all kinds of good or not-so-good spirits. It is here that the human soul is said to reside between earthly incarnations. The celestial or causal level appears to be the realm of Platonic forms, angels, deities such as the Christ, Buddha, Vishnu, and Shiva, and other assorted nondual entities (duality still occurs at the subtle level but not the causal level). The boundless, formless, or ultimate level does not contain particular beings or entities at all; it is undifferentiated and unified.

Consciousness can expand—grow in inclusiveness—through all of these levels. In what is called channeling (the transmission of messages from the spirit world), our consciousness can expand to the astral or causal levels as we connect with particular spirit guides or "ascended masters." When consciousness expands to the universal, formless level, we experience complete unification and oneness because there is no longer any boundary between personal awareness and the most universal awareness. The personal ego dissolves into a boundless unity, the Buddhist nirvana.

Toward a Single Map of Consciousness

Different cultures and traditions have somewhat different maps of the inner domain—for example, the Buddhist bardos or the shamanic lower, middle, and upper worlds. In the West we have psychoanalytic, Jungian, and transpersonal maps of consciousness. Is there a way to arrive at the "best" map? The current plurality of maps of the inner domain somewhat resembles the plurality of maps of the outer world that existed during Greek, Roman, and medieval times prior to the development of modern science. Will we eventually develop a "science" of the inner domain that will lead to a universally accepted map that everybody around the world can agree upon? What kinds of advances in our ability to impartially observe the inner domain are needed for such a science to develop? Presently, we're still at the point of defining the important questions.

For one thing, as discussed in chapter 7, we will surely need a broader definition of what constitutes valid inquiry than that presently accepted by conventional science. The exploration of consciousness depends on developed insight and intuition, not just sense experience. Ken Wilber would probably call for a highly trained and standardized group of meditators. Would this enable us to arrive at a "standard model" of the inner domain? What about a group of highly trained and gifted psychics? We might need psychics to tune in to the subtle/astral level, which seems to be their specialty, and meditators to tune in to the celestial and formless levels, since they are generally trained not to get hung up on the psychic level. Which of the psychics or meditators' "observations" are we to accept as valid? Presumably the observations they could all agree upon and that could be replicated. Consensuality and replicability across different sources would seem to be the minimum criteria necessary to validate observations of the inner domain.

If a science of consciousness is possible, it will differ from present-day science in some fundamental ways: It will use intuitive and visionary experience of the inner domain of consciousness as its basis for "observation." Moreover, it will somewhat modify the high standards of interobserver agreement and replicability required by present-day empirical science. Again, though not impossible, strict consensus about the inner domain of consciousness is harder to come by than consensus about the outer world of sensory experience. Clearly, personal and cultural interpretations affect inner experiences of consciousness more than outer experiences of the physical world. Nonetheless, it seems likely that humanity will gradually approach a single, universally accepted map of the psyche and consciousness. Eventually, the various models—philosophical, theological, and metaphysical—of today will be seen as early, culturally distinct mythologies that attempted to fathom the depths of consciousness.

Further Aspects of a New Map: Transpersonal vs. Personal Self

Understanding the various levels of consciousness (the conscious, personal unconscious, collective unconscious, and supraconscious aspects of awareness) just described is an important initial step in elaborating a new map of the psyche. Another key step lies in the distinction between the transpersonal self and the personal self.

Transpersonal Self

Transpersonal literally means beyond the personal—what lies beyond our ordinary, everyday experience of life and ourselves. The *transpersonal self* refers to the background awareness or "presence" that exists prior to conditioned thoughts and feeling-reactions. It is the formless consciousness that precedes all self-conceptions and identifications. It is that which is capable of observing the contents of experience, while existing apart from the stream of particular thoughts, feelings, and sensations that make up ongoing experience. Carl Jung referred to the transpersonal self as the "Self"; Roberto Assagioli, the founder of psychosynthesis, called it the "Higher Self." It is related to the concept of the soul in Judeo-Christian theology. These various conceptions suggest that the transpersonal self has several features:

- It is the silent witness, the "inner observer" within us that is capable of observing our stream of experience. While it can observe the content of awareness, it cannot stand behind or observe itself. It cannot be an object of awareness since it is the source of awareness itself. (This idea—of the transpersonal self as an inner witness—is an important concept in Buddhist psychology.)

- For Carl Jung and Roberto Assagioli, it is the integrative function of the psyche. In this aspect, the transpersonal self accounts for a person's capacity to integrate unconscious and conscious aspects of personality. The transpersonal self is also able to embrace and integrate conflicting subpersonalities, such as the inner child and adult aspects of our psyches. The transpersonal self, in this aspect, is always seeking wholeness. It manifests itself in behavior to the extent that a person functions as a whole being (body, mind, and soul integrated as a whole).

- As a metaphysical construct, the transpersonal self also includes the soul that precedes birth and survives death. In Eastern philosophy, especially Hinduism, it is the aspect or entity that exists through a series of reincarnations (in each incarnation the soul projects through a different body and personality). The soul grows through its many incarnations until it has run the gamut of possibilities on the earth; it then returns to other dimensions—"planes" in Hinduism or "bardos" in Tibetan Buddhism—to complete other experiences. The ultimate destiny of the soul is unification (actually reunification) with Deity or God. Issues or patterns that the soul has to work out over many lifetimes are called sanskara or karma. These generally correspond to the most salient conflicts or issues, whether intrapsychic or interpersonal, that a person experiences in the present.

Personal Self

In contrast to the transpersonal self, the *personal self* is the concept our mind forms of ourself. It consists of the vast number of concepts, images, attributes, roles, identifications, and stories we have constructed about ourself over a lifetime. It is the self-concept or "me" that we are continually aware of and strongly identified with. Specifically, it is pure awareness (the transpersonal self) identified with a multiplicity of forms. A popular term for the personal self in spiritual literature is the *ego*. This is not exactly the same as Freud's ego, which is an executive function that permits us to mediate among the competing demands of the id, superego, and outer environment. Rather it is a self-concept—a set of constructs, images, and stories we hold and maintain about ourselves. This ego is who we are to ourselves.

Human beings are not content just to be—to merely experience the ongoing stream of conscious experience. Each of us has an inherent need to define the essential mystery of what we are in specific terms. It's difficult for us to go through our lives—especially in relationship to others—as mere beings. Instead, we seek to fill our formless existence with content—to construct a "me" or personal self. According to Eastern spiritual traditions (especially Buddhism), it is this personal self that keeps us separate from our essential nature, which is formless and beyond definition. This essence is what we brought with us into this world, before we identified with our mothers and fathers, with their values, and with our culture's norms. Upon entering the world we were as close to pure consciousness as is possible in a human life, albeit contained within a tiny human body with its own natural urges, desires, and instincts. The dependency of an infant does not obscure the fact that the infant is still close to expressing the pure radiance of the formless ground of all existence (call it nirvana, divinity, or God), for it does not yet have boundaries set up by specific identifications, that is, by a personal self.

Though we come into the world close to pure consciousness, the moment of birth renders us separate. The very act of birth is itself a profound separation. As we mature, we come to feel separate from our parents, separate from our siblings, separate from our peers at school, and separate from the society in which we develop. Most significantly, we become separate from our deepest selves. None of us grows up with the unconditional acceptance, love, and approval that we yearn for. So we learn to hold back and disassociate from those aspects of ourselves that are not deemed acceptable—or perhaps not understood—by our parents and our society. We do not grow up close to our essential being, but as the child of our parents and a member of our society. Who we become is based on our internalization of parental and societal expectations, values, and approved roles.

This separation, both from others and ourselves, leaves us with a feeling of emptiness. When we feel empty, it is simply human nature to fill the emptiness in hopes of making ourselves feel more complete.

So the personal self tends to identify deeply with various persons, enterprises, and things. Whatever we value the most, be it family, career, love relationships, accomplishments, roles, property, our bodies, or specific positive or negative images of ourselves, that is what holds the personal self together. To the extent any of these strong identifications is diminished, our ego may feel profoundly lost or bereft, because its very existence is dependent upon these identifications. Again, whatever you value or identify with the most is a clue to what deeply constitutes your personal self.

Ego identifications limit us to a specific set of self-imposed images and roles. Yet we seem to need them. They enable us to reduce the totality of what we are down to a manageable size and shape that fills or completes us. We acquire self-definition to feel as though we are a "somebody." This helps us to feel better oriented in our everyday dealings with ourselves, others, and the world.

Dynamics of the Personal Self

Our personal self, or ego, tends to separate us both from our essential being and from everyone else. (Again, at the depth of consciousness, we are deeply interconnected with others and ultimately all things.) This allows for the possibility of being threatened by otherness—that which is not ourselves. The need to protect or defend ourselves from others (people or things) perceived as threatening is the origin of self-will and the need to be in control. It is also the origin of fear.

Because the ego perceives itself as separate from others and the world, it strives to keep everything under control. Thus self-will is a manifestation of our separation from our innermost being—and ultimately a separation from the pure consciousness that underlies everything. Were we to let go and be fully in alignment with our innermost being, we would recognize that we are radically interdependent with everyone and everything that exists. We would understand that our own being, like all other discrete beings, is simply an aspect of a single reality (the ultimately formless Godhead). We would see that we are all facets of one diamond, different reflections of one Source.

Disidentifying with the Personal Self

Eastern religions, particularly Buddhism and Hinduism, define the spiritual quest in terms of relinquishing or disidentifying with the personal self in order to abide in or align with the transpersonal self. Ego identifications are understood as obstructions to our true identity—the pure beingness or presence that underlies all discrete thoughts, images, and concepts we might have of ourselves. Suffering results from our attachment to and identification with things that are ultimately transient. The end of suffering—referred to as "liberation" or "enlightenment"—is the release of ego identifications to such an extent that all that remains is what has always been there in the first place: the transpersonal self, the formless presence that is the ground of all experience.

Disidentifying with the personal self literally means we do not define ourselves (actually our consciousness) through a particular self-concept, role, subpersonality, belief system, thought, or emotional pattern. We are able to stand outside of these mental constructions (in sixties jargon, "head trips") and create enough space around them so that they do not claim or run us. Instead of identifying with them, we take a step back and impartially witness them.

It's important to distinguish between disidentifying with your ego and denial or repression. This distinction is frequently misunderstood. When you disengage from your ego, you do not ignore, deny, or repress painful parts of yourself—parts that are angry, fearful, sad, guilty, or compulsive. Rather, you stop resisting these states and instead impartially witness them. In fact, you still fully experience all of your thoughts, feelings, painful sensations, desires, impulses, and motivations, but without reacting to or judging them other than simply observing them just the way they are. Instead of identifying with them, you develop the ability to notice what is going on internally and say: "Oh, this particular (thought, feeling) is up right now. That's interesting." You may be stuck in a particular thought or feeling for a while, but you have the ability to stand back from it. Sooner or later you will relax into the spacious awareness of your transpersonal self. The popular term for this capacity to witness the ongoing content of consciousness is "mindfulness."

Both Buddhism and Hinduism advocate meditation as the "royal road" to disidentifying with the personal self or ego. Consistent practice of meditation reinforces our inherent connection to the transpersonal self and gradually loosens the connection to the ego's conditioned patterns of thinking and reacting. Over time, meditation can lead to the liberation of our innermost being from the suffering stemming from identification with our personal self and ego attachments. (Chapter 22 offers a further introduction to meditation.)

To sum up, disidentifying with the personal self implies the ability to embrace all of our thoughts, emotional reactions, self-images, and roles, while being able to move fluidly from one aspect of ourselves to another. We do not get stuck or overidentify with any one of them in particular. If you find that you are stuck in a particular emotional reaction pattern or looping set of thoughts, relax and allow yourself to just be with it—to observe it—in the present moment. Simply being with your immediate experience, observing it nonjudgmentally, and letting time pass (sometimes a long time) may allow this to happen. If you allow yourself to be mindful of your ongoing experience long enough, eventually everything you have pushed back over a lifetime will come up to be processed and released. Practicing meditation regularly will enhance your ability to be mindful of your experience.

Transpersonal States and the Path to Liberation

In mystical states our personal sense of ego boundaries and identifications tends to drop away. A direct experience of unity or oneness with a larger reality—variously described as nirvana, cosmic consciousness, enlightenment, or salvation—becomes possible. Both Eastern religions and the mystical traditions within Judeo-Christian religions encourage the cultivation of these states.

The Eastern path to liberation—through disidentifying with ego—was brought to the West in the twentieth century. Early teachers from India, such as Paramahansa Yogananda and Maharishi Mahesh Yogi (founder of transcendental meditation), did much to disseminate its basic teachings in Europe and the United States. Later, American teachers, such as Ram Dass, Jack Kornfield, and Jon Kabat-Zinn, were influential in bringing meditation to a wide segment of the population. More recently, Eckhart Tolle has developed an articulate, westernized version of the basic teachings about mindfulness and relinquishing the ego that has had a wide appeal (2005).

The Role of Transpersonal Psychology

No discussion of a new map of the psyche would be complete without mentioning transpersonal psychology. For more than thirty years, the field of transpersonal psychology has attempted to explore the transcendent aspects of human experience in a systematic way. The field considers itself a "fourth force" in psychology, in addition to psychoanalysis, behaviorism, and humanistic psychology. Unlike theology and metaphysics, transpersonal psychologists use the experimental and clinical methods of mainstream psychology to study mystical, unitive states of consciousness as well as the further reaches of human development, beyond ego and ego adaptation. They strive to integrate the insights of modern psychology with the world's contemplative traditions, especially those of the Far East. Ken Wilber's hierarchical stage-theory of human development is a central model within the transpersonal field at this time. Apart from Wilber's theories, the field encompasses a diversity of studies, including Hindu and Buddhist psychology, shamanism and Native American healing, meditation research, adult spiritual development, psychedelic peak experiences, diagnosis and treatment of spiritual problems and pathologies, deprogramming of former members of cults, dying and near-death experiences, past-life regression, and many other topics.

Transpersonal psychology is presently eclectic because it is still in an early stage of development. In the present century, however, it is likely to become a primary source for the new model of the psyche described in this chapter. A comprehensive sampling of the field can be found in the *Journal of Transpersonal Psychology*, published quarterly since 1970.

One exception to transpersonal psychology's eclecticism is Ken Wilber's previously mentioned developmental theory of consciousness, probably the best-known attempt to date to unite Eastern and Western psychological conceptions into a single paradigm. Wilber's model is elaborated in a variety of books, such as *No Boundary* (1979), *The Atman Project* (1980), *Up from Eden* (1981), and *A Brief History of Everything* (1996).

Conclusion

For the past few decades, a new model of the human psyche has been emerging. Forerunners of this model include teachings of ancient Hinduism and Buddhism as well as the twentieth century writings of Carl Jung and Roberto Assagioli. This model goes beyond the Freudian distinction between conscious and unconscious minds to propose a supraconscious mind that transcends the boundaries of the personal self. The supraconscious mind reflects archetypal and universal aspects of consciousness associated with collective humanity and the cosmos at large.

The supraconscious mind is also intimately associated with the transpersonal self, referred to by Jung as the Self and by Assagioli as the Higher Self. The transpersonal self has been variously associated with the inner observer that stands behind the conditioned mind, with the organizing function that integrates disparate parts of the psyche, and with the traditional concept of the soul.

Other aspects of the emerging model of consciousness reflect traditional Buddhist psychology, particularly the notions of identifying and disidentifying with the personal self or ego. Ego identification limits our consciousness to the set of stories, attributes, and investments that make up our self-concept. From a Buddhist standpoint, this is a construct that has no ultimate reality. (Many non-Buddhist spiritual traditions, however, posit an individual soul that persists beyond earthly life and/or for multiple lifetimes.) The ego's hold is released when we let go and align with the pure consciousness of our innermost nature instead. Mindfulness meditation is a potent practice for disidentifying with the ego, but ego transcendence can also occur through prayer, ritual, hypnotic trance, and spontaneous or drug-induced mystical experience.

The field of transpersonal psychology has investigated the dimensions of the psyche beyond the ego for the past thirty years. Though still quite eclectic in its studies, transpersonal psychology provides a foundation for a possible science of consciousness independent of the culture-based formulations of the worlds' religions. A systematic framework for understanding both personal and transcendent aspects of the psyche has been proposed by Ken Wilber. However, a universally accepted framework for understanding the inner domain of consciousness still lies in the future. The following two chapters provide a few further steps in this direction.

10

Life-Force Energy: A Step Beyond Physics

What we speak of as the "life force" in everyday conversation is not recognized by mainstream science. Life force cannot be observed or measured directly, so science does not (yet) view it as a legitimate part of nature. Biophysical studies of electrical processes within the cell, and recent studies of communication between cells via photons, examine visible correlates of the life force, but not the life force itself. Notions that attempt to account for the self-organizing and self-maintaining properties of living organisms—such as Rupert Sheldrake's theory of morphic fields (1981)—are discredited by conventional science. Yet the energy of life is so much a part of us, and so obviously present, that denying its existence would be absurd. We can sense energy in being cared for and loved by another human being, even if we are not directly touching that person. Our life-energy level or vitality fluctuates according to whether we are sick or well, and changes from morning to evening. That we work off excess energy through exercise and take in life energy from sunlight and food seems obvious. Still, the energy we are so intimately in touch with doesn't fit easily into any of the four categories of energy permitted by physics: electromagnetic, gravitational, and strong and weak nuclear forces. It appears to be something else; what it actually is remains a mystery. Science sidesteps the life force because it lacks an adequate explanation for it.

While our present level of technology does not have the apparatus to detect the life force directly, apparently our human perceptual faculties do. We have the capacity to perceive energies and forces that are seemingly above or outside the physical world as presently understood by science. What these capacities are, however, is not clear, although one finds references in esoteric literature—for example, in the works of Rudolph Steiner—to "subtle senses" and "subtle sense organs." This doesn't really tell us much. What constitutes a subtle sense? Are subtle senses related to what Hindu and other metaphysical traditions speak of as the "third eye" or sixth chakra? Whether they exist or not, subtle senses are a convenient way to talk about the human ability to perceive subtle phenomena beyond the ken of the physical senses.

Throughout human history, only the Western scientific worldview has neglected to explore and examine the life force in detail. Names for this force abound in other cultures, ranging from *ki* or *chi* in Japan and China to *prana* in India. Several ancient societies mapped the distribution and flow of life force throughout the body thousands of years ago. Of these, the Chinese acupuncture meridian system and the eastern Indian nadi and chakra systems are probably the best known. Both of these systems detail elaborate pathways in the body through which subtle life energies flow.

Detecting Life-Force Energy

Recent times have seen a few preliminary attempts to investigate these ancient systems in an objective manner. A Japanese scientist, Hiroshi Motoyama, has developed a device that apparently locates and measures energy flow through acupuncture meridians. Using this device (called the "apparatus for meridian identification"), Motoyama has found streams of ions flowing in the interstitial layer of tissue just beneath the surface of the skin (1981). What is remarkable is that these streams of ions correspond exactly with the location and distribution of acupuncture meridians mapped out thousands of years ago. (It's important to recognize that these electric ion streams are not equated with life-force energy in and of themselves; rather, they are physical markers that appear to parallel and mirror the flow of subtle energy.) The strength of chi measured by an acupuncturist's pulse diagnosis corresponds exactly with the strength of charged ion flows measured by Motoyama's device. This offers us some preliminary scientific support for the existence of a subtle life-force energy and the channels of its flow identified long ago by Chinese medicine. The exact nature of this energy, however, and its relation to physical, electromagnetic energy, remains a mystery.

Motoyama has also developed another device—the chakra instrument—for detecting and measuring the activity of the seven chakras (Gerber 2001). *Chakras* are subtle energy junctions or centers; they have been part of Indian spiritual practice and Ayurvedic medical theories for three thousand years. A fairly detailed understanding of the chakra system (as part of the energetic anatomy of the person) has also spread in the West during the past forty years (see, for example Anodea Judith, 1996). Motoyama's chakra instrument is able to detect the numbers of photons (units of light) being emitted at the location of each chakra. Meditators and yogic adepts who have "awakened" their chakras appear to emit substantially higher numbers of photons than ordinary people. Also, by focusing on a particular chakra, an individual can greatly increase the number of photons it emits. (Again, this device is looking at an electromagnetic correlate or marker of subtle-life energy—not the energy itself.)

In short, Motoyama and certain other progressive scientists have provided some preliminary evidence, not for subtle energy itself, but for electromagnetic signatures of it. To date, mainstream science has simply ignored these initial findings. This trend is likely to change as more research appears and funding for such research increases.

The Human Biofield

While Eastern medicine has explored the centers, points, and channels in the physical body directly associated with the life force, Western metaphysics, drawing from Eastern concepts, has described an energy field, or "energy body," surrounding the physical body. This field is sometimes referred to as the human aura. A more recent, quasiscientific term for it is *biofield*. The biofield can change in relative size, intensity, and even color. Scientific instruments easily detect electromagnetic fields surrounding living organisms and, in fact, surrounding inanimate objects as well. What they cannot detect, however, is so-called subtle anatomy, such as chakras and meridians. Nor is it possible to scientifically detect colors in the biofield that correlate with emotional states and personality traits. Yet thousands of intuitive individuals commonly report "seeing" colors around people that reveal their emotional states and personality. What do we make of this? It certainly appears to be a form of intuitive or paranormal knowledge outside the compass of ordinary sensory-based observation. Replication and consensus among independent intuitive observers would afford such phenomena credibility, much in the same way replication and interobserver agreement among scientists bestows credibility on empirical knowledge. Specifically, with respect to the human biofield, the objectivity of any observations about a particular individual would gain credibility if several independent intuitive observers agreed on the intensity, quality, and colors of that subject's biofield. (Popular intuitive healers, such as Rosalyn Bruyere and Barbara Brennan, have done interesting preliminary work in this area.)

What is the nature of the subtle fields surrounding human beings? What kind of "stuff" is the life force made of? It's clear that the electromagnetic fields around the body (as well as ion-mediated charges conducted by neurons) are a measurable part of the physical world. However, more subtle phenomena, such as chakras, meridians, or auric colors perceived in the biofield, are a different matter. Are they physical or nonphysical? Are they *supraluminal* (faster than the speed of light) components of some cosmic energy spectrum that both includes and transcends the physical world—or something entirely different? Faster than light energies would require a radical revision of current physics, which, following Einstein, has maintained that the speed of light is the speed limit for all known phenomena. (One yet-to-be-proven interpretation of nonlocal phenomena in physics is to assume that they involve supraluminal processes.) Whatever the life force is composed of, it must represent a type of energy or energy field that is different from the four basic forces that make up the world studied by physics.

Levels of the Biofield

In esoteric traditions from Vedanta to theosophy, the biofield is often said to consist of different levels or different "subtle bodies."

Acupuncture meridians and chakras refer to the first level, often called the *etheric body*. Other levels proposed by esoteric literature include astral, mental, causal, and spiritual levels or bodies. These various levels are not separate but interpenetrate, merging with each other. They can be understood as different frequency bands (somewhat like different frequency bands on a radio) progressively more refined or of higher frequency. It is commonly proposed that the different levels vary only in their relative vibratory rates. The notions of vibratory rates and frequencies seem to imply that these various levels consist of some kind of energy. However, as mentioned, it is not the kind of physical energy we ordinarily understand, since these levels or domains exist independently of the four types of forces or energy fields known to physics. Except for the etheric body, they even appear to transcend physical space. They are more related to the interior aspect of the world associated with the mind, psyche, and consciousness.

A Matrix for the Life Force

Do the subtle bodies (astral, mental, causal) spoken of in esoteric literature provide the matrix of the life force? If so, we are left with a deep paradox: How do these so-called subtle bodies get anything done? How do they order and orchestrate life? How do they act on the physical body while existing outside of three-dimensional space? As Kant recognized long ago, it's difficult for us to imagine how anything can do anything outside of space or time. Nonspatial action is hard to imagine. Action without duration (time) is even harder. However, in either this century or the next, physics may be able to offer us a coherent account of a multidimensional universe in which both spatial and nonspatial dimensions exist and interact. Current models of superstring theory already require multiple dimensions beyond the four-dimensional space-time view of the universe popular in the twentieth century.

Brief Descriptions of the Subtle Bodies or Fields

Though at this time they remain highly speculative, it is worth examining the nature of the various subtle bodies that may form the foundation of the life force. The following descriptions are drawn from a variety of sources, ranging from early accounts by theosophists such as Rudolph Steiner and Annie Besant, to a modern account presented by physician Richard Gerber in his book *Vibrational Medicine* (2001). Keep in mind that a future science of consciousness may dispense with the notion of subtle bodies altogether, as the existence of an invisible, nonphysical body is paradoxical, if not contradictory. It may be that the concept of a *field* will be employed instead, and we will speak of subtle fields— perhaps along the lines of Sheldrake's morphic fields—that orchestrate and direct life processes. One advantage of the field concept is that it may be able to straddle both sides of the fence between physical phenomena and consciousness.

Etheric Body (Field)

The *etheric body* is an invisible duplicate of the physical body that is thought to exist at a higher frequency than the physical level. It functions as a matrix or template for the development of the physical body. It's sometimes referred to as the "etheric double."

In Ayurvedic medicine, the etheric body is described in terms of prana, nadi, and chakras. In Chinese medicine it's described in terms of chi, meridians, and points along meridians that can be manipulated to increase the flow of chi.

Rupert Sheldrake refers to something like the etheric body of an organism as a *morphic field* (1981). He argues that the persistent organization of all living things, from single cells up to complex organs like the brain, as well as entire organisms, is governed by these morphic fields. For example, during fetal development, cell differentiation—into various types of tissue—is governed by an individual's genetic code. The etheric body's template then guides the various different types of cells in the emerging fetus to their appropriate spatial locations. Conventional biologists reject Sheldrake's notions, arguing that morphogenesis will eventually be fully explained through the operation of genetic, and biochemical processes. Yet intuitives who claim to have observed fetal development maintain that they can "see" the etheric body as it appears early in pregnancy and then functions as a "mold" that guides the development of the fetal body.

The etheric body has never been photographed directly. The *phantom leaf effect*, however, offers indirect evidence for it. It is possible to amputate the upper portion of a leaf, destroy the amputated portion, then electrically photograph the remaining leaf. The resulting image reveals the fully intact leaf as it appeared before the upper portion was amputated. The portion of the leaf that appears where it should be missing is called the "phantom leaf"—much like the phantom limb that an amputee may experience—and is believed to reflect the etheric body or template of the leaf. Some scientists have disputed the phantom leaf effect and claim that it is an artifact of the particular photographic technique (Kirlian photography) used to capture the effect. If the effect turns out to be able to withstand scientific scrutiny, however, it will be the most direct evidence available for the existence of something like an etheric body.

The etheric body also assists cells to reassemble into the appropriate configuration during wound healing. It helps the normal cellular reproductive systems to direct the right cells to the right locations in order to fill in missing tissue.

Of course the concept of the etheric body is quite controversial. Mainstream medicine and biology believe it is simply a convenient fiction invoked to explain processes that science will eventually be able to explain. The question is how science will perform this feat, since what we readily perceive and describe as the life force does not lend itself to explanation in terms of electromagnetic or any other known physical force.

Astral Body (Field)

The *astral body* is the basis for the qualitative aspects of our feelings. On a physical level, emotional reactions are identified objectively with the activation of limbic brain centers and the autonomic nervous system. The subjective, qualitative aspects of our feelings, however—the qualities we actually experience when we feel sad, happy, anxious, angry, and so on—reside in the astral energy field, or body. Such qualities cannot be objectively located anywhere in space.

The astral body is not as strongly attached to the physical body as the etheric body, and appears able to move around somewhat independently of the physical body. Robert Monroe's out-of-body travels are sojourns of the astral body (1994). Part of human consciousness appears able to move into the astral body and move about in the dimension in which the astral body "resides." This can occur in the form of out-of-body experiences when a person is awake, and is believed by many to be common at night during dreaming.

During a near-death experience, consciousness may withdraw into the astral body. Thus a person may be able to "see" their physical body—perhaps being resuscitated—from a remote vantage point. After being revived, individuals are often able to report specifics of procedures done on their "lifeless" physical body, which they couldn't have possibly seen with their actual eyes.

If we accept the existence of the astral body, then emotional disturbances are due not only to neuroendocrine imbalances in the brain as proposed by neuropsychiatry; or to etheric body disturbances as dealt with by acupuncture, homeopathy and, more recently, energy psychology; but also to disturbances in the astral body or field itself. There are probably reciprocal influences, both top-down as well as bottom-up, among the various levels of the human energy system. Just as faulty beliefs and irrational thoughts can affect emotional, etheric, and physical levels, so can physical imbalances in the nervous, endocrine, and immune systems affect subtler levels.

At death, the astral body—and any subtler bodies that inform it—detaches from the physical and etheric bodies and continues to have an existence on what is referred to as the astral plane in theosophy, heaven (or hell) in Judeo-Christian tradition, Summerland in some of the Native American traditions, and the bardos in Tibetan Buddhism.

Dualism still exists at the astral level. Less advanced souls (in an evolutionary sense) are believed to reside at lower astral levels, while more advanced/evolved souls reside at higher astral levels. Many different spiritual philosophies believe in the notion of multiple levels of the astral dimension. Those that propose there are demons (for example, Swedenborg and fundamentalist

Christianity) consign them to the lowest astral levels, otherwise known as hell, Hades, or the underworld.

Mental Body (Field)

This is the realm of language, intelligence, and—at higher levels—intuitive wisdom. From a scientific standpoint, the left hemisphere of the brain is responsible for these functions, but our subjective experiences of thinking, problem-solving, and both deductive and inductive logic exist at the level of the mental body. Metaphysically, the mental level of reality is involved wherever intelligent order exists, from the organization of atoms to galaxies, as well as in nonphysical beings such as angels. In Sanskrit, the entire spectrum of this intelligent order is referred to as the *manasic plane.*

The mental body is powerful because it is the seat of our core beliefs and assumptions, which have an enormous influence on our perception, emotional life, and behavior. The beliefs we hold about ourselves, others, our environment, and life in general, largely create the reality we inhabit.

Emotional disorders often have their origin in the mental body. At this level, mistaken, fear-based beliefs can create various kinds of emotional imbalances and conflicts in our astral/emotional body, which can ultimately work their way down to physical disease. Modern psychotherapy works with the mental body when utilizing a cognitive approach: changing dysfunctional beliefs about self and others is assumed to help promote both emotional and physical well-being. On the other side, psychotherapists also encourage people not to deny or repress their emotions through excessive rational control, which can lead to conflict. Free expression of feelings—in an appropriate fashion—is important for health and well-being. Wholeness depends on an integration and right balance between the astral (emotional) and mental bodies.

Causal Body (Field)

The *causal body* is a close counterpart of what has been called the soul. It's called "causal" because, from the level of the causal body or the so-called causal plane, it is possible to see the "true causes"—the spiritual causes—of ailments. In indigenous cultures, shamans treat health problems at this level. When we speak of the "condition of a person's soul"—whether it is open or closed, fearful or love-based, innocent or malevolent, hopeful or crushed—we are referring to the causal body.

The deepest desires of our soul originate at the causal level. When we hold to these desires and believe deeply in them, they tend to manifest at the mental, emotional, and physical levels, as do all causes which begin at this level. When we ask the question, what is the higher purpose of a sickness, mishap, or negative event, we attempt to evaluate the situation from the causal level. The causal level has to do with the larger or spiritual purpose of events rather than the ego's perception of them.

The causal body also contains a record of all that has been experienced in both a person's current life as well as other life-times, forming the basis for experiences that come to light in past-life regressions. Thus, the causal body is the ultimate basis of our individuality; it is beyond the ego identity of this lifetime or any other. Unresolved experiences carried from one lifetime to the next (such as traumatic imprints, conflicts, or guilt about wrongdoings) are retained in the causal body. In Vedanta philosophy, these unresolved experiences and the patterns of behavior they result in are called *sanskara*. Sanskara sometimes manifest physically in the form of birthmarks or physical defects; sometimes they may manifest emotionally in the form of fears or phobias that appear at an early age, seemingly without cause.

The symbolic or larger meaning of what happens in a person's life occurs at the causal level. Often this is also called the archetypal level. This is the vantage point from which we search for the "higher purpose" of life events. Learning to interpret the symbolic meanings of dreams is one way to access this level. We can analyze wakeful experiences similarly.

A common contemporary belief is that we can create our own personal reality. If we truly wish to manifest a personal intention, it must be held at a place deeper in our innermost being than just the mental level. When we consistently hold an intention at the level of our soul or causal body, it has a greater likelihood of manifesting—especially if it is in harmony with the rhythm or flow of universal, archetypal forces and does not conflict with personal karma or anyone else's karma. Miracles originate from the causal level or from even higher levels.

Celestial or Spiritual Body (Field)

The *celestial body* is an individual's divine spark. It is that innermost, deepest part of our being that is pure love and radiance. Ultimately it is that part of God or the Godhead that projects through a person's individuality. It is eternal and entirely indestructible. When Jesus said, "I am the Light of the World" and "the Father and I are One," he was fully identifying with his spiritual body. Any of us can do the same; when we do, we may experience mystical states of awareness or cosmic consciousness.

The celestial or spiritual realm is beyond all polarities and dualities. It is the residence of angels, archangels, and other angelic entities, such as those spoken of in the Judeo-Christian tradition as thrones, dominions, powers, seraphim, and cherubim. These beings (and numerous others, with various names, depending on the religion involved) exist in complete resonance and alignment with the Godhead or Source, so their activity can be said to be the same as or identical with the cosmic expression, flow, or movement of the Godhead.

The celestial or spiritual body is the highest level at which the Godhead is differentiated or divisible. The goal of spiritual evolution is to eventually return to this level.

Ultimate Level

The *ultimate level*, is referred to in Buddhism as the Void, is not really a body or a field as it is beyond all form and differentiation. It cannot be described or conceived. However, the most profound mystical states of which humans are capable—those where our ego entirely dissolves into a universal unity—are said to provide access to it. It is the wholly transcendent aspect of the Godhead prior to any differentiation. In the *Tao Te Ching*, Lao-Tzu describes this level in these terms: "The name that can be named is not the eternal Name. The Nameless is the origin of Heaven and Earth." Very little more can be said about it.

The status of these various subtle bodies or fields within the human biofield remains controversial at best. Although long established in esoteric traditions such as theosophy, they have largely been ignored by mainstream science. They are presented in this chapter not as a definitive statement of the nature of reality, but as intimations of where we might look for an understanding of the life force and ultimately consciousness itself. Living creatures clearly have capacities not adequately explained by present-day physics and biology, such as self-organization, self-maintenance, and intentionality. Whatever force or field is responsible for these properties will ultimately be explained through a deeper understanding of the various domains or dimensions of consciousness.

Conclusion

The "energy" of life cannot be fully explained in terms of the four known forces of physics: electromagnetism, gravity, strong and weak nuclear forces. Ancient healing arts such as Chinese medicine and Ayurveda have studied the distribution and dynamics of the life force—referred to as chi and prana, respectively—in great detail, providing models that explain how it works in both health and disease. Some initial correlations have been found between measurable biophysical phenomena and these ancient models: ion streams correlate with acupuncture meridians and photon streams with the physical locations of chakras. Yet our knowledge remains rudimentary at best. A model of multiple bodies—or perhaps better, fields—within the human biofield (etheric, astral, mental, causal, and celestial) provides an intriguing (though provisional) way to connect the physical body to the more subtle, non-physical substrate or substrates of the life force. This particular model originated in ancient Vedanta philosophy, was carried forward by theosophy, and has been utilized by Ken Wilber in his developmental theory of consciousness.

On the surface, the life force seems obvious to us in our everyday experience. Yet a full conceptual grasp of what it is, whence it originates, and how it interfaces with measurable biophysical processes in the body awaits future breakthroughs in our understanding.

11

Understanding Consciousness*

Consciousness is notoriously difficult to define. Its ineffability is remarkable, even paradoxical, given that it is so intimately connected with our moment-to-moment experience. To attempt to understand it, we can start by defining consciousness as a state or quality of being that is characterized by sentience and subjectivity. *Sentience* can be defined as the capacity to feel or be aware of, however dimly, anything within or beyond our immediate experience. At the very least, we can say animals and humans have the capacity to experience their environments; inanimate things like tables and chairs do not. *Subjectivity*, in turn, can be defined as the capacity to have a point of view from the inside out. Objects are things and events perceived as external without any internal point of view. In contrast, a subject is something that can have a point of view toward an object; it is the seat or locus of a point of view.

As a subjective phenomenon, consciousness is *interior* to things—not in a spatial sense of being physically inside, but in an ontologically distinct sense of "from the inside out." Teilhard de Chardin expressed it as the "within" of things (1959); philosopher Thomas Nagel described it as the "what it feels like from within" (1998). This is an important point. The interiority of consciousness is not the spatial interior of anything we might regard as an object. It is an ontologically distinct category: a state of being, directly experienced from the inside out. Objects are perceived by a conscious subject as distinct from that subject. But consciousness, in

* **Note:** This chapter offers a somewhat more philosophical exploration of consciousness and may not be of interest to all readers.

its essence, cannot be an object unto itself, because it is a state of being. We can be aware of our thoughts and feelings the moment after we experience them (in fact, they are actually very recent memories). Yet that which is aware—the seat or source of our awareness—can only ever be. It is fundamentally a state of being and cannot, in the moment of experience, be an object unto itself.

The solution to the perennial mind-body problem isn't to regard mind or consciousness as *merely* subtle energy or nonspatial stuff that somehow mysteriously interacts with the brain. As discussed earlier, this is the solution Descartes proposed four hundred years ago, and it's fraught with problems. No matter how subtle, energy or stuff can never constitute an interior point of view. Energy, perceived as an objective process, can never reason or intuit or feel happy or sad. Mind and consciousness *as experienced* are categories of being—we can "be" our experience directly, but it does not occur as an object of our sensory faculties. The difference between brain and mind is not a matter of different types of substance but one of ontologically distinct points of view: on the outside versus from the inside out.

If there is a solution to the mind-body problem, it is likely to be some form of *monism*: mind and body as flipsides of a common coin. The physical brain is the exterior aspect that we observe as physiological and biochemical processes. Mind is the subjective counterpart that is experienced as a stream of thoughts, feelings, and sensations. Whatever the stuff—or, better, process—is that underlies both mind and body remains a mystery. There are, though, certain concepts from the objective side that seem to correspond rather closely to what happens on the subjective side. The concept of a *field*, for example, can be applied to both physical and subtle energy fields as well as to the notion of a "field of consciousness." If there is a point of correspondence between objective brain processes and the subjective stream of consciousness, it may lie in events/processes described in terms of fields.

Sentience and subjectivity aren't the only distinguishing characteristics of consciousness. Other characteristics include:

Intentionality: the ability to refer to or be *about* something else. A typical state of consciousness such as believing, doubting, or hoping is about something. Ordinary physical objects such as lamps or chairs are not about anything.

Purpose: the capacity to aim toward a goal. Purpose is closely related to intentionality. We can assign purpose to a physical object such as a chair, but it does not make any sense to regard the chair in and of itself as aiming for any goal. Physical objects without consciousness do not pursue goals.

Self-agency: the capacity to direct oneself. What is conscious has the capacity to move itself internally. It is self-directing and self-organizing. Though it may be influenced by external factors, it can be said to be its own source of causation. As such, it may be said to have the capacity for choice.

Meaning: the capacity to have import or significance. Subjective experience has meaning to the subject who is experiencing it. Meaning is not ordinarily a property of what we view as objective events and processes. Meaning is experienced from the inside out.

The Reach of Consciousness

What is the extent of consciousness? Is it confined simply to the human brain? Descartes thought so, excluding consciousness in the sense of a mind even from animals. If consciousness is characterized foremost by qualities such as sentience, subjectivity, and self-agency, how far down the evolutionary scale does it extend? Are worms conscious? Are plants conscious? If so, in what sense? It would appear that organisms all the way down to bacteria display self-agency. How a bacterium might experience subjectivity or sentience isn't clear but is certainly within the realm of possibility.

In his recent book, *Radical Nature* (2002), Christian de Quincey argues that consciousness extends beyond living organisms, all the way down to the most minute elements of physical reality, such as molecules, atoms, and even subatomic quarks. He maintains that to say consciousness is an emergent phenomenon that appears only at higher levels of organization leaves a significant question unanswered. It does not tell us where consciousness comes from or how something ontologically distinct from objective nature—something with properties of subjectivity and sentience—could ever occur.

For consciousness to suddenly appear out of nowhere would, de Quincey argues, require a miracle—it would be a bit like suddenly pulling a rabbit out of a hat. Thus, the argument goes, consciousness must be an inherent aspect of things all the way down to microentities such as atoms and subatomic particles. If this is true—if there is indeed an interior or subjective aspect to everything—then in some sense atoms and even electrons are capable of experience and sentience, although perhaps in a way that is only dimly comparable to human experience. In taking this position, de Quincey echoes Alfred North Whitehead, who developed a cosmological model in which all processes, down to the most microscopic, are capable of *prehending*—taking into account—other processes and events. De Quincey calls his point of view *radical naturalism* and points out that it has numerous predecessors in the history of philosophy—the lineage of *panpsychism*—in which mind, consciousness, and subjectivity inherently inform matter at all levels.

Consciousness at the most minute level is suggested by the fact that quantum events are acausal. The inherent indeterminacy of quantum processes implies that the exact moment an electron jumps orbit, or a radioactive particle is emitted from an atom, is entirely random—which may be interpreted as saying it's entirely uncaused. This is Niels Bohr's view and that of most quantum physicists. Only Einstein took the position that "God doesn't play dice," arguing that there must be underlying causes that are invisible or undetectable. Could it be that Einstein was right, but not in the way he might have supposed?

If quantum particles are in some sense "conscious" and their behavior is not caused by any discernible forces, could their behavior be self-caused? This is the position of philosopher Arthur Young, who argues that describing an event as uncaused, amounts logically to saying that it is self-caused. Ultimately this is to say that the particle in some sense "chooses" to come into existence—that is, it is self-determining, one of the essential characteristics of consciousness (de Quincey, 2002, 27). The notion that quantum events in some way "choose" their behavior is a radical idea indeed—and probably not one that most quantum physicists would accept.

The idea that consciousness is the interior aspect of all phenomena in nature implies not only that it goes all the way down to the most minute levels but also that it goes all the way up. This fits with Lovelock's original Gaia hypothesis (1979): the view that the entire earth is an intelligent, self-organizing, and in some sense "conscious" being. (Lovelock later softened his original idea, claiming that the notion of the earth as a conscious being was only a metaphor.) Considered from this view, the bizarre weather patterns of the past decade are the earth's response to the imbalances in the atmosphere created by global warming, ozone depletion, deforestation, and other environmental hazards.

On an even larger scale, the entire solar system can be understood as having an interior, subjective aspect. In astrology, the configuration of planets at any given time implies a meaningful, archetypal pattern (each planet represents a particular astrological archetype) that is reflected—or imprinted—on anything that is created or comes into existence at that particular time. For example, individuals born when the planets Mars and Saturn are in opposition (180 degrees apart), may frequently experience obstacles to action, since Mars is the archetype of action and Saturn is the archetype of contraction or restriction. Those who believe in astrology see the entire solar system as a cosmic mandala that plays out different archetypal patterns as the planets change their relative positions. But meaningful patterns are something we ascribe to subjects, not objects. So the solar system may have both an objective aspect (astronomy) and a subjective aspect (astrology). Before the Scientific Revolution, there seemed to be some recognition of this—many of the finest astronomers (Johannes Kepler and Tycho Brahe, for example) were also astrologers. (More will be said about the question of astrology's validity in chapter 16.)

Beyond the solar system is the Milky Way galaxy; beyond that, galaxy systems or clusters. If consciousness goes all the way up, there must be a sense in which even these enormous systems are conscious, self-organizing, and have a subjective interior aspect.

A Radical View of Consciousness

The idea that consciousness exists at all levels, from the most minute to the most macro phenomena—a concept often referred to as panpsychism—is not new. Nevertheless, it challenges the prevailing scientific worldview, which, following Descartes, limits mind or consciousness to the human brain, or perhaps more broadly, to the brains of living organisms. This more radical view holds that any self-organizing system—whether molecule, plant cell, the earth, or a galaxy—is a system that both exhibits self-agency and is influenced by objective, external causes. Self-agency is one of the attributes of consciousness. By implication, all such systems thus have both an interior, subjective aspect and an objective, observable one. Perhaps Aristotle had it right when he posited that everything in nature could be characterized not only by material and efficient causes (the outer, objective explanations typical of science) but also by what he called a final cause (a particular purpose or goal).

To accept such a radical view of consciousness is to fundamentally change the way we look at the world. Nature is understood to be conscious at all levels. From here it is only a small step to viewing nature as enchanted or sacred. If all levels of nature have intrinsic purpose and value, nature is clearly worthy of our deep respect.

The desacralization of nature that occurred with the Renaissance and Scientific Revolution is thus reversed. Nature is *not* simply a neutral object to be analyzed purely objectively (though science has done a good job of describing and explaining it in this way). It is also a sacred being, deserving our reverence. We are called to live in balance and harmony with that which is the matrix of our very existence. Many indigenous cultures have never given up this view.

Consciousness and the Life Force

What is the relationship between the life force and consciousness? Are all life forms, including viruses and plants, conscious? Are only living things conscious—or does consciousness extend (as suggested above) beyond what is typically considered alive? If we subscribe to radical naturalism, consciousness includes far more than what is motivated by the so-called life force. If any self-organizing system can be said to be conscious in some sense, then viruses and plant cells are definitely conscious. But, then, following the same reasoning, so are protons, atoms and molecules which also exhibit self-organization. Should we thus say atoms and molecules are alive? It would seem to make more sense to restrict the terms "life" and "life force" to biological entities alone, which includes the entire evolutionary sequence, from algae, viruses, and bacteria up to primates and humans. Biological organisms and plants can be said to be alive. Atoms, molecules, and galaxies are not, as they are not, strictly speaking, biological in nature. However, they may still in some sense be viewed as conscious, and can be said to have characteristics such as self-agency and even subjectivity in some sense. Thus, consciousness may be far more inclusive than the life force.

This distinction between consciousness and the life force also brings clarity to discussions of the survival of the soul after death. Restricting the concept of life to biological processes allows us to say that the soul is not, in a biological sense, alive after death, but that it continues to be conscious—that its consciousness goes on. Thus consciousness can, in some sense, survive physical death, even though life does not. If we stick with these definitions, angels and spirit guides are certainly conscious and capable of influencing us, but they are not the kind of beings that we can speak of as alive (at least in the biological sense). If we speak of them as "living" spirits, then we have changed the definition of life, extending it to any being that can act, whether that being happens to be physical or nonphysical (outside of four-dimensional space-time). While these definitions are somewhat arbitrary, it would seem simpler and more logical to restrict the notion of life to biological entities alone.

Consciousness and Freedom

Is consciousness free or is its activity strictly determined? In the worldview we inherited from Descartes, Newton, and the Scientific Revolution events are causally determined. Although quantum physics has revised our notion of causal determinacy at the microscopic level, we still tend to assume that events at the macro level are subject to the law of cause and effect. At least for nonliving phenomena, such as the weather, the motion of falling objects, and the operation of machines, we assume that each event in a sequence of events is the outcome of preceding causes.

However, when we consider human beings—and, for that matter, animals—we encounter a problem. As conscious beings, we believe we freely choose our behavior from moment to moment. Most of the time we see ourselves as free agents who act in a purposeful, intentional way. If our behavior were entirely determined by prior causes, we would be like robots. We would not be free—everything we did would result mechanistically from all of the causes that were acting on us at any moment in time.

But when we look closely, it appears that each of our actions *is*, in fact, determined by—or flows out of—the thoughts, feelings, motivations, and impulses that occur immediately before we act. In turn, these thoughts, feelings, motivations, and impulses are the effects of previous thoughts, feelings, and motives that are influenced both by our current goals, intentions, feelings, moods, and dispositions and by the cumulative history of our entire life experience and everything we have learned. Are we really free after all—or is each of our actions the result of a myriad of influences, both past and present?

Herein lies the famous philosophical dispute of determinism versus free will. *Determinists* believe that our subjective feeling of agency or free will is an illusion, and argue that everything we do is determined by numerous subjective as well as objective conditions and influences. *Volitionists* take the opposite tack. They maintain that determinism cannot be true because it contradicts our most intimate experience: the ability to choose freely what we do. Volitionists give experience primacy over logic: our subjective experience of personal freedom takes precedence over the logic of causal analysis.

However this either-or dilemma—either our behavior is completely determined or we are completely free—leaves us with some problems. On the one hand, if everything we do is entirely causally determined, then it would seem we are like robots, our notion of free will illusory. This not only contradicts our experience, it undermines the entire basis of moral responsibility, ethics, and law. Our entire legal system would make no sense if our actions were strictly determined. We would have no personal, moral responsibility, and our notions of ethics would be illusory.

On the other hand, total freedom—if everything we do is entirely free and unconstrained—would contradict our experience that much of what we do is influenced by past conditioning, preferences, goals, and expectations, all of which we have learned. Even the writing of this book is not completely free and unconstrained: it follows from an intention to record ideas on this subject, and these ideas, in turn, have been acquired over years of reading and reflection.

So there appears to be something wrong with casting the dilemma in terms of strict determinism and complete freedom. It would seem the answer lies somewhere in between. What if it were possible that in each moment our behavior is both relatively determined and relatively free to varying degrees? But how can this be? How can free will and determinism both be true? We can we avoid contradiction here by making two key assumptions; if you accept these assumptions, then an important conclusion follows.

Self as Its Own Cause

The first assumption is that the origin, locus, or source of human action—which we can call the *self-as-agent*—is its own cause. We are, after all, conscious beings, and a defining attribute of consciousness is self-agency. This self-as-agent is not the effect of prior causes. In every moment it is consciously choosing; its choices are not strictly caused by anything prior to the self's acting as agent. Each act of choice by the self-as-agent is a spontaneous act of volition at the moment of choice. Furthermore, there is no distinction between cause and effect. The self choosing is both cause and effect simultaneously. In fact, one definition of self-as-agent is a point or place in the universe where cause and effect are the same—where the actions or effects of the self are caused by that same self.

If the above is true, then in a sense we are like gods. Each of us is a unique source of volition in the universe, and, as such, we are ultimately responsible for what we do. The nineteenth-century German philosopher Johann Gottlieb Fichte expressed this idea in referring to consciousness as "self-positing itself" (de Quincey 2002, 100). In the twentieth century, Alfred North Whitehead developed the idea further in his notion of the self as a "creative agent positing itself from moment to moment" in a world of objects (de Quincey 2002, 100).

Influence vs. Total Causal Determinism

The second assumption is that a distinction can be made between influence and total causal determination. Even though we are choosing our behavior from moment to moment, our choices may be influenced by a diversity of factors, including our goals, intentions, motives, feelings, needs, and moods, as well as numerous outside circumstances (my turning on the air conditioner, for example, is influenced by the room being too hot). Self-as-agent can be influenced by all sorts of things, but that does not for a moment diminish the fact that it chooses how to respond to these influences. It does not react reflexively, like a machine—it responds. Thus it can be said to be "responsible." A motorboat's motion may be influenced by current, turbulence, and wind, but that does not change the fact that its own motor is playing a large role in its motion. So each choice we make is influenced by a host of factors, but is not entirely determined by them.

A critical point here is that our choices can be influenced by inner and outer factors to varying degrees. All of us have at some time felt like we were acting on automatic. When we drive a car, many of our actions—turning the wheel, braking, and accelerating—seem to be relatively automatic because they follow from habits conditioned over years of driving. When we first learned them as teenagers they were not automatic; now they are. In a real sense, our behavior while driving is more robotic because it occurs automatically or reflexively without our having to think too much about it. At the other end of the spectrum, when we paint a picture, compose a letter, or engage in any other creative activity, there is relatively more freedom from moment to moment— though, to be sure, past learning and conditioning still enter into our behavior. Creating something as you go along entails a greater degree of freedom than driving on the freeway, though both are a synthesis of free choice and influence from past conditioning. The only perfectly free behavior would be one that is in total alignment with the rhythm, flow, or movement of the entire universe, cosmos, or God. If we were completely enlightened, like Buddha or Jesus Christ, our actions would not be influenced by the history of our personal conditioning, or even our heredity, but would flow from the fully spontaneous, creative flow of the cosmos itself. It is no accident that spiritual enlightenment is often referred to as liberation or total freedom, not only from the external influences of the physical world, but also from conditioned patterns of thought, feeling, and behavior.

Our degree of personal freedom is relative. The more we align ourselves with our innermost essence (our soul, the Dharma, the Tao, or the Way), the more our actions begin to take on the attributes of complete creativity, spontaneity, and freedom. Conversely, the more we act out of prior conditioning, the more our action is influenced and constrained by our history and past. In any given moment, the amounts of freedom and constraint contributing to our action will vary, depending on the degree to which we are in attunement with our true essence—and therefore the intelligence of the universe—and living beyond the dictates of our ego self. This ego self is simply a construction based on our cumulative experience in this life as well as the traits we inherited from our forebears.

To sum up, in each moment human behavior is both freely chosen, and, at the same time, constrained or influenced by a variety of internal and external conditions. Each of us responds—rather than reacts reflexively—to the circumstances of each moment. Since we respond, we can be held responsible for what we choose. Our behavior can be said to adhere or not adhere to the ethical dictates and principles that serve to hold society together. As long as we respond rather than merely react in an automatic way, we can be held accountable. Thus, ethics and the legal system do have relevance, although outer circumstances are often taken into consideration when evaluating the magnitude or degree of a person's responsibility for a given action.

Conclusion

Consciousness is widely discussed these days, yet defining what exactly it is can be daunting. To begin with, it's not something observed in the outside world, it's something we can only experience subjectively, and only in the present moment. Yet it appears to have a visible influence on natural systems, orchestrating a coherence that allows systems such as cells—or entire organisms—to maintain their integrity.

Consciousness is not just a property of living systems but extends all the way down to the quantum level and all the way up to the universe as a whole. To say that it just appears at a certain level of biological complexity (the materialist viewpoint) begs the question of where did it come from in the first place. Physical and chemical processes, no matter how complex, do not produce feelings and moods; the two are categorically different. If consciousness survives physical death, consciousness itself must then be something nonmaterial, transcending biological life and life forms.

Freedom of choice is an attribute of consciousness. Although our freedom is constrained by multiple influences affecting us at any given moment, we have the capacity to reflect and enact a creative response, exercising a higher degree of freedom than if we were to just reflexively react.

Consciousness is distributed throughout the universe; each point or locale of consciousness responds to its surroundings with the intention of maintaining itself. At the same time, all points of consciousness are deeply interconnected parts of a seamless whole.

12

The Universal Context

In the twentieth century, humanity began to study its own subjective awareness through the field of psychology. Prior to this, the primary focus of scientific inquiry had been the outer world of nature. Proponents of psychoanalysis and other schools of depth psychology sought to understand emotional disorders in terms of the dynamics of components of the psyche: id, ego, superego, defenses, drives, needs, self-concept, motives, persona, archetypes, and so forth. Behavioral psychology examined habits and behavioral patterns established by conditioning or reinforcement. Other branches of psychology studied functions of the mind such as memory, sensation, perception, and cognition. The intent was to understand human beings—their capabilities, behavior, development, conflicts, and problems—through an analysis of various subsystems or processes within the total spectrum of human functioning.

Social psychology enlarged the field of inquiry. Group psychology and family systems theory/therapy sought to understand the individual in the context of small groups. The study of group dynamics, social perception, interpersonal attraction, or shifting alliances and hierarchies within the family system, all provide a deeper understanding of how individuals function in—and are affected by—groups. Sociology and anthropology enlarged the context of inquiry further still to include a person's society or culture. To understand socialization is to explain how individuals' personalities or behavior are shaped by the culture in which they live. While these disciplines often take an entire society or culture as their unit of study, their major thrust is to understand how people function in and are affected by the larger culture into which they are born.

Each of these disciplines has attempted to explain religion in terms of its own territory. Freud viewed religious beliefs as infantile fantasies, and religious motivation as a wish to return to maternal symbiosis. Although Jung's view of religion was much less reductive, in his published writings he always treated religious processes and experiences as strictly psychological phenomena. Sociology and anthropology regard religions as cultural constructs developed to provide a meaningful view of the world and encourage social cohesion. Religions are thus social institutions that serve very specific societal functions; the question of their intrinsic validity—if even relevant—lies outside the purview of social science.

What is the context in which religion itself operates? It seems evident that if we are to understand religion on its own terms—and not just seek to explain it in terms of psychological or sociological constructs—then the proper context would be the Cosmos. Religion focuses on the individual's experience of and relationship with the Cosmos. Cosmos does not mean just the physical universe. Certainly religion is not talking about our relationship with galaxies or the Big Bang. A more accurate definition of "Cosmos" would be all that exists—reality in its broadest reach or totality. As discussed in previous chapters, such a reality contains a lot more than just the physical universe—however grand that may be—for it encompasses values, meanings, qualities, and the full scope of what is implied by the concepts of the mind and consciousness. We are talking about a multi-tiered universe that has the physical universe as its outward visible aspect (the object of science) as well as subtle and conscious aspects that we cannot directly observe through our senses but can experience subjectively.

To raise spiritual or religious questions, then, is to raise questions about our experiences in the context of—and in relationship with—the cosmos in its totality, what might be called the *universal context*. Strictly speaking, it might be called the *universal subjective context*, the most inclusive context of reality "from the inside out." In different words, the universal context is the entire Cosmos viewed as a subject rather than an object.

Religions have explored and sought to understand this universal context for thousands of years. However, they typically codify original revelations into cultural belief systems and then create institutions and customs around these beliefs. Prophetic revelations about the cosmos are structured into specific sets of beliefs, practices, and customs that then become a particular creed, such as Christianity or Hinduism. Eventually factions develop, leading to a variety of different sects or denominations within the original religion. Each religion has its own history that can be, and has been, readily studied by the social sciences.

The Experiential Core of Religions

The mystical or prophetic core of each religion retains a direct connection with the Cosmos—the universal context—because it remains grounded in direct spiritual experience. Such experiences may be shaped by cultural categories (Sally may have a vision of Jesus while Sita has one of Shiva), but they don't tend to be encrusted in dogmatic beliefs or used to prescribe how people should behave. In its essence, the mystical, experiential core of religion precedes culture and is often referred to simply as spirituality. Thus spirituality can be defined as the individual's direct experience of and relationship with the cosmos at large. Various religions and metaphysical systems refer to this ultimate reality as God, Allah, Brahma, the Creator, the Infinite, Nirvana, the Divine, Cosmic Consciousness, Source, the One, and so on. The name differs according to culture or tradition, but the context referred to remains the same.

Because this direct experience arises from intuitive and visionary faculties rather than the senses, an empirical science of the universal context is probably impossible. Replicable experiences of spiritual realities—equally apparent to everyone—are not easily available. Since the time of Francis Bacon, science has been based on repeatable sensory experience of the external world; developing an objective science of spiritual realities would thus be difficult. Most likely, though, we would not even want to, because to recast the sacred and numinous into the object language of science would be to flatten it—to squeeze the awe, beauty, mystery, and grandeur out of it. What would be left would be a gross reduction of the inherent quality of spiritual experience. We can certainly study comparative religions in a dispassionate way, but this will not lead to any *spiritual* understanding, which is acquired experientially through insight and revelation—what in times past was referred to as *gnosis*. However, as suggested in chapter 8, a degree of cross-cultural consensus on certain fundamental attributes and dimensions of mystical experience may be possible. (This idea is explored both later in this chapter and in the following one.)

A Continuum of Contexts

The universal context can be viewed on a continuum with less inclusive contexts, such as culture, society, and family. It is simply the most inclusive context for understanding ourselves, our lives, and our development and destiny in this world. It exists one step further out from the contexts implied by anthropology, sociology, and psychology.

Spiritual/religious inquiry shares with the social sciences a participatory approach to knowledge, but one applied to the context of the entire cosmos rather than a specific group or culture. Because knowledge of the universal context arises fundamentally from direct inner experience, we can experience it apart from any particular culture-based religion. It is there for any person to become aware of and investigate prior to codifying it in terms of a specific religious faith or metaphysical system. Its existence and operation continue quite apart from all human attempts to interpret it.

If the universal context is on a continuum with cultural, social, and psychological contexts—and is not, therefore, something radically separate from these—then spiritual growth is on a continuum with personal psychological growth. Just as there are concepts and principles that help to illuminate psychological growth (what we might learn in an undergraduate psychology courses or at a personal growth workshop), so there are concepts and principles that can help to illuminate spiritual growth.

Each of us can choose to adopt these concepts from specific religions or from other metaphysical ideas that have developed outside of any particular religion. We can draw on Christianity or theosophy, Judaism or Kabbalah, Buddhism or A Course in Miracles. Some of us may choose to draw on concepts and principles from a variety of sources. Whatever spiritual conceptions we choose to believe (for example, notions about personal karmic lessons, redemption and grace, the law of attraction, or manifestation of our soul's intentions), they are personally validated because they can help us make sense of our personal spiritual experiences and their meaning in our life. That is, they are validated existentially, rather than empirically, as in science. For each of us, the final criterion for accepting or rejecting a particular spiritual principle or concept is whether it helps us to understand and make sense of our personal life experience. It does not serve us to adopt beliefs that conflict with our life experience or gut feeling simply because we were raised in a tradition that told us to believe them.

The Validity of Spiritual Experience

Do spiritual conceptions have any validity beyond a single individual or group's particular point of view? Postmodern relativism would say no. It views religious and metaphysical frameworks simply as cultural constructs that function to help a group or individual make sense of the world. We create these frameworks to explain the cosmos and guide our actions toward each other, but beyond that, they have no inherent validity. This is also the position taken by conventional science.

The emerging new paradigm questions the postmodern point of view. It proposes the possibility of spiritual knowledge—gained through insight, intuition, and revelation—that refers to something true and valid; something just as real as the trees, mountains, and stars that we can see with our own eyes. The universal context is just as real as the physical universe studied by the hard sciences. It is simply the interior aspect, or interiority, of that universe, much as the content of our thoughts and feelings is the interior aspect of the brain's processes. The universal context is, in a sense, consciousness on the largest scale.

As mentioned previously, replicable experience and consensual validation of the universal context is harder to come by than observations of the outer world. Yet points of consensus are possible; eventually they are likely to be achieved cross-culturally by culture-free explorations of this realm. This is already beginning to happen in fields such as transpersonal psychology and transpersonal philosophy. Such fields treat the universal context as a topic for disciplined study and systematic investigation.

At present, an enormous number of religions and metaphysical systems attempt to describe the universal context. If what they are all referring to is ultimately real, can we ever arrive at one, uniform body of knowledge such as exists for the natural world in science? Probably not any time soon. Understanding the universal context through existential insight, intuition, and revelation is always likely to be more subjective (subject to cultural and individual interpretation) than apprehending the physical world through our five senses. Although some cross-cultural consensus is likely to be achieved, it won't be at the level possible in the physical sciences. A plurality of paradigms seems inevitable, at least for the foreseeable future. In fact, for any domain that relies on participatory forms of knowing—such as empathy, intuition, or revelation—there is always going to be more divergence in perspective than in the hard sciences that rely solely on replicable sense experience.

Sensory forms of knowing are, by nature, more concrete and easier to agree upon than more participatory, intuitive forms of knowing (though they are also ultimately interpretive and fallible, as the history of science repeatedly demonstrates). Having a plurality of religious and metaphysical frameworks for understanding the universal context is not that different from having a plurality of paradigms for understanding culture or individual personality in the social sciences. Theology, sociology, and personality theory in psychology all rely on participatory forms of knowing. Thus all three endeavors have multiple paradigms for understanding their respective phenomena of interest. Just because different theological or religious frameworks are more interpretive does not make them false or mythical, as conventional scientists have often argued. Freud and Jung had quite different interpretations of the dynamics of individual personality, but their disagreement did not render their interpretations false or mythical.

Conclusion

Spiritual inquiry, like inquiry in the social sciences, explores realities that have their existence confirmed through insight, intuition, and, in the case of the universal context, vision or revelation of the subtle domains. These domains are not in physical space; they are a part of the consciousness or interiority of the Cosmos—the

Cosmos "from the inside out." Postmodern relativism would argue that religious and metaphysical conceptions are merely cultural constructs that do not point to any ultimate reality. The position taken here is that there is an underlying universal reality to which these various conceptions refer. Most important, clues to this reality can be found in the points of convergence and consensus that exist across different religious and spiritual systems of understanding. For each of us individually, personal truth comes from whatever conceptions help us to better understand the spiritual dimension of our experience and its relevance to personal life. Yet the emerging worldview intimates that there is also a universal truth. This is a truth that can be revealed by points of consensus within the various attempts to understand the universal context. Reality itself has a unique spiritual face or aspect that lends itself to such understanding.

While we are still a long way from a universal, consensual understanding of the universal context (a variety of theologies and religions with differing beliefs are likely to be around for a long time), many more people embrace a universal spirituality now than even a hundred years ago. The long march toward a universal spirituality has begun. Some of the steps that have already been taken will be discussed in the following chapter.

13

Toward a Universal
Spiritual Perspective

Aldous Huxley referred to the common spiritual core that underlies all of the world's religions as the *perennial philosophy* (1945). He defined it as "the metaphysic that recognizes a Divine Reality substantial to the world of things and lives and minds; the psychology that finds in the soul something like, or even identical with, Divine Reality; and the ethic that places man's final end in the knowledge of the immanent and transcendent Ground of all being" (Woodhouse 1996).

The perennial philosophy, developed over several thousand years, falls into two distinct traditions with overlapping general principles. One tradition springs from Eastern and Western mystics and spiritual teachers, and is often supplemented by philosophical insight and reflection. The other tradition consists of secret societies, occult wisdom, and mystery schools only marginally connected with organized religion. Both traditions share a paradigm that encompasses some conception of divinity; the notion of irreducible dimensions beyond the physical; a belief in the interconnection of all things; and the idea that the ultimate purpose of life is spiritual evolution.

In the East, the perennial philosophy arose from the experience of the ancient yogis of India, was partially systematized in the *Upanishads*, and was later refined in the *Bhagavad Gita*, the *Yoga Sutras* of Pantanjali, and by Shankara in his *Crest Jewel of Wisdom*. It has come down to us in recent times through the writings of Sri

Aurobindo in *The Life Divine*, the teachings of Ramana Maharshi, and Lama Govinda's *Foundations of Tibetan Buddhism*.

In the West, the perennial philosophy can be traced back to Plato's theory of forms in *The Republic*, Plotinus's *Enneads*, kabbalistic thought in the *Zohar*, and Meister Eckhart's *Sermons*. It was elaborated philosophically in Spinoza's *Ethics* and Hegel's *Phenomenology of the Mind* and was carried forth in the twentieth century by William James's *Varieties of Religious Experience*, Aldous Huxley's *Perennial Philosophy*, Huston Smith's *Forgotten Truth*, and, more recently, the voluminous writings of Ken Wilber.

The esoteric tradition—that of the secret mystery schools—dates back to Pythagoras and in ancient times included Gnosticism, Kabbalism, and the Essenes. During the Renaissance, groups such as the Rosicrucians and Masons emerged. More recent examples, from the eighteenth through twentieth centuries, include Swedenborg's teachings, spiritualism, theosophy, and the work of Alice Bailey.

New Age spirituality of the late twentieth century, which flourished in the 1980s and early 1990s, is in a category by itself. It has made its own contribution to the perennial philosophy through channeled teachings such as *A Course in Miracles* and the writings of Lazarus, Emmanuel, Sanaya Roman, and Neale Donald Walsch.

It seems likely that in the twenty-first century, various forms of the perennial philosophy will gain an increasingly wider following. Up until the last fifty years, a majority of people identified spiritually with a particular religion rather than a universal form of spirituality associated with either a mystical philosophy or a specific esoteric school. While this is still largely true throughout the world, during the New Age movement in America and Europe a large number of people departed from established religion, adopting spiritual perspectives and practices that crossed the boundaries of Eastern and Western traditions. It's likely that this move from religion to spirituality will continue to broaden during the present century. Over a longer time period—perhaps several centuries—humanity may gradually evolve away from highly defined traditions toward a more universal spirituality. It's unlikely, though, that religions will disappear altogether. Cultural and national differences will probably always lead to a variety of religions. Yet the boundaries between different religious traditions and paradigms will continue to become more fluid as human consciousness evolves and more people move away from the dogmatic and primitive notion that "there is only one right way, and it's our way."

The Shape of a Universal Spirituality

As a universal spirituality begins to emerge, what shape might it take? There are some who would like to place it on a continuum with science. Just as we presently have natural and social sciences, we could imagine *noetic* sciences that seek to understand the more subtle and transpersonal aspects of consciousness and the cosmos at large. As more people come to agree on the reality of processes and phenomena such as ego-transcendence, the soul, survival after death, and karma and reincarnation, humanity may develop a consensual, worldwide body of spiritual knowledge similar in acceptability to that of the natural and social sciences.

Up to a point, such an approach is fine—and indeed, may eventually occur, encompassing what has traditionally been called metaphysics: those aspects and dynamics of reality that exist beyond the physical universe as presently understood by science. Where its usefulness may be limited is in dealing with the experiential and ethical dimensions of present-day religion, which often focus on a personal relationship with deity and how we should ultimately behave toward one another rather than the metaphysical structure of the subtle domain. As discussed earlier, science and religion may ultimately be partially integrated in some future understanding of the complete structure of reality. Yet there are aspects of science and religion/spirituality that will continue to remain separate because they refer to very different types of basic questions: descriptive questions versus normative questions. Personal salvation and the act of forgiveness toward others are not the stuff of science.

Dimensions of a Universal Spirituality

What are the dimensions of the perennial philosophy—the common spiritual core or transcendent unity that exists prior to all religious differences? A universal spirituality might be expected to answer three basic questions:

- What is the nature of reality?

- What is the meaning and purpose of human life?

- How should we as humans act toward each other?

What follows is a provisional attempt to suggest how a universal spirituality might begin to answer the first two of these questions. The third question will be explored in the next chapter.

Nature of Reality

A universal spirituality is likely to include at least the following basic assumptions about the nature of reality or the cosmos at large:

Everything Is One

At the highest level of reality, things are not separate. The distinct objects and events that we perceive ultimately emanate from one source. Apparent dualities, such as good and evil, light and dark, and male and female, prevail at our level of existence but are transcended at the highest level of reality. It is through consciousness, not the material forms of objects, that all things are interconnected. By implication, all of humanity—indeed all living things—are emanations of one Source.

Every Separate Object Partakes of Consciousness

Reality is intelligently ordered at all levels, from subatomic particles to the Cosmos as a whole. Wherever an organized whole exists—be it an atom, molecule, crystal, cell, organ, organism, culture, race, species, planet, solar system, galaxy, or the entire universe—consciousness is active in both establishing and maintaining the integrity of that particular unit of reality. Organized wholes are not created by the purely mechanistic processes studied by science; rather they require an intelligent ordering principle that is both inherent in and transcendent of physical reality. Mystics have referred to this principle as Cosmic Consciousness, Spirit, Essence, Logos, and the Ultimate Ground. Religions use names such as God, Allah, Brahma, and Yahweh. Because everything in the universe is not just objective but also subjective, and in some sense conscious, most religions and spiritual paths view the entire universe as holy or sacred. The universe is not a meaningless object (though science treats it as such for the purpose of mechanistic-causal analysis); rather it is meaningful, enchanted, purposeful, and deserving of our reverence. The wonder that we feel when looking up at the stars at night is a reasonable response to a sacred universe.

Reality Consists of Multiple Dimensions Which Exist Beyond the Physical, Space-Time Dimension

Throughout history, religions have described a realm beyond the physical, referring to it by different names, such as heaven, nirvana, bardos, or Summerland. Both esoteric spiritual philosophies, such as Vedanta and theosophy, and modern spiritual philosophers, such as Huston Smith and Ken Wilber, speak of multiple dimensions beyond the physical, for example, the subtle, causal, and ultimate levels of reality. All of these ideas share the notion that there are nonphysical dimensions of reality that exist beyond space-time. Many religions hold that various types of nonphysical beings exist in these dimensions, such as angels, devas, spirit guides, various kinds of positive and negative spirits, as well as disembodied human beings such as ghosts. Because science cannot give a coherent account of how such dimensions could exist—or how they might relate to space-time reality—many scientists dismiss the idea of nonphysical dimensions. However, anyone who believes in the survival of the human soul beyond physical life must assume that such dimensions exist. This idea is required by the previously described notion that all things are one at the highest level of reality, and would be a fundamental tenet of any universal spirituality.

Reality in General—and Humanity Specifically— Is Always Evolving

Duality and a multiplicity of forms evolved out of the one ultimate ground or God. As time passes, all apparently separate beings gradually evolve in the direction of reunification with their source. God first differentiates into the many and then, over eons, gradually reintegrates the many back into the one. Most, though not all, religions assume an evolutionary view of the cosmos. Hinduism specifically describes this evolution and involution of deity; most religions and spiritual paths simply describe the desirability of spiritual progress and being "right with God," "aligned with God's will," or "unified or one with God." This raises the next question that a universal spirituality needs to answer: What is the purpose of life?

Purpose of Human Life

Does life have an ultimate purpose beyond mere gratification of the ego's basic needs for survival, security, comfort, love, belongingness, self-esteem and recognition? Most religions and spiritual paths maintain that we are here to grow through life experience—to become more loving, compassionate, tolerant, patient, and kind. Many religions center around an individual who illustrates ideal behavior, such as Jesus, Buddha, Mohammed, or Krishna. These individuals are commonly believed to be replications or emanations of the divine on earth. So basically human beings are here to grow and evolve—to become more "Godlike," as demonstrated by God's exemplars. Yet isn't this just an extension of the final principle described in the previous section? Are we not here to evolve toward becoming more like, aligned, or unified with divinity, because that is the direction in which everything is ultimately going?

In an evolutionary cosmos, everything originally evolved out of God and is ultimately returning back to God. When our personal life is growing in this direction, we are in alignment with the natural direction or flow of the universe. When we are not— when we are acting from a place of fear, anger, greed, prejudice, envy, or jealousy, for example—then we are out of alignment or flow with the natural direction of the universe. Typically we find that being out of alignment does not feel very good (at least not for an extended time) even though our ego inclinations may have led us that way. So the purpose of life, first and foremost, is simply to evolve toward being in alignment with the natural flow of the universe—to grow toward increasing unification with God, Spirit, or Source. Our purpose is also to learn from mistakes that lead us away from this flow. In this light, life is a classroom for growth in consciousness—for the development of wisdom and the capacity to love.

The tasks and challenges that come up in life, and our responses to them, do not have eternal repercussions (at least not for religions that take an evolutionary view of human spiritual destiny). Nor do they have no meaning at all. They are more like lessons in a school, lessons to which we apply ourselves, and which we try to master as best we can. Each lesson is repeated until it is mastered. As we master lessons, new ones are put before us. This "earth school" is thus a place where each of us can learn and grow; it's not our final dwelling place. Eventually it's time to leave the classroom and move on.

Conclusion

This chapter has briefly considered the first two questions that a universal spirituality needs to answer: the nature of reality and the purpose of human life. Core assumptions about the nature of reality common to many religions parallel those of the emerging worldview described in this book. They imply a universe that is conscious, evolutionary, and purposeful—a universe that contains subtle dimensions beyond the physical world. As for the purpose of life, most religions propose that we are here to grow in our capacity to be loving and compassionate, realizing qualities demonstrated by great spiritual teachers such as Jesus and Buddha. The purpose of our lives is to transcend our own personal selves and connect with something larger, whether the needs of others or the consciousness of the universe as a whole.

The next chapter looks at the third and final question: whether there can be a spiritual foundation for ethics.

14

Natural Ethics

What is the ultimate basis for ethical human conduct? Postmodernism's answer is that there is no ultimate basis. Our behavior is simply guided by the values and mores of our particular culture. A universal, culture-free basis for ethics is impossible. Each culture creates its own moral standards and laws. Cultures may clash because their values and morals differ. The emerging paradigm, with its universal spiritual perspective, offers a different answer. It suggests that there is a basis for human conduct that transcends different cultural prescriptions and resides in the nature of the Cosmos itself. Ethical conduct arises naturally from our innermost relationship with the Cosmos—the universal context previously described.

In brief, a *natural ethics* locates the ultimate basis for ethical conduct in a natural order inherent in the workings of the universe. It is distinct from *ethical relativism*, which regards ethics as a construction of human culture, and *consequential ethics*, which assigns value to human conduct based on good consequences. Natural ethics is not a new idea. One of the best-known proponents of natural ethics was Thomas Aquinas, who proposed that the foundation of ethics lay in the rational order of the universe established by God. According to Aquinas, humans freely choose to participate in that rational order—or to go against it—based on whether their conduct is rational or irrational. Aquinas then took some pains to define the nature of "rational" conduct (Murphy 2008).

In modern times natural ethics has fallen out of favor. For many of us, ethics is no longer based on universal principles inherent in the cosmos but rather on some form of social utility. Humans make up their own ethical conventions in order to maintain social order and cohesion. What we should do is based on our society's conventions of socially adaptive behavior, codified in our society's set of laws. There are no universal ethical principles apart from a given culture's particular set of norms. Both our legal and criminal justice systems are based on this view.

Unconditional Love: An Inherent Quality of the Cosmos

The emerging worldview restores a universal and spiritual foundation to ethics, resulting in a type of natural ethics. The basis for right conduct is found neither in human convention (ethical relativism) nor in theological views such as those of Aquinas. Instead, the universal principle of unconditional love—or compassion—becomes the basis for human behavior across cultures. *Furthermore, unconditional love is not merely a human sentiment but understood to be inherent to the workings of the Cosmos.* This is only possible if the Cosmos is not merely the physical universe but an intelligently ordered, conscious field of potential—a conscious order that includes love as an inherent aspect.

Unconditional love is a universal value that appears to transcend culture. All religions emphasize the fundamental importance of unconditional love as a basis for ethical conduct. From the first two commandments of the Old Testament to Buddhist injunctions to act with compassion and lovingkindness, unqualified love (epitomized in the Greek concept of *agape*) is the principle that seems to stand above all others in governing our conduct toward our fellow human beings. In our actions toward others, the operative question from a spiritual standpoint is, "What is the most loving thing to do?" In some instances this may require what is often called tough love—the setting of a limit or boundary to protect others from harm or to protect someone from harming himself. To be sure, the "most loving thing to do" may sometimes require taking a firm stand rather than allowing yourself to be abused.

A majority of the world's religions believe unconditional love is a fundamental attribute of the Godhead or Divinity. Buddha exhibited the Godhead through his perfect compassion; Jesus exhibited the Godhead through his perfect love and forgiveness. Pure unconditional love is, at the very least, a major aspect/archetype of divinity, along with perfect truth, beauty, peace, and joy. Many would say it is the most fundamental aspect of divinity. Mystics such as Meister Eckhart have said that the entire universe would fall apart if it were not for the love of God.

Most religions propose that we each contain a spark or element of divinity within the deepest part of our being. Jesus said that the kingdom of God is within each of us. The Hindu concept of Atman or Self implies the same thing. In Buddhism, beyond the self-concept or ego-self is the One (the unity of all things). So we are left with the following syllogism: if perfect love is a fundamental attribute of the cosmos or of Divinity, and the deepest, most fundamental aspect of our being is unified with the cosmos or with Divinity, then it is within our innermost nature to be unconditionally loving.

Unconditional Love as the Basis for Ethics

While conventional ethics may view unconditional love as an external standard to live up to, spirituality regards it as an innate potential of our innermost being. The more we are able to align ourselves with that place of perfect love within ourselves, the more we will naturally be inclined to act in a loving way.

This can be summed up simply: the ultimate basis for ethical conduct is just to be who we truly are in our very innermost being. We simply act from our authentic self. If we strive to bring ourselves into alignment with the divinity within, through spiritual practices such as prayer, meditation, ritual, and worship, we will naturally embrace divine love and naturally act in a loving way toward others—as well as toward ourselves.

It follows that the ultimate basis for ethics lies not in standards devised by humanity. Nor is it relative to culture. Different cultures may have different values and standards regarding human conduct, but they all share the basic value of cultivating love and compassion toward others. This is expressed in the fact that every religion throughout the world has its own variation of the golden rule, or "do unto others as you would have them do unto you." The ultimate basis for ethics is simply to express unconditional love by being who we truly are.

Being who we truly are—aligning with divinity within—generally feels good. Ultimately it feels better than just about anything else. Beneath all of our ego goals and aims, beneath all of the fear, anger, prejudice, and narrow-mindedness that come from cultural and familial conditioning, we all want to live and express our innermost nature, to live in attunement with the divinity within. So the highest form of action—the most ethical way to proceed in any situation—is simply to act with love, *which at the deepest level is what we are naturally inclined to do anyway* (although we may not be aware of this if we are coming from a more superficial ego perspective).

Conclusion

In summary, to act ethically toward our fellow human beings is simply to be and act as we want to naturally at the deepest, spiritual level of our being. Because the ego often acts out of fear, hurt, avarice, envy, self-righteousness, or a sense of competition rather than cooperation, it may attempt to cajole us otherwise. Yet in our heart of hearts, the most ethical way to behave toward others—and ourselves—is to express unconditional love. This is completely natural when we act from a place of authenticity.

Thus, ought ultimately reduces to is. When we live from our innermost spiritual truth, there are no "oughts" or "shoulds" to which we need subscribe. Rather, we simply enact, in our everyday actions, the forgiveness, tolerance, and love of the Christ, or the compassion and lovingkindness of the Buddha. As humanity moves toward a future where cooperation among all people is increasingly needed, each of us can become a force for peace by embodying the innate compassion that is our essence.

15

Unity of Consciousness: The Interconnection of All Minds

The idea that all minds are joined is a long-standing precept of Eastern philosophy as well as Western mysticism. The Atman or Self of Hinduism refers to a universal consciousness that underlies each individual's personal awareness. In Buddhism, relinquishing the ego allows a merging of personal awareness with a primal state of consciousness that is formless but universally present. In the West, Jesus referred to the unity of all human beings in his statement, "Even as you do it unto the least of them, you do it unto me." In the words of Meister Eckhart, the great Catholic mystic, "When is a man in mere understanding? When he sees one thing separated from another. When is he above mere understanding? When he sees all in all" (Woodhouse 1996, 213).

Common to all of these perspectives is the idea that at the foundation of each individual mind is a universal consciousness that pervades the known cosmos and beyond. Each individual's consciousness is embedded in—or is an emanation of—an infinite mind. If this is true, then at the deepest level all minds are joined. At the ultimate level, our separate minds are in communion with one another and with the consciousness of the cosmos at large.

This underlying, unitary consciousness is roughly equivalent to what is referred to as the *supraconscious mind* in chapter 9. Other terms for it include "cosmic consciousness" and the "universal mind." Such a universal consciousness cannot be equated with the Godhead, which is forever ineffable and beyond description. However, we can speculate that it is one of the loftiest points at which the Godhead manifests into form. Perhaps cosmic consciousness is itself the highest level at which form first enters into existence out of the ultimate ground that is beyond form.

Evidence for Unitary Consciousness

Paranormal events offer evidence for a unity of consciousness. The phenomenon of mental telepathy, for example, seems to demonstrate that minds are joined. The essence of telepathy is that one mind receives information from another mind without any verbal or explicit communication. Common examples of telepathy include:

- Knowing what someone is going to say before he speaks

- Knowing who is calling when the phone rings

- Feeling uneasy or distressed when a loved one is suffering, without knowledge of the fact and no matter how far away she is

- Having a strong mental, emotional, or physical reaction at the time of a loved one's death, no matter how far away it occurs

Another indication of a unitary consciousness is the way in which people are affected by major world events. When a disaster of worldwide proportions occurs, many people feel affected, even when they are not following the news on TV or in the newspaper and perhaps do not even know about the event. Such an event seems to color the mood of people all over the world, whether they have knowledge of it or not.

The existence of both telepathy and the universal psychic effects of global events is supported not just by anecdotal reports, but by a considerable amount of carefully done empirical research.

Telepathy Experiments

Several generations of research support telepathy (Radin 1997). The best-known series of experiments were conducted by Joseph Banks Rhine at Duke University from the late 1920s through 1960. Rhine had a deck of twenty-five cards displaying five distinct symbols. A "sender" would pick up one card at a time, concentrate on its symbol, and then "send" it mentally it to a remote person, or "receiver." The receiver would then try to guess the correct sequence of symbols the sender sent. Randomly, a receiver should match five out of twenty-five symbols correctly. Across a total of four million trials and thousands of experiments reported in more than a hundred publications, receivers frequently exceeded the expectations of random chance. Rhine's experiments were carefully designed to avoid methodological flaws, and they provided the first significant body of evidence in favor of paranormal processes. However, they could not determine whether the receivers were using telepathy or clairvoyance to identify the symbols on the cards.

More recently, evidence supporting telepathy has come from *ganzfeld experiments*. In this type of experiment, a subject sits in a comfortable reclining chair and listens to white noise while wearing translucent hemispheres over her eyes. A ten-minute relaxation sequence is played through headphones in order to reduce external stimulation so that the subject's mind can quiet down and attend to faint impressions, some of which may be psychic in origin. In a separate room or building, a sender views one of four pictures, randomly selected, and attempts to send it to this receiver. After this is done, an independent observer asks the receiver to rank the four pictures according to how well each one matches her perceptions during the ganzfeld session. If she ranks the picture actually viewed by the sender as first, then the session is scored a hit; otherwise it's scored a miss. By chance, the experiment should result in a correct match between sender and receiver once in every four sessions, for a 25 percent hit rate. Two meta-analyses of all known ganzfeld experiments in 1985 found that twenty-three of twenty-eight studies obtained greater-than-chance hit rates (Radin 1997, 79). When the results for all twenty-eight studies were combined, the odds against chance for the combined results were ten billion to one. Between 1985 and 1987, ganzfeld experiments were improved methodologically to a point where most skeptics could not find fault. Studies were independently replicated in eight different settings around the world. By the end of the 1990s, the vast majority of studies reported hit rates in the range of 30 to 35 percent—well beyond the 25 percent chance hit rate. The odds of all these results occurring by chance were over a trillion to one.

Thus the experimental evidence for telepathy/clairvoyance is robust. Anyone who makes a fair and thorough appraisal of the evidence, with full attention to experimental methodology, is compelled to conclude that information is either being transferred between sender and receiver (telepathy), or between stimulus and receiver (clairvoyance), in a manner that cannot be explained by present-day science. There are no known laws of physics that can explain the acausal, nonlocal nature of paranormal processes.

Field-Consciousness Experiments

Even more compelling is the evidence for group consciousness effects, often referred to as *field-consciousness* effects by investigators. A series of experiments, pioneered by Roger Nelson at Princeton University and replicated by Dick Bierman at the University of Amsterdam, have investigated this phenomenon (Radin 1997, 157). Dean Radin has also conducted this type of experiment, reporting his results in his widely respected review of paranormal research, *The Conscious Universe* (1997). Field-consciousness experiments suggest that the mental focus of groups of people—ranging from a small number in a workshop to more than a billion watching the same television program—can have consistent effects on the physical world. The broad implication is that there appears to be a fundamental interconnection not only among all minds but indeed among all things.

Field-consciousness studies measure the impact of group consciousness by the behavior of random phenomena—in particular, random-number generators—during events in which a group's attention is focused on a common object or event. Random-number generators simulate the process of tossing a coin, generating zeros and ones randomly at the rate of four hundred tosses every six seconds. Normally, over an hour or longer, the numbers of zeros and ones very closely approximate the expected 50-50 split. However, when random-number generators are observed during times when a large number of people are all focused on the same thing, the ratio of zeros and ones typically departs from that expected by chance. For example, a study that observed random-number generators during the 1995 Academy Awards broadcast—watched by approximately a billion people across the world—found that the machines behaved in a significantly nonrandom fashion during the broadcast as compared with the hour preceding and the hour following the broadcast. The odds against this being the result of chance exceed one hundred to one (Radin 1997, 164). Similar results have been observed during other events that drew the attention of many millions of people around the world at the same time, such as the opening ceremonies of the Olympics, and the hours following the 9/11 disaster in 2001 (Radin 2006, 203).

Field-consciousness experiments imply that something like a group consciousness—a unity of minds—exists, and that it can exert an influence on physical events. This suggests not only an interconnection of minds but a potential interconnection of all things, mental and physical. Summarizing the results of field-consciousness experiments, Dean Radin notes, "The common link between mind and matter, as observed in these experiments, is order. Order expressed in the mind is related to focused attention, and order in matter is related to decreases in randomness" (1997, 172). He goes on to note that the experiments provide evidence for Jung's concept of *synchronicity*—a nonrandom, meaningful correspondence between mental and physical events. (Synchronicity will be discussed further in the following chapter.)

What are the broader implications of these group consciousness effects? On the negative side, does the anger and despair of millions of impoverished and disenfranchised people throughout the world have a disruptive effect on the collective consciousness of mankind? Alternatively, does the existence of millions of people meditating and raising their consciousness have a collective positive effect, as New Agers often believe? One might wonder whether the collective consciousness of our planet is skewed more in a negative or positive direction at this moment in history, and also how major world events might affect that consciousness. Consider the difference between the energy—the "feel" of things—on worldwide holidays, such as Christmas or Easter, and on the days following natural disasters, such as the east Asian tsunami of December 26, 2005. The difference is easily noticed.

The Parallel Between Paranormal Events and Nonlocality in Physics

In physics, the existence of nonlocal events is well accepted. The spin of one particle changes in a way that is identical to that of a distant particle, and at exactly the same time, so that it's impossible that any information could have been transmitted from one particle to the other. Such a connection is acausal and instantaneous, meaning it cannot be explained in terms of any physical causes operating between the two particles—hence the term "nonlocal event." Separate particles that exhibit a nonlocal connection are often spoken of as "entangled" or intimately tied together in an acausal way. Physicist David Bohm theorizes more generally that we cannot fully account for the universe in terms of discrete particles or fields; instead, everything must be interconnected at a deep level—what he calls the *implicate order*—underlying the visible universe of ostensibly separate things (1980).

Paranormal processes—telepathy, clairvoyance, and precognition—suggest the existence of nonlocal events in the global field of consciousness. It appears that information can be mediated nonlocally between two different points in the field of consciousness apart from the constraints of space and time. Clairvoyance over vast distances overcomes limitations of space; precognition of future events overcomes time. The mechanism of such events is unknown but transcends ordinary causality as well as the four types of forces known to physics. Instead, the connections appear to be synchronistic, in Jung's sense of the word: they are based on a correspondence of subjective meaning, not a mechanistic causal relationship. They occur along lines of personal significance rather than causal sequence. One mind instantaneously picks up on something important happening to a loved one at a distance (telepathy occurs more often between people who are personally connected in some way). An event foreseen in the future is typically of personal significance to the one who sees it.

Can paranormal processes—and ultimately consciousness itself—be explained in terms of quantum physics, or any future form of physics? Dean Radin believes this may eventually happen. A popular proposal in recent years (for example, Laszlo 2004) has been that non-local paranormal processes—and the self-organizing capacity of consciousness itself—are integrally associated with the zero-point field of empty space, in which quantum wave fluctuations are observed to spontaneously appear and disappear. One difficulty with this hypothesis is that the zero-point field occupies space; it is also the ground state of known types of particles or forces in physics (such as electromagnetism and strong and weak nuclear forces). As long as it is conceptualized in terms of constructs of physics—or in cosmology as the so-called dark energy—the zero-point field cannot fully account for the attributes of consciousness, especially symbolic meaning and intentionality. Thus, to view it as the *ultimate* basis for consciousness is unsatisfying and leaves us with a subtle form of materialism. At the very least, consciousness needs to be intrinsic, or more likely antecedent, to the zero-point field. The zero-point field may turn out to be a type of medium or a mediating field through which consciousness acts in interacting with physical reality.

Questions remain about the very possibility of fully accounting for paranormal processes in terms of entangled quantum phenomena or dynamics of the zero-point field. Physics, by its very nature, studies observable physical phenomena in space-time. Paranormal processes, on the other hand, occur in the domain of consciousness. Consciousness is not localizable in space; we can only experience it directly by being it. Whether physics will ever fully grasp and explain consciousness is an open question. Perhaps consciousness can only be understood on its own terms. From a scientific standpoint, we may be able to create models of how it might work, yet if consciousness isn't localizable in space-time—and thus isn't something we can empirically observe—we may never be able to fully account for it scientifically. As Kant pointed out long ago, it is very difficult for us to even conceive of natural phenomena except in terms of substance, space, and time. At best, then, entangled minds in telepathy parallel entangled particles in quantum physics. Perhaps they offer us two different lenses—at the micro and macro level—through which to appreciate the ultimate unity and interconnection of all things.

Some Implications

The existence of a unity of consciousness has some important implications. If all minds are deeply interconnected, then each of us can be described as a "cell" in the collective "body" of human consciousness. If this is so, then each of us has the potential to make a contribution to the whole. Whatever each of us does to heal our own awareness—to cultivate peace within ourselves—will have some impact, however small, upon the whole of humanity. A large number of us living at relative peace with ourselves, may well be able to cause a ripple effect for the world at large. On the other hand, the larger the number of people on the planet living in stress, despair, or violence, the more chaotic or turbulent the collective consciousness of humanity is likely to be.

Furthermore, if an underlying unity of minds does indeed exist, then all differences among human beings due to gender, age, race, ethnic group, culture, nationality, and religion are relative. At the deepest level we are all one and the same—all emanations of the same consciousness. Whatever we do, for better or worse, to another person, we do to ourselves. So the golden rule—the moral imperative found in all of the world's religions to "do unto others as you would have them do unto you"—may in fact reflect the fundamental structure of reality.

Conclusion

Acting with love and compassion toward our fellow human beings is not just a universal moral imperative. It follows directly from the inherent structure of reality, in which all consciousness—though seemingly separated by discrete physical bodies—is actually one unified field. The gradual awakening of a global consciousness in our time is a step toward a wider recognition of this truth. By moving beyond self-interest to care for the environment and all humanity, each of us can begin to embody this deep connection to the whole world.

16

Symbolic Connections: The Role of Esoteric Disciplines in the New Worldview

A central idea discussed in earlier chapters is that the cosmos is enchanted—infused with consciousness at every point at which an organized whole exists, from atoms to cells to galaxies. What we consider subjective—the meaningful context of human experience—is not confined to human consciousness but extends throughout and beyond the physical world we observe with our senses. Indigenous cultures have always understood this. Most have approached the subjectivity or interiority of nature through pantheons of deities that govern and oversee the course of natural events.

Human consciousness is embedded in and inextricably linked with a much larger consciousness of the universe. This is a foreign concept to the contemporary scientific-materialist worldview that regards the universe as neutral and meaningless. Throughout much of the twentieth century, only a few innovative thinkers ventured outside the limits imposed by mainstream science. One of these was Carl Jung, who in his later years developed the concept of synchronicity (1973).

Synchronicity refers to an acausal correspondence between the human psyche and the outside world. A synchronicity is a meaningful connection between an outer event in the objective world and an inner, psychological theme within a person or group's consciousness. There is no sharp distinction between subject and object. Instead, inner meanings are connected seamlessly with outer events; the two are bridged by archetypes.

An *archetype* is an innate symbolic form that unconsciously structures human experience and behavior at both the personal and collective level. In the context of synchronicity, Jung proposed that archetypes were autonomous patterns of meaning that operate simultaneously in the psyche and the external world, bridging inner and outer. The subject-object distinction is transcended: archetypes are meaningful patterns within the soul or psyche of the Cosmos itself, of which our personal consciousness is merely a small part.

For example, when you can't decide whether to pursue a new job opportunity or not, while driving to work you may spot a personalized license plate that says, "Go for it." At that moment something may click deep within you that resonates with this sign, and you may decide to apply for the job. Or you might be thinking about researching a particular topic when a friend calls to mention a new book he just discovered that pertains to that exact topic. Many of us are familiar with such everyday coincidences that do not seem to be just coincidences.

Synchronicity and the Cosmos

The concepts of synchronicity and archetypal correspondence are taken to a new level by Richard Tarnas in his book *Cosmos and Psyche* (2006). A cultural historian and philosopher, Tarnas is best known for his first book, *The Passion of the Western Mind* (1991), considered by many one of the most compelling and insightful histories of Western thought ever written. His newer book takes a radical step forward, making the case for a symbolically (archetypally) meaningful cosmos. Building on the work of Jung, Tarnas expands archetypal psychology, presenting evidence for synchronistic correlations of historical events with astrological alignments of planets, particularly Saturn, Uranus, Neptune, and Pluto. The sheer volume and uncanny consistency of such correlations across several historical periods may open the minds of those previously skeptical of astrology.

Astrology has spent much of the last three hundred years in disrepute. The Scientific Revolution sought to divest nature of any shred of inherent meaning beyond that ascribed to it by the laws of science. As a result, all systems of human thought that invest the cosmos with symbolic meaning are disparaged by science as mere projections of human fantasy onto a physical universe that is fundamentally neutral to human affairs. As recently as 1988, more than a hundred Nobel laureates signed a petition condemning astrology as superstitious and unscientific.

Much of this skepticism is based on the false view that astrology asserts that the planets have a causal effect on human personality and the course of world events. Since there is no known force or emanation from the planets that could affect the course of worldly events, astrology is thought to be nonsense. However, any serious student of astrology knows that astrology has never claimed that the planets cause personal and social events. Instead, it claims there is a *synchronistic correspondence* between the two. The universe is viewed as an integrated whole in which patterns are replicated on multiple levels. In such a universe the microcosms of human personality and life events can meaningfully correspond with the positions of planets in the solar system. However, planets are understood not in their outer aspects but with regard to their symbolic, archetypal meanings—what astrology has focused on for more than two thousand years. Tarnas articulates this idea well: "A more plausible and comprehensive explanation of the available evidence would rest on a conception of the universe as a fundamentally and irreducibly interconnected whole, informed by creative intelligence and pervaded by patterns of meaning and order that extend though every level, and that are expressed through a constant correspondence between astronomical events and human events" (2006, 77).

This point is simply stated in the Hermetic axiom, "as above, so below." Planetary positions do not cause any meaningful patterns of events; rather, their alignments reflect the condition of cosmic archetypal dynamics at any given time. For believers in astrology, this implies a potent extension of Jung's concept of synchronicity: psyche and cosmos (specifically, in this case, psyche and the solar system) are integrally related in a way that has not been appreciated by the modern scientific mind. The significance of astrology, and its ability to symbolize human experience, has been appreciated by many great minds prior to the advent of modern science, including Plato, Aristotle, Ptolemy, Plotinus, Aquinas, Dante, Kepler, and Goethe. In modern times, Jung used astrology extensively in his practice with patients, although he prudently left this out of his published works.

To give one example of this synchronistic correspondence, throughout history the conjunction—co-occurrence in the same position relative to Earth—of the planets Uranus and Pluto has been associated with periods of social ferment and revolution. (Astronomy's recent demotion of Pluto to a quasi-planet does not affect its symbolic, archetypal meaning within astrology.) Such a conjunction happened during the 1780s and 1790s, the period of the French Revolution. It also recurred during the 1960s, a decade of widespread social and political change and often destructive upheaval. Tarnas's book offers a considerable amount of evidence that the conjunction or opposition (180 degrees opposite) of these two planets is consistently accompanied by historical periods characterized by revolution and rapid social change.

Conjunction and opposition alignments between other planets are associated with historical periods that bear a different archetypal stamp. For example, the period associated with the conjunction of Uranus and Neptune that occurred between 1985 and 2000 reflected a synthesis of the two planets' archetypal meanings. Uranus is associated with the principles of change, rebellion, freedom, liberation, and technological innovation. Neptune is associated with the transcendent, spiritual, ideal, symbolic, and imaginative dimensions of life, as well as with the dissolving of boundaries and the dissolution of ego structures. According to Tarnas, one of the many indications of the Neptune-Uranus conjunction in the 1990s was the pervasive shift toward global consciousness—the breakdown of barriers to communication throughout the world—fostered particularly by the technical innovation of the Internet. He cites scores of other developments toward the end of the century that reflect a synthesis of the Neptune and Uranus archetypes in a way that is distinct from the Pluto-Uranus synthesis that happened during the 1960s (419-451).

What are we to make of Tarnas's extensive documentation of correspondences between specific planetary alignments and the archetypal "flavor" of culture, politics, and society that occur during the time of alignment? Any serious reading of his book leads to a conviction that these correspondences have credibility—

and that astrological alignments and meaningful cultural events do mutually implicate one another on an archetypal level.

Archetypal Knowledge

To appreciate the possible relevance of astrology in understanding human and societal behavior, we need to approach it from a mode of knowing quite different from the linear, rational methods of science. Seeing astrological correspondences requires a more holistic, intuitive mode of knowing—an "archetypal perception" or "archetypal knowing" that can discern a symbolic consistency among a variety of superficially different characteristics or events. Jung's student James Hillman refers to this as developing an archetypal eye: the capacity to recognize archetypal patterns in the complexity of one's personal life experience or the great events of history and culture (1975). Those who cannot or will not develop this more global, intuitive mode of knowing—who remain confined to the linear, deductive reasoning characteristic of science—will have difficulty comprehending and ultimately accepting the deeply symbolic nature of astrological correspondences. For such a person, skepticism is to be expected. Thus Tarnas's portrait of a deeply symbolic cosmos requires an expanded epistemology that honors intuitive, symbolic modes of knowledge. As discussed in chapter 7, the emerging new worldview can be expected to grant equal credibility to intuitive, participatory forms of knowledge as to sensory, empirical knowledge.

When such an epistemology becomes more widely accepted, all of the esoteric, divinatory arts are likely to regain their former credibility. Not just astrology but also numerology, the I Ching, and the Tarot will all be seen as vehicles for revealing the archetypal or symbolic meaning of any given instant in time. The pattern of the coins thrown in the I Ching, or the layout of cards of the Tarot, synchronistically reveals the archetypal dynamics of the moment in which the act is performed. The meaning that is revealed is not literal but highly symbolic; it should be appreciated as suggesting the archetypal potentials that exist at a given moment in time rather than predicting specific future events. Jung, who was interested in all of the divinatory arts, conveys this in his statement,

"Whatever is born or done at this particular moment of time has the quality of this moment of time" (Tarnas 2006, 57).

Conclusion

Divinatory practices such as astrology and the Tarot have their place in the emerging global paradigm shift. They do not appear to make sense from a strictly rational, scientific perspective. However, we can comprehend and appreciate their utility by developing a highly intuitive mode of knowing that is able to "see" the archetypal patterns of meaning that these systems reveal. As such, these esoteric systems can be useful tools for understanding both individual lives as well as societal trends. They reveal the way an individual or society's destiny will unfold, based on the way the archetypal stage is set at the moment the chart is cast or the cards are laid out. The correspondence between the symbolism revealed by these practices and how events then transpire is not coincidental but synchronistic. It implies a conscious universe—a universe in which all levels of phenomena are intimately interconnected through that very consciousness. At each moment, the Cosmos, in its subjective aspect, has a unique, archetypal configuration that can be profoundly revealed by these long-practiced arts.

17

Implications of the
New Worldview

The preceding chapters have outlined several aspects of the world-view emerging today. Fundamentally, this worldview involves re-envisioning the universe as a conscious, organized whole. The universe in its entirety, from atoms to galaxies, is understood to be conscious, deeply interconnected, and intelligently ordered.

At first this might sound like a return to a primitive form of animism—a throwback to precivilized modes of perception. In fact, it's quite different. Animism and early religions saw the phenomenal world as influenced by a plurality of deities that fought among themselves and could be hostile to humanity. Often it was necessary to appease or propitiate these deities by ritual and sacrifice. By contrast, the emerging worldview is fundamentally holistic. There is only one consciousness or spirit pervading all things. Everything we behold is a manifestation of this one universal cosmic intelligence.

This is not a new view. In the history of religions, it has been associated with pantheism. However, while pantheism generally equates the visible world with God, the emerging worldview goes beyond this. Consciousness is both immanent in all phenomena as well as transcendent. It is not only the ground of all that is, it also interpenetrates the phenomenal world. In the history of philosophy, this view is called *panentheism*; it was held by Plato, Plotinus, and Spinoza, among others.

What are the implications of a universe that is radically interconnected and conscious? How does such a view affect our perception not only of the world but of ourselves and each other? What follows are just a few of the obvious implications.

The Development of a Respectful and Cooperative Relationship with Nature

Seeing the entire universe as a conscious order restores sacredness to the world. The sacred is not just an invisible, inscrutable other beyond our perception, not just something in which we can only have faith. It belongs to everything we see—stars, mountains, trees, animals, fish, insects, rocks, soil, cells, molecules, and atoms. It is as immediate as a flower, mountain, or child standing in front of us.

When we see nature and the universe as sacred, we cease to exploit them for selfish ends. The thrust of the Industrial Revolution over the last 150 years has been to exploit and dominate nature, predominantly for economic gain. The results of such exploitation are well known; these include global warming, deforestation, desertification, massive loss of species, widespread pollution, and rapid depletion of natural resources.

Our planet is facing an unprecedented crisis. Present patterns of economic growth and consumption cannot continue without essentially destroying and depleting the earth to the point at which it will no longer be able to support life. As the global environmental crisis intensifies over the next few decades, we will be forced to assume a more caring, respectful, and cooperative relationship with our planet. Even from a purely economic standpoint, this will be necessary. Humanity can no longer arrogantly assume that nature is simply a neutral resource available for unlimited exploitation.

An Increased Sense of Connection and Communion for All Peoples

Personal identity is beginning to move away from self-perception as a separate, autonomous ego toward a greater sense of participation and interrelationship with others, nature, and the cosmos. The twentieth century was characterized by alienation. Many forces associated with industrialization and urbanization were separative—disconnecting the individual from self, family, community, nature, and spirit. The twenty-first century will see these splits begin to heal. The individual as a unique autonomous ego against the world will be replaced by an awareness of increasing interconnectedness. Lifestyles and values will shift to allow people to feel greater kinship with people of all races and cultures, as well as with animals and plants. Ultimately we will see our own lives as integral parts of the cosmic order, our own projects and purposes as fulfilling the creative intentions of the universe. In traditional religious terms, our personal will and divine will more easily align and harmonize.

Greater Compassion for All Beings

If we see ourselves all as interdependent parts of one seamless whole, we can begin to overcome gender, racial, and cultural barriers, and embody the golden rule—to indeed treat our fellow humans as we would treat ourselves. The injunction to love one another in Christianity—or to exercise lovingkindness for all living things in Buddhism—is simply a logical consequence of a consciousness where we recognize we are all highly interdependent parts of a single organic whole. Whatever we do to another, we in effect do to ourselves.

Decline of Consumerism

If nature is nothing more than a repository of unlimited resources, without any sacredness, then we have only material acquisitiveness to justify our lives. Having more and getting more become preoccupations and ends in themselves. Shopping malls and commercial websites become our places of worship. We look to material wealth and personal property to assuage the emptiness of a life and world devoid of any other significance.

On the other hand, as we come to see the world as increasingly sacred—and not forever expendable—we can learn to live more lightly upon it. Unabated consumerism can be replaced by a tendency to purchase goods that are not only simpler and more durable, but also sustainable. As goods and resources become more scarce, consumerism is being replaced by renewed interest in intangible values: love, reverence, compassion, generosity, charity, and so on. Self-worth is increasingly gauged on the basis of who we are rather than what we have.

The Valuing of Intuitive Knowledge

In the new worldview, intuitive ways of knowing—including empathy, insight, and even mystical revelation—are afforded equal credibility as the sensory, empirical knowledge on which science is based. We come to appreciate that the cosmos can only be fully understood when we use both our senses and our intuitive faculties. Decision-making at all levels is based not just on rational analysis but on wisdom, which requires insight often gained through alignment with a higher dimension of consciousness.

A Natural Ethics

Ethics will no longer be viewed as a cultural construction relative to each society's interpretation of which rules and laws promote social order. The ethical relativism of the twentieth century is gradually being replaced by a natural and universal ethics, based on a culture-free perception of a spiritual universe. If all human beings are part of one sacred whole, then compassion, generosity, and kindness toward all beings—animate and even inanimate— follows logically. Whenever a moral dilemma arises, the operative questions become, "What is the most loving thing to do?" and, "What is the most compassionate choice for everyone involved?" Morality is based not on particular social mores but on a universal respect and compassion toward all life.

Emergence of a Global Consciousness

While ethnic, religious, and cultural diversity will always be a part of our world, human beings are increasingly coming to respect these differences within a broader vision of a common humanity. Many of us are beginning to look beyond our social and national identities to regard ourselves instead as members of a deeply interconnected, planetary civilization.

Conclusion

The global shift described in this book so far is about a change in vision—the way we perceive the world and our relationship to it. Yet the shift does not end there.

For a shift in consciousness to be truly relevant, it needs to be more than just intellectual or perceptual. Each of us needs to take it into our hearts and our everyday lives. We need to *feel* and *act* as though nature is conscious and sacred, as though all human beings are part of one, interdependent whole. The remainder of this book is about embodying the new shift—taking it into action.

18

Making the Shift:
From Vision to Action

Up to this point, the global shift has been discussed in largely conceptual terms. The emphasis has been on a shift in worldview—a new perception of reality—that is needed at the present time given the global challenges humanity is facing. The remainder of this book, beginning with this chapter, examines the global shift in more personal terms. What does it mean to make the shift personally, in terms of your own beliefs and values? *What can each of us actually do in our day-to-day life* to support and align with the emerging worldview?

This chapter asks you to reflect on where you stand in making the shift with respect to:

- Concepts and perceptions about the nature of reality (as described in chapters 4-17)

- Personal values

- Practical actions

Conceptual Shifts

The following is a summary of the major conceptual shifts described in previous chapters:

Nature is conscious and exhibits attributes of consciousness at all levels, from atoms to galaxies: The cosmos does not behave like a machine but is a self-organizing, evolving entity. As a conscious being, it is fundamentally sacred.

Reality is larger than the observable, physical universe, and contains multiple nonphysical dimensions: What is real is not limited to the physical universe observable through human senses. There are other, subtle domains that can be perceived through insight, intuition, and revelation. Current unified field theories in physics, such as superstring theories, also imply a multidimensional universe.

Knowledge based on intuition is just as valid and necessary as empirical knowledge based on the senses: Empirical science reveals the causal, mechanistic order of nature understood through the senses. The humanities and religion explore the interior aspects of nature that are primarily grasped through intuition and revelation. Both are necessary for a complete understanding and explanation of the Cosmos.

Fundamentally all of us are joined as one; nothing is independent of any other thing: All of us are united in consciousness at the deepest level. We are united not just as the collective consciousness of humanity but literally with all that is conscious throughout the universe. The religions of the world have attempted to grasp and articulate the underlying reality that there is only one, unitary source for everything.

Feminine values of interdependency, cooperation, and respect for the earth are a central part of the new worldview: Long-dominant masculine, patriarchal values are being integrated with reemerging, traditionally feminine values. Competition will ultimately be superseded by interrelationship and cooperation as the dominant ethos governing relations among different peoples of the world.

The basis for ethics is not found in socially constructed rules relative to each culture but in the natural order of the universe: To act in a loving, compassionate way is merely to live in alignment with the inherent order of nature (Cosmos) and our own soul as a part of that nature. Ought reduces to is: what we ought to do is simply live to the best of our ability in harmony with our innermost being, which coincides with the conscious intelligence of the universe

(Logos in Greek philosophy, Divine Will in Christianity, Dharma in Buddhism, the Tao in Taoism).

Reflections

Take some time to think about how you feel about the perceptual shifts just listed. Do they resonate or make sense to you? Are they already a part of your current belief system? Do they seem difficult to grasp or improbable? Use the following guided reflections to further define where you personally stand in regard to some of the major conceptual shifts described in this book.

Conscious Universe

Imagine a world where all things are in some sense conscious—not just humans and animals, but trees, rocks, clouds, streams, rivers, and mountains. How would you feel about such a world?

Now imagine that you can come into conscious "dialogue" with the other entities of this world—again, not only with other animal species, but with a tree, rock, cloud, or a mountain. Picture yourself sitting quietly in the middle of a forest or by the ocean at sunrise or sunset. What is the nature of the communication or messages you might receive from your surroundings?

Now suppose that the entire planet is a conscious being. All of its intricate, interrelated ecological balances and cycles function in unison as an organic whole. If you embrace such a view, how does this affect your attitude toward the earth?

If the earth is actually a type of conscious, living being, how do you feel about the extensive damage that humanity has done to the environment in the past one hundred years? What might you be willing to do personally to help the earth?

Now try on the idea that the entire universe is a type of conscious being. Suppose that our solar system, the Milky Way galaxy, and even the galaxy cluster of which our galaxy is a part are all intelligent entities with some form of consciousness and intention. How does this change your view of the cosmos as a whole? How does your perceived relationship with such a cosmos change?

Multidimensional Universe

Suppose that there are indeed other dimensions of reality beyond those of the physical, space-time universe. Suppose the entire physical universe is just a small subsystem within a larger matrix that mostly exists outside of space-time. Does this seem likely to be true to you? How does this idea change your understanding of and feeling about the cosmos? What do you imagine the dimensions of the universe outside of space-time to be like?

Now suppose that part of your own consciousness exists outside of space-time. Imagine that your immediate, conscious stream of awareness is actually rooted in something that transcends space-time. If so, your physical body is merely a projection into space of something that ultimately exists outside of space. How does this idea affect your sense of who or what you are? If you are much more than your physical body, then what are you? If a part of you exists outside of space-time, where do the boundaries of your individuality lie?

Finally, if you believe there is a nonphysical aspect of your being (call it the soul, if you wish), then imagine that it existed before your body was born and continues indefinitely after you die. How does this affect your feelings toward physical death? What do you believe about the nature of personal existence after the death of the body?

Unity of All Consciousness

Imagine that your mind is seamlessly joined, at a deep level, with the minds of your family, significant others, and friends. When someone you care about is in distress or experiencing excitement or joy, that person's experience subtly registers somewhere in your consciousness—perhaps even percolates into your conscious awareness. How does it feel to be so intimately connected with your loved ones and friends? Do you mind the possibility that their experiences may subtly impact your own stream of experience, whether you are aware of it or not? Does this connection feel comforting, or does it feel like a violation of your personal boundaries?

Now try on the idea that your consciousness is connected to the greater consciousness of your community, city, state, country, and ultimately the global consciousness of humanity at large. If a major event occurs that impacts people throughout your country or all over the world, suppose that it impacts your consciousness, whether you are informed of it or not. How do you feel about the possibility that the collective mood of your country or the world may impact you, whether you are aware of what is going on or not?

Finally, imagine that some of the awarenesses with which your own awareness is connected are neither human nor animal, but instead associated with so-called spirit guides or subtle beings. Is the prospect of having a deep connection with subtle beings—beings that you may or may not even be aware of—comforting? Or does it seem intrusive?

Synthesis of Science and Religion

The emerging worldview regards science and religion as two complementary ways of understanding the same cosmos. Science investigates the outer, objective aspect of the physical universe, while religion or spirituality fathoms the inner, existential aspects of that same cosmos—particularly the relationship of individual consciousness to the universal consciousness of the entire cosmos. Thus science and spirituality don't ultimately conflict, they are just concerned with different aspects or faces of the same reality. Does this seem plausible to you? Do you feel there is a genuine conflict between science and spirituality?

Some scientists propose that scientific knowledge will eventually evolve to the point that religious and metaphysical ideas will be entirely replaced. Science will provide a complete description of all aspects of reality, and present-day religious ideas will be relegated to folk concepts or mythologies of merely historical interest. What do you think of this proposal?

Many religious thinkers maintain that there are several types of questions about reality that science will never be able to answer. For example, they doubt that science will reveal the meaning of human existence or the ultimate foundation for ethical behavior. What is your opinion? Will science ultimately provide us with a satisfactory account of the meaning of human existence or the basis for acting ethically toward others?

Value Shifts

Human beings are not, of course, purely mental creatures. Shifts in perception and belief are inevitably accompanied by changes in *values*. The way we view the world profoundly affect our priorities and values—and ultimately the ways we behave. However, it cannot be said that shifts in perception and worldview necessarily *cause* shifts in values or behaviors. Our beliefs, values, and behaviors are interwoven and tend to shift concurrently and synergistically. Many people, in fact, are likely to make basic shifts in values—and behaviors—without necessarily embracing the worldview shifts described above.

What are some of the fundamental shifts in values likely to accompany the global consciousness shift described in this book? An abbreviated, partial list follows:

Increased reverence and respect for the earth and all forms of life upon it: The earth is understood as a sacred matrix in which we are deeply embedded, rather than something to be exploited for material gain.

Increased compassion rather than prejudice toward peoples whose race, nationality, religion, ethnic group, or economic status differ from our own: This means acceptance and respect for all human beings as part of the same planetary community, deserving of equal rights to health, livelihood, safety, and prosperity.

Greater priority given to personal and spiritual growth than to materialistic values of acquisition and consumption: We focus increasingly on finding peace and presence within ourselves rather than striving for outer material success. This means recognizing the importance of aligning our personal life with the rhythm and flow of the earth, and indeed the larger Cosmos.

Embracing nonlinear, intuitive ways of knowing the world: Such ways of knowing are understood to offer deeper insight into the symbolic or interior face of the Cosmos, in contrast with sensory ways of knowing that provide information about the outer, objective face. While reason and logic have their place, intuition offers additional, often uncanny guidance for problem solving.

Honoring unconditional love and forgiveness as the highest values in all of our relations with others: If we are all one, then to harm another person is to harm oneself. Thus we come to recognize that the operative question in any interpersonal situation is truly: "What is the most loving thing to do?"

A shift toward such values is already evident in many places. Concern about the state of the global environment is much more widespread than it was even five years ago. Humanity has also moved a long way from the racial and ethnic prejudices of the past (such as Nazi Germany), though in certain parts of the world there is still a long way to go. In the West, interest in personal healing and spiritual growth dates back to the focus on Eastern mysticism in the 1970s, and has increased in the past twenty years through widespread interest in holistic health, yoga, and meditation. Intuitive ways of knowing are gaining credibility through humanistic and transpersonal psychology, popular interest in "channeling" and listening to inner guidance, and the focus on insight in creative problem-solving. While religions have always emphasized the primacy of unconditional love, compassion, and forgiveness, these values now also enjoy widespread recognition in popular movements such as the twelve-step programs, nonviolent communication, and New Thought churches such as Unity and Science of Mind.

Further Reflections

As you think about the values just described, consider where you stand in your own personal evolution with respect to each value. To what extent does your daily life—your lifestyle, activities, and personal relationships—reflect these values?

Use the scales below to reflect on where you stand in "making the shift" toward values compatible with the new worldview. In each scale, a value associated with the new paradigm is contrasted with a value associated with the old paradigm. In looking at where you stand, don't be too quick to judge yourself if you don't fall near the new-paradigm end of each scale. Most of us these days are still transitioning from the old to the new. Many of us would find living at the extreme and rejecting all old-paradigm ways wholesale to be impractical. You may feel better striking a balance between old- and new-paradigm values rather than living at the edge.

Lifestyle

Materialism/Acquisition . . . . Personal/Spiritual Growth

Consumerism. . . . . Concern with Sustainability

Complexity . . . . Simplicity

Life in the fast lane. . . . . Self-Care

Interpersonal Relations

Competition . . . . Cooperation

Self-Interest. . . . . Concern for Others (family, friends, coworkers, community, and planet)

Cognition (Thinking Style)

Rational/Analytical. . . . . Intuitive/Visionary (the goal is to balance and integrate both poles)

Self-Concept*

Self-Focus . . . . Letting Go of Self

Independence. . . . . Interrelationship

*Self-focus versus letting go of self refers to how much you feel caught up in yourself and personal dramas, as opposed to perceiving yourself and your life as part of a larger whole. (A more detailed description of this can be found in chapter 9.) Independence versus interrelationship is similar: Is your life primarily about you and your personal destiny or is it more about being a part of relationships and larger networks of people?

Motivations for Making the Shift

What kinds of circumstances can motivate us to make a shift in consciousness compatible with the emerging worldview? What follows are some of the more common motivators. Consider which ones, if any, have been instrumental in your own life:

Life Crisis

After a personal crisis or other life challenge, you may become more focused on inner development rather than material concerns and goals. For example, as a result of a life-threatening sickness, you may make some major modifications in your diet, simplify your lifestyle, and take up the regular practice of yoga and meditation. Or after being laid off from an unrewarding corporate job, you may decide to live with less income and get involved with a nonprofit organization striving to help the environment.

Burnout with Material Values

At different ages, many people reach a point where they feel exhausted by a lifestyle focused on consumption, status, and material goals. Concerns about how you look, the house you own, and where you live lose their former importance. After realizing that the pursuit of material goals does not bring you peace of mind, you may start to search within. Carl Jung described a need to shift values during the "second half of life," from outward achievement in the world to a more inner-directed focus on personal and spiritual development. It's possible that such a trend has accelerated in our time, so that people are now making this transition at an earlier age.

Peak Experiences

You may experience a heightened state of awareness or epiphany in which you come to appreciate the importance of the whole of humanity over your individual concerns. For example, after witnessing the birth of a child you suddenly see the preciousness of all life. In such an experience, you might also catch a glimpse of the entire earth or universe as a conscious being, of which you are but a small, interdependent part. Such experiences may enhance your perception that you are a fundamentally spiritual being having a physical experience on earth—or that your life has a larger purpose beyond personal ego needs. Following such an experience, you may decide to focus more on spiritual growth or get involved with organizations seeking to help the environment or correct social injustices.

Peer Influence

Friends or loved ones may adopt values associated with simplicity, sustainability, concern for the earth, or compassion for human suffering, influencing you to make similar shifts.

Education

We are surrounded these days by books, magazines, and media presentations that provide information about the global crisis, environmentally friendly practices and lifestyles, and alternative approaches to health and personal growth. As you learn more about pathways to healing yourself as well as the earth, you may naturally feel moved to shift your values in that direction.

From Values to Action

While changes in basic perceptions and values are essential to the shift our planet needs, they cannot go far without corresponding actions. Thus a critical question arises: *What can each of us actually do in our daily lives to embody the global shift?* How can each of us personally help bring about a new world in which the beliefs and values listed above are honored? How can we put into practice the perceptual and value shifts needed to help our planet survive the major crises it is currently facing?

One way is to start with ourselves. The global shift ultimately begins with each of us, one person at a time. Each of us is a "cell" in the collective consciousness of humanity. By working on personal healing and inner peace, each of us contributes in a small but unique way to promoting the healing of the planet. In being more at peace with ourselves, we affect many others, both through our example and through our actions. So the very first step each of us can take to promote a global shift is to engage in practices that lead to greater personal peace, healing, and spiritual growth. *It is from a foundation of such inner peace and healing that each of us can develop the compassion and sense of social responsibility to move beyond ourselves—to do what we can to help the planet.*

Some of the many ways you might cultivate inner peace and healing include:

- Simplify your life by, for example, living close to where you work or combining errands so that you make only one trip to the mall per week.

- Learn basic communication skills that promote compassion and understanding in your relationships with family, friends, work associates, and others.

- Transition your diet away from processed foods toward organic, whole foods.

- Take time out from cumulative stress to relax every day.

- Have a daily exercise routine that helps to discharge tension.

- Visualize and deeply affirm a goal, such as finding your "right" employment or relationship, or optimum health.

- Reframe your attitude toward a negative experience by reflecting on what it may have taught you.

Another way to take action is simply to do things that help the earth and socially disadvantaged people. This includes both personal lifestyle choices that directly help the planet as well as contributing time and/or money to organizations that deal with environmental and social problems.

Examples of personal lifestyle choices that can help the earth include:

- Improve the energy efficiency of your home (for example, through proper insulation, reducing use of heat and air conditioning, using compact fluorescent light bulbs, and purchasing energy-efficient appliances)

- Drive energy-efficient vehicles, such as hybrids or compact cars, as well as driving less

- Over time, shift your diet away from meat toward vegetarianism (meat production industries are very energy and water intensive)

- Recycle paper, glass, metal, and plastic

- Engage in socially responsible investing

- Reduce consumption of luxury items

Beyond changing our lifestyles and habits, we help when we:

- Contribute time locally to help impoverished, hungry, or homeless people

- Contribute financially to nonprofit organizations striving to ameliorate global problems such as climate change, loss of biodiversity, inhumane treatment of animals, overpopulation, and third-world poverty and disease

- Sign petitions and vote for political candidates who are concerned about the environment and the serious problems that the planet is confronting

Conclusion

The final six chapters of this book enumerate several transformative practices that can lead to personal healing as well as help humanity and the planet. These are by no means the only practices that can facilitate personal and planetary healing. Yet collectively they offer several pathways to bring your personal life into closer alignment with the emerging global shift. As you read about these practices in the next few chapters, notice those you are already doing and then consider which additional ones you might be willing to embrace.

Transformative Practices:
An Introduction

A global shift in consciousness takes place one person at a time. Ultimately it begins with each of us cultivating healing and peace in our personal lives. Each of us is a microcosm of the planet as a whole. The planet's current travails are suffered in an endless variety of ways by each of us individually. The "body" of humanity begins to heal as each "cell" in that body heals. If we are all deeply interconnected, then cultivating our own inner peace is a gift to the whole of humanity. Our personal healing can have a ripple effect that we can't even imagine. As each of us develops more harmony in our personal life, we become an example for others to follow the same path.

Over the next six chapters, several pathways for cultivating inner peace and healing are described. While the practices presented are certainly not all-inclusive, they are among some of the more helpful ways to positively transform your life and ultimately that of others. In embracing these practices, you align the course of your personal life with the higher purpose of the conscious universe described in earlier chapters of this book.

The six transformative practices described call you to:

- Simplify your life

- Build peaceful relationships

- Care for your body

- Practice meditation

- Think larger

- Take action

These practices help reduce stress and promote personal healing. They also help bring you into alignment with the natural rhythm and intelligence of nature and the universe. Throughout this book it has been emphasized that the universe (including Earth) is not a passive object but a conscious, intelligent, intentional *process*. All whole systems in the universe—from atoms to cells to galaxies—exhibit a type of consciousness and intention. Moreover, all of these systems are interlinked and involved in a common evolution. By cultivating personal healing and peace, you can align better with your own innermost self—which, in turn, links you with the larger consciousness of which your inner being is a part. At its deepest level, your innermost consciousness is not separate from the consciousness of the planet and the cosmos at large. The two are deeply interconnected.

What is this "universal consciousness"? If this term seems too impersonal or abstract, you can substitute more traditional religious terms such as God, Spirit, or Higher Power; in truth, words are just words, and the ultimate reality behind everything surpasses any concept or name that can be given to it. When speaking of the new worldview that is emerging, this book speaks of the consciousness or "intelligence" of the universe (a universe that contains dimensions beyond the physical universe studied by science) to emphasize that earth and cosmos are not just passive objects of scientific explanation and control. Whether you wish to think of the ultimate ground of reality as a universal cosmic consciousness, or in more personal terms such as God, is a matter of personal preference. Whatever that infinite reality is, it's large enough to be both impersonal and personal. It's something that can be both abstract and with which you can also have a very personal relationship. That it can be both may seem paradoxical, but only to our limited minds. (As suggested earlier in this book, the conscious universe is likely one or two steps down from the ultimate ground of everything, so that it is an *expression* of that ground rather than being identical with it. Whatever is ultimate is ineffable.)

For purposes of the practices described in the next few chapters, keep in mind that not only can they bring you inner peace, they can also align you with the larger evolutionary processes of the earth and cosmos. On a practical level, certain practices that are personally helpful are also helpful to the planet. For example, by simplifying your life, you can save yourself stress and give yourself more time to enjoy personal relationships and to be simply present (quiet) with yourself. At the same time, you will be aligning with the planet's needs by consuming less, conserving resources, and lightening your environmental footprint. On a more subtle level, some of these practices, by reducing stress and helping you to be more at peace, open you to higher sources of inspiration, creativity, and guidance. The more your consciousness is unfettered by stress—such as that caused by denied emotions or habitual mental patterns that lead to fear, frustration, or resentment—the more open you will be to inspiration, guidance, and energetic empowerment from beyond your ego, from the conscious universe or God.

Such inspiration and guidance can be highly personal, or it can impel you to serve other persons, organizations, or causes larger than yourself. In fact, your life is not really just about you and your needs. As you align with the conscious universe, you begin to embody the universe's purposes and are motivated to fulfill its needs.

To sum up, the practices described in the following chapters promote health and peace in your own life as well as help you to align with the larger needs of the planet. By undertaking each practice, you lessen personal stress while at the same time contributing to the global shift in consciousness needed on the planet at this time.

19

Simplify Your Life

Living more simply is a potent way to change your life. To do so is to live more consciously and with a minimum of needless distractions. It is to establish a more direct and unencumbered relationship with all aspects of your life: family, work, community, nature, the environment, and yourself. Simplifying your life gives you more time to be present—present with your own innermost self and present for the important people in your life. A simple way of life also benefits the planet. When you decrease your acquisition and consumption of goods, you use less of the earth's precious resources. Reducing your energy consumption helps to mitigate climate change. A simpler life aligns you with the shift in consciousness—the new values and actions—needed on the earth at this time.

The first part of this chapter focuses on simplifying your life in general. It enumerates a variety of ways to reduce complexity and create more time to do what nourishes your soul, such as spending time with loved ones or expressing your innate creative potential. The second part of this chapter, "Simplicity and the Planet," focuses on the environmental benefits of living a simpler life, including specific steps you can take to reduce your personal carbon emissions, decrease your consumption, and live more sustainably.

Simplifying your life does not mean living in poverty. Poverty is involuntary and disabling, whereas choosing to live simply is voluntary and empowering. Simplicity is finding the right balance between austerity and excess. It's somewhere between the log cabin in the forest and the estate in the suburbs. Simplicity can be achieved in an urban or rural environment. Above all, simple living does not mean doing away with modern comforts and conveniences to prove your ability to live apart from twentieth-century technology. Gandhi made an interesting statement about denying the material side of life: "As long as you derive inner help and comfort from anything, you should keep it. If you were to give it up in a mood of self-sacrifice...you would continue to want it back, and that unsatisfied want would make trouble for you" (Elgin 1993, 32).

No precise formula defines what constitutes living simply. Each of us is likely to discover our own ways to reduce complexity and unnecessary encumbrances.

One View of the Simple Life

In *Voluntary Simplicity* (1993), Duane Elgin notes that people who choose a simple life tend to:

- Invest the time and energy freed up by simpler living in activities with their partner, children, and friends (walking, making music together, sharing a meal, camping, and so on)

- Work on developing the full spectrum of their potentials: physical (running, biking, hiking, and so on), emotional (learning the skills of intimacy and sharing feelings in important relationships), mental (engaging in lifelong learning such as through reading or taking classes), and spiritual (learning to move through life with a quiet mind and compassionate heart)

- Feel an intimate connection with the earth and a reverential concern for nature

- Feel a compassionate concern for the world's poor

- Lower their overall level of personal consumption—buying less clothing, for example (with more attention to what is functional, durable, aesthetic, and less concern with passing fads, fashions, and seasonal styles)

- Alter their patterns of consumption in favor of products that are durable, easy to repair, nonpolluting in their manufacture and use, energy-efficient, functional, and aesthetic

- Shift their diet away from highly processed foods, meat, and sugar toward foods that are more natural, healthy, simple, and appropriate for sustaining the inhabitants of a small planet

- Reduce undue clutter and complexity in their personal lives by giving away or selling those items that are seldom used and could be used productively by others (such as clothing, books, furniture, appliances, or tools)

- Recycle metal, glass, and paper and cut back on consumption of items that are wasteful of nonrenewable resources

- Develop personal skills that contribute to greater self-reliance and reduce dependence upon experts to handle life's ordinary demands (basic carpentry, plumbing, appliance repair, gardening and so on)

- Prefer smaller, human-scale living and working environments that foster a sense of community, face-to-face contact, and mutual caring

- Participate in holistic healthcare practices that emphasize preventive medicine and the healing powers of the body when assisted by the mind

- Change transportation modes in favor of public transit, carpooling, smaller and more fuel-efficient autos, living closer to work, riding a bike, and walking (32-35)

Some Ways to Simplify Your Life

Below are a few suggestions for simplifying your life. This is a partial list and by no means complete. Some are changes you can make immediately, while others require more time and effort. Remember: one goal of living a simple life is to free yourself from commitments that deplete your time, energy, and money without meeting your essential needs or sustaining your spirit. The other goal is to lighten your impact on the planet by consuming less resources and living more sustainably.

Downsize Your Living Situation

Smaller living quarters offer several benefits: For one thing, you are much less likely to accumulate large amounts of things when you don't have sufficient room for them. Also, a smaller space takes less time to clean and maintain and is typically less expensive. Finally, your energy use and cost will be less in a smaller place.

Let Go of Clutter

We live in a time of unprecedented abundance. This makes it easy to accumulate stuff that has no real value or use and only creates more clutter. Take a look at your stuff and decide what is useful and worth keeping and what is simply taking up space. As a general rule, to reduce clutter get rid of everything you haven't used in more than a year—except, of course, items that have sentimental value. Be sure to dispose of electronic devices such as old computers, stereos, and TVs properly, by donating or recycling them (contact your local recycling center for more information). If you just put them in the trash, they will end up in landfills where they will leach toxic metals into the groundwater and atmosphere.

Do What You Want for a Living

Doing what you truly want can require time, risk, and effort. It may take one or two years to acquire the retraining or retooling you need to begin a new career. Then you may have to work at an entry-level position before your new line of work meets your financial needs. However, the time, effort, and disruption are usually well worth it.

Doing what you want for a living feels good because when you do so, you align yourself with your highest purpose or personal mission in the world. Because your highest purpose originates from your deep inner wisdom, aligning with it can empower you to contribute to something larger than just your own personal needs. In living your highest purpose, your life can become part of the global shift happening on the planet at this time.

Reduce Your Commute

Reducing or eliminating your commute to work is one of the most significant changes you can make to simplify your life. Negotiating rush-hour traffic on a daily basis adds considerable complexity to your life. Reduce your commute by moving closer to where you work or choosing to live in a smaller town. At the very least, if you have to commute over a long distance, try to arrange for flexible work hours to avoid rush hour. At this time many Americans work out of their homes, and the number is rising. If there is a consulting service or computer-based job you can do out of your home, you can join them.

Reducing your commute not only lessens personal stress, it helps the planet by conserving energy and reducing your carbon output into the atmosphere.

Reduce Exposure to TV and Computer Screens

How much time do you spend in front of a screen each day? These days the ordinary American household has two to three TVs, each typically with forty to nine hundred channels. As if this were not enough, more than a hundred million American households have computers offering a potentially endless array of games as well as Internet access to millions of websites. Granted, there are many good programs on TV, and the Internet is a wonderful tool for communicating information; the concern is the sheer complexity of having so many options, all of which involve a passive stance of either witnessing entertainment or absorbing information. Life in front of the screen can be more than just a distraction; it can be a hindrance to building a deeper connection with nature, others, and yourself. Time in front of the screen is best ruled by moderation. Quality time with loved ones as well as quiet time just being present with yourself offer you a better opportunity to be in harmony with the rhythms of life.

Live Closer to Nature

The hectic pace of modern life is sometimes associated with feelings of disembodiment. This disconnection can be aggravated by situations that involve being literally disconnected from the earth, such as riding for a distance in a car, being high up in a tall building, or flying. It may also be aggravated by situations that bombard you with so much stimulation that your awareness becomes scattered or dispersed, such as a grocery store, shopping mall, or social gathering.

Taking a walk in the woods or a park is a simple act that can help reverse these feelings of disembodiment. Being in close proximity to the earth—its sights, sounds, smells, and energies—can help you to remain more easily connected with yourself. Choosing to live in such a setting, if possible, allows you to enjoy a connection with the earth—a connection that much of modern civilization seems to have lost—on an ongoing basis.

By spending more time in nature, you're also likely to feel more reverence for the earth, and thus be more inclined to make choices to protect it.

Tame the Telephone

There are people who believe they should answer the phone virtually every time it rings, regardless of the time of day or their current mood. Whether it's a creditor, a sales solicitation, or a cantankerous relative, these people feel it is an almost sacred obligation to answer every call. But answering the telephone—and this includes your cell phone—is optional. You can always let your voice mail or answering machine answer it for you, and then return calls when you are ready to give your callers your full attention. If you are engaged in a project or activity that you find rewarding, there is no need to drop it to take a call that does not require your immediate attention.

Delegate Menial Chores

How many menial chores would you delegate to someone else if money were not an issue? Delegating even just one activity you don't like to do can make a difference in the sense of ease you experience in your day-to-day life. If money is an issue, is there something your children can learn to do just about as well as you? Can you allow other family members to help with the cooking, yard upkeep, or housecleaning?

Delegating can open up more time to stop action, relax, and be present with yourself. Quiet, reflective time offers the opportunity to slow yourself down to the speed of life, putting you in touch with sources of wisdom and peace deeper than your conditioned mind.

Learn to Say No

No is not a dirty word. Many people pride themselves on always being able to respond positively to the needs of friends, family, and coworkers. The problem with this consistent helpfulness, is that its end result is exhaustion. Sometimes we can become so busy taking care of others' wants and needs that we have no time or energy to take care of ourselves. When someone asks you for your time, effort, or anything else, think about whether saying yes serves both your highest interest and the other person's highest interest.

Other Ways to Simplify

There are many other ways to simplify your life. For example, you can reduce the amount of junk mail you receive by writing to an organization called Stop The Mail at Box 9008, Farmingdale, NY 11735. You can also reduce junk mail by registering with the Mail Preference Service at dmachoice.org. Reducing junk mail saves paper and ultimately trees. Similarly, by calling and placing your name in the Do Not Call Registry (donotcall.gov), you can cut down on unwanted phone calls. Also consider eliminating all of your credit cards except for one or two. (Having at least one card can be handy for making telephone or Internet purchases or renting a car.) By doing so, you can save yourself a lot of monthly bills and annual fees by eliminating most of your other credit cards.

Simplify Your Life Questionnaire

Take some time to think about ways to simplify your life. To help you do this, ask yourself the following questions:

- On a scale from 1 to 10, with 1 representing a high degree of simplicity and 10 representing a high degree of complexity, where would you rate your present lifestyle?

- Have you made any changes in your living arrangements in the past year toward simplicity? If so, what were these changes?

- What changes toward simplifying your life are you willing to make in the next year?

Review the following simplification strategies and decide which ones you would be willing to try or initiate in the next two months.

- Reduce the clutter in your home

- Move to a smaller house

- If practical, move from a major metropolitan area to a smaller town

- Move closer to shopping resources so you can do all of your errands quickly

- Combine errands so that you make fewer trips (this helps both you and the environment)

- Buy less clothing, with attention to what is functional, durable, and aesthetic rather than fashionable

- Drive a simple, fuel-efficient car

- If practical, replace driving with walking or riding a bike (again, helps both you and the environment)

- Reduce dependence on your TV

- Reduce dependence on outside entertainment (movies, plays, theater, concerts, or nightclubs)

- Reduce magazine subscriptions

- Stop newspaper delivery

- Stop junk mail

- Pay your bills by automatic debit to your checking account (this both saves you time and wastes less paper)

- Stop answering the phone whenever it rings

- Use an all-in-one printer, copier, fax and scanner (simpler than four separate machines and uses much less energy)

- Reduce your commute (if possible, walk or ride your bike to work)

- Work where you live

- Tell your friends you no longer do Christmas gifts (or cards, for that matter)

- Take one suitcase if you vacation and only pack essential clothes

- Take your vacation near or at home

- Reduce your consumption of luxury and designer items; favor products that are durable, easy to repair, made locally, and nonpolluting

- Take steps to get out of debt

- Keep only one or two credit cards

- Consolidate your bank accounts

- Delegate busywork (for example, yard work, housecleaning, tax preparation)

- Simplify your eating habits to include whole, unprocessed foods

- Buy groceries less often, in bulk

- Make water your drink of choice

- Pack your own lunch

- Learn to say no

- Stop trying to change people

- Stop trying to please people—be yourself

- Dispose of all items you don't really need (when possible, give them away or recycle them)

- Do what you truly want for a living

Some of these changes can be made quickly; others involve a lengthier process. It may take a year or two, for example, to arrange your life so that you are doing something you truly enjoy for a living or working out of your home. To reduce clutter, put aside things you think you won't need for a year in a locked closet or storage compartment. At the end of the year, if you have not given them any thought during that time, let them go. Learning to say no and to stop always trying to please others often requires that you learn how to be more assertive. There are classes, workshops, and books that can help with this.

Simplicity and the Planet

Living a simpler life will not only give you more time to be present with yourself and others, it will also help align you with the needs of the earth. This can happen in at least two ways:

- By reducing your energy and fuel use, you reduce your carbon footprint and help mitigate global warming

- By consuming less and recycling more, you use less of the earth's precious resources

Conserve Energy and Reduce Carbon Emissions

What can each of us do, individually, to help mitigate global warming? More than you might think. Quite a few things, both within and outside of your home, can make a difference. Not all of them are simple to do, but they are all compatible with a simpler way of life.

The following are some practical actions you can take to diminish your energy use and indirectly reduce the amount of carbon dioxide you are responsible for producing. A number of these actions are based on a list on the climatecrisis.net website, a site developed by Al Gore to introduce his popular documentary *An Inconvenient Truth*. It's clear that if a substantial number of Americans adopted even some of these measures, the emission of CO_2 into the atmosphere by the United States would be significantly reduced.

- Replace regular incandescent light bulbs with compact fluorescent bulbs, which use about 60 percent less energy. Remember to turn off lights when you are not using them. One widely quoted statistic suggests that if every American household installed just one 75-watt compact fluorescent bulb, it would be equivalent to taking one million cars off the roads in terms of reduced carbon emissions.

- Turn your thermostat down 1 or 2 degrees in the winter and up 1 or 2 degrees in the summer, reducing the energy use of your furnace and air conditioning system. Ideally, set your thermostat to 75 degrees in the summer and 68 degrees in the winter. In the winter, open blinds to let in sunlight; in the summer, close blinds to block heat. This will reduce the demand on your heating and air conditioning systems.

- Clean or replace filters in your furnace or air conditioner. Even better, replace your disposable filter with a permanent one that can be washed and reused.

- Choose energy-efficient appliances when making new purchases. Use the Energy Star label as a guide when selecting appliances such as refrigerators, clothes dryers, stoves, dishwashers, televisions, clothes washers, microwaves, and computers (listed in order of energy usage).

- Wrap your hot-water heater in an insulation blanket. Set the thermostat on your water heater to between 120 and 130 degrees. Consider choosing a tankless, "on-demand" water heater when it's time to replace the appliance.

- Use less hot water by installing low-flow showerheads and washing clothes in cold or warm water.

- Run your dishwasher on its energy-saving setting, and only when it is full.

- Turn your TV, stereo, DVD player, computer, and other appliances off when not using them. You can reduce your energy use even further by plugging multiple appliances or office equipment into one or more power strips. Most appliances use a small amount of electrical current even when turned off; turn off the power strip, and they will use no current. When you want to use them again, simply turn the strip back on. Unplug seldom-used appliances entirely.

- Though it involves a cost upfront, insulate and weatherize your home. Properly insulating your home can reduce your power bill by 25 percent or more in the winter. Within a few years you will recoup your initial cost. The Consumer Federation of America (consumerfed.org) has more information on how to insulate your home.

- Recycle your waste. Recycling even half the waste you produce (paper, glass, plastic, metal) can save a considerable amount of CO_2 per year.

- Buy recycled paper products. It takes 70 to 90 percent less energy to make recycled paper, and helps save the earth's forests.

- Switch to alternative energy sources, such as solar water heaters, for part or all of your home's energy needs. Again, upfront costs will be recovered within a few years through energy savings.

- Buy foods that are locally grown and produced. The average meal travels 1,200 miles from the farm to your plate. Buying locally saves fuel costs. Avoid specialty produce shipped from other continents.

- Buy fresh rather than frozen foods. Besides being healthier to eat, fresh foods take much less energy to produce.

- When possible, buy organic foods. Organic soils capture and store carbon dioxide at much higher levels than conventionally farmed soils.

- Avoid heavily packaged products. You can save a significant amount of carbon dioxide per year simply by cutting down your garbage by 10 percent.

- Reduce the number of miles you drive by walking, biking, carpooling, or taking public transportation.

- Keep your car tuned up and your tires properly inflated. Regular car maintenance increases fuel efficiency and reduces carbon emissions.

- When you buy a car, purchase a more fuel-efficient vehicle such as a hybrid or compact car. You can save more than a ton of carbon dioxide a year by buying a car that gets three miles per gallon better mileage than your current one. With rapidly increasing fuel prices, you will save a lot of money as well.

- When you buy a new computer, consider buying a laptop. Laptops use significantly less power than desktop models.

- If possible, fly less. Air travel produces large amounts of carbon emissions. If you must fly, purchase carbon offsets from reliable organizations such as carbonfund .org.

- Have an energy audit or rating performed for your home. Usually conducted by your local utility company, this will help you to identify areas where you can make cost-effective improvements in energy efficiency.

- Ask your utility company to provide a detailed break-down of the sources of electricity it provides. If you can choose among companies, go with the one that relies most on alternative energy sources (wind, solar, hydropower, or energy from plant matter).

Reduce Consumption of Nonessential Material Goods and Conserve Resources

Each of us can practice ecological simplicity by downsizing our consumption without sacrificing basic life comforts. As suggested in the first part of this chapter, this means buying products that are lasting, reliable, and nonpolluting in their manufacture and use. It also means reusing items that are functional rather than always buying the latest or newest replacement. For example, you can simply upgrade the operating system on your existing computer rather than replacing your computer every two or three years.

Also, look for goods that are labeled as environmentally friendly. As described above, you can buy new appliances that are Energy Star–certified. Eco-labeling identifies products derived from sustainable forest practices, products that utilize energy-efficient technologies, and products that constitute sustainable food choices. A good place to start is the Center for a New American Dream (newdream.org). Their website offers extensive recommendations on eco-friendly products in a variety of categories, ranging from clothing to appliances. Particularly helpful are the comparative energy-efficiency ratings presented for household appliances, vehicles, electronics, and other consumer items. Another good resource for buying ecologically friendly household furnishings, clothing, garden supplies, and sundries is ecoshoppe.com.

Finally, try to buy local when you can. Purchasing produce from your local farmers' market not only gives you fresher fruits and vegetables than you're likely to find at your commercial grocery store, it also reduces the energy consumption of long-distance transport.

Sustainable consumption is an important part of living more simply. Buying into the materialistic values of mass-market advertising not only ignores the desperate condition of the planet but often complicates your life. Living simply means buying less of what you don't really need. It means focusing on the intangible values of life found in family relationships, friendships, and creative activities rather than on passive entertainment and the acquisition of material goods.

A more extensive list of ways to conserve important resources such as water and trees can be found in chapter 24, Take Action. Detailed guidelines for recycling paper, plastic, aluminum, and glass, as well as electronic devices you no longer need, can be found there too. While these actions may not always be simple to do, they are compatible with a simpler lifestyle that values conservation over consumption.

Conclusion

Living more simply means cutting through what is trivial to opt for what is essential in life. In doing so, you both live more authentically with yourself and others, as well as live more lightly on the earth. Large numbers of people making the shift to simplify their lives will have important implications for the planet. The resulting conservation of critical resources and reduction in energy waste and carbon emissions will help create a more viable future for humanity. The shift begins with each of us. Consider what changes toward a simpler and more sustainable life you might be willing to make at this time

20

Build Peace in All Relationships

By working toward peace in your relationships, you acknowledge a principle, integral to the emerging worldview, that all human beings are ultimately part of the same consciousness. At the deepest level, we are all interconnected. What you do to another, you do to yourself. For centuries, people have been divided along lines of national identity, race, religion, and ethnicity—divisions that have led to tremendous conflict. In the twentieth century alone, nearly a hundred million people died as the result of major or lesser wars. In the future, diminishing resources and climate change may lead to increased conflict between the haves and have-nots around the globe. There can be no peace without a worldwide shift in consciousness toward an understanding that we are all part of the same humanity—a common brother- and sisterhood. As conditions on the planet become more challenging, the need for each of us to build peace in all our relations will increase. The emerging new worldview asks us to begin to identify ourselves as global citizens instead of defining ourselves by race, religion, nationality, or ethnicity. Earth is facing many challenges; it is time for us to wake up and join one another, to understand that we are all in this together.

Learn Peaceful Communication Skills

World peace begins with peace in our own personal relationships. The quality of our life and the lives of others is profoundly
influenced by our capacity to live harmoniously with our family,
friends, coworkers, and acquaintances. Communicating in a
manner that builds peace requires an awareness of certain skills.
The following brief outline, based on several different guidelines
for constructive communication, provides a short summary of
some of the more important skills that lead to more harmonious
interpersonal relations. If you're interested in learning more about
peaceful communication, you may want to consult classic works
on communication skills such as *Nonviolent Communication* (2003)
by Marshall Rosenberg and *Messages* (1995) by Matthew McKay,
Martha Davis, and Patrick Fanning. Nonviolent communication
has become a worldwide movement, with teachers and workshops
offered in most major cities. For further information, contact the
Center for Nonviolent Communication's website (cnvc.org).

Fundamental Attitudes for Peaceful Communication

Peaceful communication, whether with family members or
coworkers, or as a participant in group negotiations, requires bringing certain fundamental attitudes and capabilities to the table:

Respect

When you respect others, you are willing to suspend any judgments or reactions you have and take time to hear them out. Respect
requires both overcoming polarized ways of thinking that divide
people into "us" versus "them"—such as victims versus perpetra-
tors, insiders versus outsiders, and righteous versus unrighteous—
and recognizing that we are all united by a common humanity.
Each of us deserves basic respect just by virtue of the fact of being
human.

Empathy

Empathy is the ability to take another's point of view, even when different from your own. Understanding another's point of view requires putting aside your own agenda—along with any judgments—and really listening to what the other has to say, whether you agree with it or not. More than that, it requires stepping into the other's perspective and attempting to see the world from that individual's point of view, again, whether you agree with it or not.

Acceptance of Differences

Personalities and personal values differ. To build peaceful relations, it's important to be able to accept that others may have perceptions of reality that are quite different from your own. This is to be expected. In accepting that others have different perceptions—and perhaps different values—we begin to accept rather than resist them as people. Herein lies the basis for both mutual understanding, and compromise rather than conflict in resolving differences.

Owning Projections

Peaceful communication requires the ability to recognize when your perception of another is skewed by your own projections. Often we project onto another some unwanted or denied aspect of ourselves that we prefer not to acknowledge. For example, you may judge someone as angry because you have unacknowledged anger within yourself. Or you may be intolerant of someone whose decisions are based on feelings, because you tend to be very rational and deny your own feelings as a basis for decision-making.

When you find yourself judging someone, ask yourself whether you are simply projecting onto this person something you don't wish to look at in yourself. Try this especially with your partner or spouse, if you are part of a couple. If you identify traits such as anger, intolerance, overcontrol, or neediness in yourself, own them and acknowledge that they may skew your perception. Then work on seeing the other person as more complex and multifaceted than your projection. Even when the other's behavior suggests the presence of an undesirable trait, your projection can inflate its significance.

Identifying the Underlying Need

When people act in a critical or angry fashion, look beyond their overt behavior. Seek to understand what they are actually asking for—what they ultimately need. Almost always, behind seemingly undesirable behavior lies an unexpressed need. A great deal of conflict, at all levels of human relationship, is based on defending against another's behavior perceived to be angry, intolerant, or self-serving. If each of us could look beyond overt behavior and attempt to understand others' underlying needs, imagine how we might be able to avoid conflict. This constitutes an implicit paradigm shift: *from perceiving others as wrong to perceiving their woundedness and need for healing.* Expand this shift in perspective from individual relationships to relationships among ethnic groups, religions, races, and nations, and you have the basis for a peaceful world civilization built on compassion rather than prejudice.

Ability to Compromise

When faced with conflict, if you wish to preserve the relationships involved, it's essential to find a compromise in which all parties get at least some of what they want. Often this means giving up some of what you want in order to foster conflict-resolution with another person or within a group of people. Every time you are willing to let go of some of your own position for the sake of the group's vision or goal, you contribute to the new consciousness emerging on the planet at this time. In this new worldview, traditionally feminine values of cooperation, collaboration, and interrelationship are beginning to supplant older, traditionally masculine values of competitiveness, dominance, and winning at all costs.

These attitudes and capacities—respect, empathy, acceptance of differences, owning projections, looking beyond overt behavior to the underlying need, and the ability to compromise—are key ingredients in building peace rather than conflict in human relationships at all levels. The ultimate foundation for all six attitudes is the compassion and love that define the essence of the human heart. Choosing to embrace these attitudes, whether at an individual level or a government level, is to choose cooperation over conflict—and, ultimately, compassion over fear and distrust.

Communication Basics

Most likely you have been exposed to the basic skills of good communication either at school or at work. While some or all of these skills may be familiar, they are worth repeating, as they are essential to promoting interpersonal peace.

Listening

Listening well is essential to good communication. Observe the following guidelines when you listen to another.

Listen carefully to others, without interruption or judgment: This sometimes requires effort. It's easy to allow your own reactions and preoccupations to interfere with giving your full attention to whoever is speaking. Being a good listener means being able to suspend your reactions, judgments, and desires to offer feedback and just hear the person out.

When you listen to another, strive to avoid:

- Criticism and blame: "You don't ever listen to me."

- Moralistic judgments: "I don't think you're making much of an effort," "Stop acting like a victim."

- Comparisons with others: "Your sister doesn't give me this kind of trouble."

- Demands: "Take out the trash right now!" Rephrase demands as requests: "I would appreciate it if you would take out the trash as soon as possible."

Listen actively: Summarize the content of what you hear others say to let them know you've heard them. For example, you might paraphrase or summarize what another says after the person has spoken for a minute or two. Then wait for the other person to give you feedback. If you didn't quite get it right, be willing to let the other person correct you. Active listening is a skill that takes some practice to develop.

Get to the underlying need: If the other person's communication is negative (defensive, attacking, judging, complaining), help that person identify the underlying need that isn't being met. Ask, "What is it that you would like?" "What is it that you need in order to feel better about this situation?"

Propose a solution: After you have identified the other person's need, let that person know what you're willing to do in order to help get that need met.

Talking

How you speak to another—especially in situations of conflict —is just as important as how well you listen. Keep the following guidelines in mind:

Avoid blaming or attacking the other person: If you're upset with something someone did, refrain from making that person responsible. Instead, let the person know how their behavior made you *feel*. Instead of, "You don't really give a _____ about me," you could say, "When you are an hour late for our appointment, I feel unappreciated."

Take responsibility for your feelings: Take personal responsibility for your feelings rather than putting them on the other person. Say, "I felt disappointed when you didn't meet me at the time you said you would," rather than, "You really let me down," or "You don't understand me."

Avoid character attributions—refer instead to specific behaviors: If you are upset with someone's action, specify the *particular behavior* that led to your being upset. Then say how their behavior resulted in your being upset. For example, you might say: "When you didn't return my call, I felt ignored," instead of, "That was very rude of you," or "You're an idiot for doing that."

Ask specifically for what you want: Think about what it is you would like from the other person and then communicate what you want directly, in a calm manner, without demands or threats. For example, you might say, "I would appreciate it if you could return my calls," or "Would you be willing to get back to me within a few days?" Make sure that when you ask for something you are making a request, rather than a demand.

Be willing to negotiate and compromise: In order to find a compromise, you may need to use conflict-resolution skills. (The principles of effective conflict resolution are briefly described below.)

Working Principles for Effective Communication

Beyond skills for effective listening and talking, there are certain general communication principles to keep in mind, especially if you're dealing with a conflict situation.

Feelings need to be expressed before negotiation is possible: People aren't usually able to begin to problem-solve until they have had a chance to express their feelings about the conflict situation. Give them time to vent before asking them to negotiate a solution.

Postpone conflict resolution if anger runs high: Time may be needed for one or more parties to cool down after having expressed angry feelings. Sometimes it is best to postpone conflict resolution until another time or day. If you are angry, take an exercise break to help discharge your anger.

Don't let conflict fester: When possible, after a cooling-off period, come back to the problem within twenty-four hours or so.

Be aware of your tone of voice: It's often not the content of what is said but the tone of voice in which it is expressed that impacts others the most. Use a respectful rather than critical or condescending tone of voice.

Maintain a solution-oriented rather than problem-oriented focus: Keep the situation positive by focusing on the prospect of finding a solution rather than dwelling on the problem and negative feelings.

Conflict Resolution (Negotiation)

There are several time-honored steps to resolving interpersonal conflicts. These steps may follow the order in which they're listed in below or happen concurrently.

Identify the problem: Each person takes a turn stating what the problem is for them. When it's your turn to speak, use the guidelines described above for talking. Avoid blaming anyone; take responsibility for your feelings. Remember, rather than make sweeping character attributions, refer to specific behaviors that are of concern. Then explain how the other person's behavior led to your feelings.

Express feelings: In the process of stating the problem as you see it, express any feelings you have without blaming or attacking the other person.

Identify needs: Each person involved identifies what they need in order to resolve the issue.

Brainstorm solutions: Come up with as many ways as possible to allow each party involved to "win" or at least obtain some of what they want. When needs and proposed solutions conflict, be willing to negotiate the best possible compromise for everyone involved.

Agree to carry out a particular solution: Pick the best overall solution out of those on the table. Agree to when and how a particular solution will be carried out. End with something positive, like a handshake, hug, or smile.

Working Principles for Conflict Resolution

In negotiating solutions to interpersonal conflict, keep in mind the following principles:

- *Conflict is a natural part of life*: Even when we have the skills to handle conflict, conflict will continue to arise in our dealings with others.

- *We can grow through conflict*: By understanding and appreciating others' positions, we can expand our own awareness.

- *Sometimes a relationship may be more important than holding a position*: Look beyond specific positions to the importance of the relationship. Do you value the relationship more than holding on to your specific position? If so, you are ready to hear the other person's point of view and consider solutions in which both of you can win.

- *For every problem, there are usually several possible solutions*: We can learn the skills to generate a range of solutions to any given problem, increasing the likelihood of finding a solution that works for all parties involved.

- *Feelings are important*: Often it is impossible to get to the solution to a problem until everybody's feelings have been heard.

- *Sometimes everyone can win*: Remember that the purpose of learning conflict-resolution skills is to arrive at solutions where everyone benefits or obtains something of what they want.

- *Complete agreement isn't always necessary*: When complete agreement is unreachable, it is okay to agree to disagree.

Building Peace Instead of Confict

The preceding brief overview of communication skills can help you build peace in your personal relationships. The outline just described can be used as a general framework for resolving conflicts with family members, friends, work associates, or in any group negotiation situation. If you wish, make copies of it and share it with family or group members. To gain proficiency in peaceful communication, consider reading a book on the subject—or better yet, take a class or workshop on communication. If available in your area, training in Marshall Rosenberg's nonviolent communication process can help you to internalize and become competent in the skills described above. When you practice peaceful communication, you become a force for reconciliation in a world that deeply needs to overcome its differences.

Forgive Others and Yourself

Effective communication can overcome conflict and disagreement with others. Forgiveness can overcome longstanding resentments that hold individuals, groups, and even nations apart. Both are needed to restore peace among the various religious, racial, and ethnic groups around the planet. Forgiveness is especially necessary when anger runs deep or is entrenched. Humanity's five thousand years of war-torn history bears witness to the destructive effects of an "us versus them" mentality. The emerging worldview requires a fundamental shift toward forgiving old resentments and perceiving the common humanity that we all share. Forgiveness leads to acceptance and respect for all people, no matter who they are or where they are from. It is a transformative practice that each of us can cultivate, beginning at home and spreading to others in increasing circles of influence.

Forgiveness, whether of another or yourself, is one of the greatest acts of healing possible. It opens channels for love to overcome fear or resentment, no matter what has gone before. In forgiving another, you liberate yourself from the resentment and hurt you have been holding within—painful emotions that can only disrupt your peace of mind. In forgiving yourself for past and present mistakes, you come to fully accept yourself. As you do so, you make space in your life to move toward a positive future unfettered by the past.

Why is it often so difficult to forgive? One of the biggest obstacles to forgiveness is trying to forgive someone or something before you feel ready. It's impossible to genuinely forgive another when forgiveness is just something you feel you *should* do. Forgiveness can't be forced—it's an experience that emerges naturally after you have had the opportunity to acknowledge and express any feelings of anger or hurt. If you are still angry with someone, you probably won't be ready to forgive that person until you have communicated your angry feelings (either directly or to someone else). This is best done in a non-blaming way; simply let the person know what they did that made you angry (and perhaps hurt as well), without putting the person down. Afterward you may experience a heart-felt shift and come to a place of clarity where it will be possible to forgive.

If the person you need to forgive is no longer around or alive— or if you don't wish to speak to the person directly—you can work through unresolved anger and pain by writing the person a letter that discloses all of your feelings in detail. It does not matter whether you ever send the letter—what is important is expressing your unfinished feelings. Only then can you be open to the pos-sibility of genuine forgiveness. (If you write such a letter, you may find it helpful to share it with a friend.)

An important aid to forgiveness is empathy. It's easier to forgive if you can take the role of the other person and attempt to understand where that person was coming from. Forgiveness is difficult when the other's hurtful action is incomprehensible. When you don't understand a person's position, what the other did may seem arbitrary, unfeeling, or possibly cruel. In attempting to understand another's motivations, you may not agree with the person's positions or actions, but at least the person's behavior will become more comprehensible. It may be that what was done arose from considerable suffering on the other's part, in which case you may be able to feel some compassion.

Understanding the abusive backgrounds of unhappy parents who abuse their children does not condone their ugly behavior. Yet it may allow enough insight to open the door to understand-ing and eventual forgiveness. Sometimes, of course, even under-standing may not be sufficient to allow for forgiveness. In such cases it's important simply to get to a basic acceptance of what hap-pened, happened. Acceptance—saying, "What happened simply happened"—is the first step. After acceptance, you can grieve your loss and begin to put what happened in the past, where it belongs, so that you are free to continue in the present.

For example, if you were physically harmed or sexually molested by a parent, you may still be angry to the point that it is difficult to forgive. Simply acknowledging and expressing your anger about the past in the presence of a counselor or a supportive friend can help you to accept what happened. Then you can grieve your parent's inability to offer you the love and support you needed.

Perhaps you can even gain some understanding of your parent's predicament through knowledge of their childhood. Whether or not you get to forgiveness, going through such a process empowers you to finish with your past so that you can get on with your life in the present.

Coming to terms with angry or hurt feelings toward another is a difficult but powerful means to opening yourself to a greater experience of love in your life. In truth, the past cannot be changed—it can only be remembered and released. When you do reach the point where you can forgive another, you are no longer likely to be afraid of that person. Forgiveness frees you of the inner stress or turmoil you feel toward someone; it also frees the other person to make amends to you. Forgiveness is a sacred act—it reaches beyond the limitations of human personality and behavior to the spiritual essence that all of us share.

Forgiveness of yourself for past mistakes is just as critical for peace of mind as forgiveness of others. Self-forgiveness begins with acknowledging the regret you feel about past or present mistakes. Often it can be helpful to express this to someone else—or at least in a journal. The key is simply to recognize your own inherent worth. Are you ready to see yourself as still acceptable and lovable, no matter what you did? Very likely you could not have done otherwise, given the circumstances and awareness that you had at the time. Ask yourself whether you are ready to let go of what happened and move on. While forgiving others heals anger and resentment, forgiving yourself heals internal conflict and restores your faith in yourself.

Forgiveness Exercise

Think about a person—alive or dead—who hurt you or did something you find difficult to forgive. What did this person do that you find most difficult to forgive? If there are many things, start with the most difficult first.

Write a letter to this person, speaking from your heart, about your feelings. Take all the time you need and do not hold anything back; this may take several pages. Write about your feelings toward the person and your feelings about what the person did. It isn't necessary—and may not be appropriate—to send the letter.

When your letter is done, share it with someone you trust, or a professional counselor. Feel free to express any feelings that have come up in the process to the person in whom you are confiding. Give yourself at least an hour for this.

Now, think again about the person who hurt you. Do you feel ready to sincerely forgive this person yet? If you aren't ready, work on accepting the fact of what happened so that you can let go of the past and move on. Working with statements such as, "It happened and it's over," or "It's in the past and I can go on," can facilitate the process. Accept any sadness or grief you feel during this process—it's part of the healing.

If you feel you are ready to forgive, relax, close your eyes, and visualize that person (whether alive or not) standing before you. Then speak to the other person as if the person were present right now. In whatever words feel appropriate, tell the person that you forgive him for what he did. If you truly forgive the person, you will feel as though a weight has been lifted. (Note: If you need to forgive yourself for something in the past, visualize yourself and follow the same instructions.)

Forgiveness is something that happens quietly in your own heart. It cannot be forced. When you are ready to let go of anger and the desire to blame, then you will release yourself from this burden. Forgiving someone does not mean you excuse or condone what the person did, it simply means you forgive the person for doing it. Then, if you wish, you may choose to communicate your forgiveness to the person, opening up new possibilities for the relationship.

Compassion

Compassion involves being concerned about others' difficulties. You feel for others' suffering and wish that they might be free of that suffering. The path to developing compassion is simple, although not always easy. Compassion begins with acknowledging that adversity exists for everyone. Although suffering certainly is not all there is to life, no one is immune to times of hardship and challenge. Much of our current society is based on the need to deny pain and suffering as much as possible. Material consumption, TV, overeating, analgesics, and alcohol are some of the many strategies we use to avoid pain. Those persons who are ill, disabled, and elderly are consigned to places where they are largely forgotten and out of sight. The media promotes youthful vitality, beauty, and virility as ideals to strive for. Looking beyond surface appearances to acknowledge the fragility and mortality of life is where compassion begins.

True compassion requires not just acknowledging the mortality and limitations of life but opening your heart to it. The ability to do so is something that develops with maturity and life experience. Sometimes it happens only after having gone through a period of personal suffering. In the moment when you stop running from your own inner pain—letting go of persons, substances, or activities that shield you from it—you find that you have more space to open your heart. To be sure, life is full of moments of joy and beauty where your heart opens naturally, without perceiving any pain. Yet opening deeply to compassion for others often follows bearing witness to your own personal afflictions. When you have acknowledged and accepted your own difficulties in life, you can be fully present for another. Having compassion for others is a gift to yourself. In bearing witness to your own inner discomfort, you allow it to emerge and move on. You release it instead of holding it—or hiding it—within your soul.

Beyond acknowledging suffering and opening your heart, compassion requires understanding others. That means understanding the conditions that led them into their predicament. Try seeing others' situations from *their* point of view rather than your own. This particular aspect of compassion is closely related to empathy—the ability to take another person's perspective, or walk in someone else's shoes. Once you genuinely understand others' difficulties, you can stop judging them and feel concern for them instead. Even the most reprehensible behavior can be understood—although not condoned—when you fully understand the conditions that led up to it. As your capacity for compassion grows, you will learn to stop judging people so quickly and seek instead to understand them.

When you fully understand another—to the point where you're truly able to feel for the other's predicament—the person will no longer seem distant, unknown, or a potential threat. Compassion for others diminishes the possibility of feeling estranged from or afraid of them. Instead you see them as fallible human beings who have suffered, just like yourself. To be compassionate, however, does not mean you allow others to take advantage of you or wield their inner distress in destructive ways at your expense. Compassion always comes from a position of strength. It may require you to set limits, and even use force, if necessary, to redirect another away from hostile or destructive behavior. In being compassionate you hold the highest vision for another; you see her suffering and acknowledge her potential. When another person's behavior is destructive or violent, the most compassionate act you can take toward him is one that calls on him to change his ways. It means calling upon him to be true to his full potential as a human being— anything less is unacceptable. A popular expression for this form of compassion is "tough love." Concern for another's distress does not include allowing destructive expressions of that distress to hurt you. Compassion for yourself is always included in compassion for another.

Compassion Exercise

Close your eyes and take time until you feel relaxed and centered. Now think about a person you know who is experiencing physical or mental suffering. Reflect on this person's situation without judgment; allow your heart to open. Do this for two or three minutes. If it helps, you may want to silently repeat a phrase such as, "May you be free of your pain and suffering," or perhaps "May you be at peace." (Pick your own phrase if you prefer.) If feelings other than compassion arise—such as fear, despair, anger, or sorrow—allow these feelings to arise and move through. You may want to write them down if they start to distract you. When your feelings pass, refocus on the person you've chosen and allow yourself to settle down into a place where you simply feel concern for the person's ultimate well-being. In learning to perceive another's adversity without getting lost in fear or sorrow, you will begin to transform the way you relate to your own pain. Developing compassion leads to more equanimity within yourself.

Optional: Try this same exercise with someone you strongly dislike, or someone who is causing harm in the world. As you reflect on this person, make an effort to understand what kind of conditions/circumstances might have led her to behave the way she does. Even if there is no way to know the background of this individual, acknowledge that certain reasons and conditions have led her to act as she does. Reflect on the truth that hurtful behavior usually arises out of suffering—and ultimately only adds further suffering to the perpetrator's situation.

If you find judgment or anger coming up, relax, center yourself in the moment, and allow the feelings to arise and pass through. If you need to write down your negative feelings do so, but then return to the exercise. See if you can reframe the way you perceive the other person. Instead of judging the other as bad or evil, try instead seeing the person's *behavior* as unenlightened or ignorant. Imagine how this person would act if she lived up to her full potential as a human being—if she was able to heal her inner wounds and act from a position of love instead of fear.

Conclusion

Consider the impact of more people in the world practicing peaceful communication, forgiveness, and compassion. Imagine how much it might promote greater harmony among family members, neighbors, friends, coworkers, teachers, and students, as well among peoples of different race, religion, nationality, and ethnicity. The intent behind building peaceful relationships is to extend love. Without a shift toward increased love and compassion, strife on the planet will likely increase in coming years due to diminishing resources and greater disparity between rich and poor. Thus it is vital for each of us to learn and practice empathy, good listening, non-judgment, and forgiveness in our day-to-day interactions. In doing so we acknowledge that we are fundamentally all one humanity, part of a common fabric. We also practice the ancient precept common to all of the world's religions: to do unto others as we would have them do unto us. Building peace in your personal relationships is a significant contribution to the larger cause of peace on earth.

21

Care for Your Body

Taking care of your body is essential to your health, well-being, and ultimately peace of mind. How does it contribute to the global shift in consciousness needed on the earth at this time?

Each of us is a "cell" in the collective "body" of humanity. By cultivating peace and healing in your own life, you become an exemplar of healing and peace for others. We tend to underestimate our impact on those around us. At an explicit level, you can teach others about healing practices (for example, exercise, diet, relaxation, yoga, or meditation) that you have found beneficial. On a more implicit, subconscious level, the peace and balance you create in your own life subtly influences others to become more peaceful themselves. There is a learning that goes on by empathic resonance—by an unconscious communication of feelings—beyond what you might communicate verbally. Thus your own level of personal peace can entrain a similar state of calmness in those with whom you associate.

Contemporary life can often be stressful. This stress can take a variety of forms. External stress comes in the form of challenges imposed by forces outside of you, for example, environmental pollution, traffic congestion, time constraints out of your control, or difficult people. Internal stress is generated by many factors, including your attitudes, denied feelings, the amount of rest you allow yourself, and how well you care for your body. In all of its many forms, stress interferes with your connection to your innermost self—what was described earlier in this book as your transcendent or transpersonal self. By caring for your body and reducing stress, you can reduce impediments to connecting with your innermost self. In fact, you can free yourself up physically and emotionally to be in touch with the deep creativity, wisdom, and inspiration that originate in your innermost self. Certainly this can benefit you, but how does it contribute to the global shift needed by the planet?

As described in chapter 9, your innermost self is intimately connected with the intelligence of the conscious universe. Whether you call it your soul or spirit, your innermost self is your point of contact with the higher consciousness, intelligence, and intentionality of the Cosmos. By aligning with your innermost self, you allow the larger intentions of the universal consciousness or "world soul" to inspire and activate your own consciousness. (Again, you can also think of this universal consciousness in more religious terms—as a part of or extension of God.) In effect, as you link up with a consciousness larger than yourself, your life comes to be about more than just your personal ego needs. This is how something as basic as personal stress reduction can ultimately have a much larger impact.

By caring for your body, reducing stress, and creating peace in your life, you will align more easily with the deeper sources of creativity, inspiration, and guidance that empower you to fulfill goals larger than those of your personal ego. When you do, you will begin to move outside the sphere of your own needs and connect with the needs of larger groups of which you are a part. Then you will be naturally motivated to make meaningful contributions to them: whether this is raising a family, doing your best at work, or contributing to environmental and social causes in your community.

This chapter describes three common ways to nurture and care for your body: conscious diet, relaxation, and exercise. You probably already know something about these topics—indeed, you may have already incorporated healthful dietary practices, relaxation, and exercise into your life. Even so, this chapter may provide you with some new ideas to work with in caring for your physical body. Also, in the case of diet, you'll see how moving toward a plant-based diet benefits both the environment and humanity.

Conscious Diet

The human body depends on both an optimal quantity as well as quality of food. In terms of quantity, the number of calories you consume needs to be balanced with your level of energy expenditure (calorie output). Over 60 percent of adults in the United States are overweight, largely due to the combination of a high caloric diet and a sedentary lifestyle. Most weight problems are resolved not by fad diets but simply by eating healthy foods in combination with sufficient exercise.

Just as important as quantity is the quality of the food you eat. Taking care of your body means being willing to eat whole foods that are free of toxic, artificial substances. Your body also needs food that has sufficient energy to sustain and enhance its intrinsic vitality rather than deplete it. The nutrient content of food is important, but so is its closeness to nature—the less processed, the better. Fresh raw vegetables and fruits are more compatible with health than their cooked, frozen, or canned counterparts. Buying fresh, locally grown food is beneficial to your health and also benefits the planet, as it requires less transport—and therefore less carbon emissions—to get to you. The next time you have blueberries or apricots, notice if they were flown in all the way from South America.

Finally, taking care of yourself means eating food of sufficient variety to meet the full range of your body's needs. This includes complex carbohydrates such as vegetables and whole grains; fats such as oils and nuts; and proteins such as organic poultry, wild fish, and soy products.

Guidelines for a Conscious Diet

The following guidelines are intended to stimulate your thinking rather than be prescriptive. None of us has exactly the same dietary needs, so consider how relevant or important each guideline is to your life. Caffeine may or may not be contributing to your stress, even though it does for many people. Perhaps your tolerance for dairy is higher than average. Also, in social situations you may choose to relax some of these guidelines, allowing yourself to eat more sugar or meat because it is socially comfortable to do so.

Reduce Caffeine Intake

Of all the dietary factors that can aggravate tension, caffeine is one of the more potent. Many people find that they feel calmer and sleep better after they have reduced their caffeine intake. Caffeine has a directly stimulating effect on several different systems in your body. It increases the level of the neurotransmitter norepinephrine in your brain, causing you to feel alert and awake. It also produces the very same physiological arousal response that is triggered when you are subjected to stress.

Caffeine is found not only in coffee but also in many types of tea, cola beverages, chocolate candy, cocoa, and over-the-counter drugs. If you are prone to high stress, you may want to consider reducing your total caffeine consumption to one cup of coffee or one cola beverage per day. Wean yourself from caffeine gradually; consider low caffeine beverages like green tea to get you going in the morning. When possible, substitute caffeine-free herb teas or soft drinks for those that contain caffeine.

Reduce Sugar Consumption

It was not until the twentieth century that most people consumed large amounts of refined sugar. Today, the standard American diet includes white sugar in most beverages (coffee, tea, cola), in cereal, in salad dressings, and in processed meat, in addition to one or two desserts per day and perhaps a donut or a cookie on coffee breaks. Sugar may be disguised under a variety of names, including dextrose, sucrose, maltose, raw sugar, brown sugar, high fructose corn syrup, and fructose. The average American consumes roughly *120 pounds* of sugar per year.

Our bodies are not equipped to process large amounts of sugar. Continually bombarding your body with this much sugar can result in chronic dysfunction of your sugar metabolism. For some people this dysfunction leads to excessively high levels of blood sugar or diabetes. For an even larger number of individuals, the problem is just the opposite—periodic drops in blood-sugar levels accompanied by feeling lightheaded, irritable, or anxious, a condition known as *hypoglycemia*. Sugar is also known to impair immune response, raise triglycerides (blood fats), aggravate digestive disorders, and increase hyperactivity in children.

Reduce all types of simple sugar in your diet. This includes foods that obviously contain sugar, in the form of white sugar or sucrose, such as candy, ice cream, desserts, and soft drinks. It also includes subtler forms of sugar, such as honey, brown sugar, high fructose corn syrup, corn sweeteners, molasses, maltose, and dextrose. Be sure to read labels on any and all processed foods to detect these various forms of sugar.

Also consider reducing simple starches, such as pasta, refined cereals, potato or corn chips, and white bread. These foods quickly break down into simple sugar in your body. Instead substitute complex carbohydrates such as whole grain breads and cereals, vegetables, and brown rice or other whole grains.

When you feel hypoglycemic—like your blood sugar is low—try a complex-carbohydrate-and-protein snack, such as cheese and whole-grain crackers or whole-grain toast and tuna, halfway between meals. If you awaken early in the morning, you may also find that a small snack will help you sleep for a couple more hours. Instead of snacks between meals, you can try having four or five small meals per day, no more than three hours apart.

For sweetening beverages, use a healthy sugar alternative, such as stevia. Stevia is derived from a plant source and is available in most health-food stores.

Reduce Consumption of Foods to Which You May Be Allergic

Allergic reactions occur when your body attempts to resist the intrusion of a foreign substance. For some people, certain foods affect the body like a foreign substance, causing not only classic allergic symptoms such as a runny nose, mucus, and sneezing, but also a host of psychological or psychosomatic symptoms, including any of the following:

- Anxiety or panic

- Depression or mood swings

- Irritability

- Insomnia

- Headaches

- Confusion and disorientation

- Fatigue

The two most common foods in modern society that cause allergic reactions are milk or dairy products and wheat. It is casein in milk and gluten in wheat—both of which are types of proteins—that tend to cause problems. Other foods that can trigger allergic responses include alcohol, chocolate, citrus fruits, corn, eggs, garlic, peanuts, yeast, shellfish, soy products, and tomatoes. One of the most telling signs of a food allergy is addiction. We tend to crave and become addicted to the very foods to which we are allergic. While chocolate is the most flagrant example of this, take heed if you find yourself tending to crave bread (wheat), corn chips (corn), dairy products, or another specific type of food. Many people go for years without recognizing that the very foods they crave the most have a subtle but toxic effect on their mood and well-being.

An informal way to evaluate your food allergies is to conduct your own elimination test: If you want to determine whether you are allergic to wheat, simply eliminate all products containing wheat from your diet for two weeks and notice whether you feel better. Then, at the end of the two weeks, allow yourself to eat wheat, carefully monitoring any symptoms that appear over the next twenty-four hours. After testing wheat, you may also want to test milk and milk products. It's important to experiment with only one potentially allergic type of food at a time so that you don't confuse your results.

Eat Whole, Unprocessed Foods

Try to eat foods that are fresh and as close to their natural state as possible. As some say, "If it grows, eat it; otherwise don't." Whole foods include fresh fruits, fresh vegetables, whole grains, unrefined cereals, beans, nuts, seeds, sea vegetables, fresh fish, and free-range, organic poultry.

Food processing diminishes or destroys nutritional value in several ways: Initially, the food is broken down at a cellular level.

Then additives and preservatives are added to these partial and fragmented foods. Such additives further reduce the value of the food and can be potentially toxic. Artificial colors and dyes, for example, can interact with and damage chromosomes. Nitrites, added to many canned meats, are not themselves carcinogenic but can easily react with protein breakdown byproducts in the digestive tract to form highly carcinogenic compounds known as *nitrosamines*. Among artificial sweeteners, saccharin is known to be carcinogenic and aspartame (NutraSweet) may be associated with brain damage. People sensitive to aspartame may also experience symptoms such as headaches, anxiety, nausea, dizziness, insomnia, or depression. In short, you can do much to enhance your sense of well-being—and avoid potential health hazards—by replacing processed foods with whole foods whenever possible.

Reduce Consumption of Saturated Animal Fats and Increase Omega-3 Fats

Over the past fifty years diets high in saturated fats have been consistently shown to lead to increased risk of heart disease and stroke. Saturated fats are the fats that come from animal sources: beef, poultry, bacon, butter, eggs, whole milk, and cheese. These fats, when consumed in high amounts, tend to end up as plaque deposits in your arteries, which accumulate over time, producing atherosclerosis. As you may already know, saturated-fat consumption correlates more highly with heart disease than cholesterol intake. Beware of foods that are high in saturated fats, even if they are low in cholesterol.

Beyond decreasing your intake of saturated fats, it's a good idea to eat more foods high in omega-3 essential fatty acids, such as salmon, sardines, flax seeds, hemp seeds, and walnuts. It's also possible to increase your omega-3 intake by taking fish oil capsules, 1000-3000 mg per day. The standard American diet is deficient in omega-3 fats; including them in your diet will help reduce inflammation in your body, a major risk factor for cardiovascular disease. Other benefits of omega-3 fats include reduction of cholesterol, improved brain function, increased immunity, and relief from depression.

Reduce Consumption of Commercial Beef, Pork, and Poultry

Meat in general, and red meat in particular, poses a number of health hazards. It's no accident that countries low in meat consumption have lower rates of cardiovascular disease and cancer. As mentioned previously, meats are higher in saturated fats. Frequent consumption of beef, pork, and poultry increases your risk of atherosclerosis, the main cause of heart attacks and strokes. Most commercially available forms of these meats come from animals that have been fed hormones to promote weight gain and growth. There is good evidence that these hormones stress the animals, and there is reason to believe that they may aggravate stress levels in meat consumers as well. Antibiotics given to conventionally farmed cattle and poultry can also increase antibiotic resistance in consumers. Moreover, the conditions in which animals live prior to slaughter are akin to torture. Is it any wonder that commercial beef and poultry don't taste as good as they did thirty or forty years ago? If you choose to eat beef pork, or poultry, try to consume it only in organic forms.

If you are interested in reading further about the abuses of the meat industry and their impact on personal health, society, and the planet at large, it is worth reading John Robbins's excellent book *The Food Revolution* (2001) and Michael Pollan's *The Omnivore's Dilemma* (2006). (The many environmental benefits of reducing meat consumption will be discussed at length later in this chapter.)

Use Organic Produce Where Possible

Organic fruits, vegetables, and grains are grown with natural fertilizers, without pesticides and fungicides. Pesticide and fungicide residues may be present in any fruit or vegetable not labeled organic. Among fruits, strawberries, raspberries, and grapes are especially likely to absorb pesticides. Among vegetables, lettuce, spinach, and celery are highly sprayed and don't have an outer shell to protect the part we eat. Most health-food stores and many grocery stores currently offer organic produce. If available, try to buy organic vegetables and fruits whenever possible. If they aren't available in your area, you can minimize your exposure to harmful chemicals by carefully washing all fruits and vegetables before eating them.

Organic produce is not only good for you, it is good for farm workers, as organic farms offer healthier, non-toxic work environments. It's also good for the planet, because less herbicide, pesticide, and synthetic fertilizer end up in the atmosphere and bodies of water.

Eat More Vegetables

Vegetables are an excellent source of vitamins, minerals, and fiber. In an era where many people eat on the run and the standard diet is replete with sweets, soda pop, and snack foods, vegetables have become less popular. Yet this is likely an acquired dislike (most babies like vegetable baby foods), and can be unlearned. As you start to remove unhealthy foods from your diet, you may discover how tasty vegetables can be when they are fresh and properly prepared. Their natural flavors often seem to come out best when vegetables are only lightly steamed.

Buy vegetables that have been grown locally, if possible. By doing so, you help the planet. Produce that has been transported long distances requires a greater use of fuel and results in increased carbon emissions.

Increase Fiber in Your Diet

Fiber consists of the indigestible parts of plants you eat. A certain amount of fiber is necessary for the proper functioning of your intestinal tract. When you don't eat enough fiber, you are likely to be prone to digestive and intestinal problems. Fiber can be found in grains, bran, fresh vegetables, and fruits. To increase the amount of fiber you eat, try bran cereals or add bran to your favorite cereal. In general, try to eat ample amounts of fresh raw vegetables and fruits. It's a good idea to have at least one mixed salad containing several different raw vegetables per day.

Chew Your Food

Apart from what you eat, the *way* you eat has an impact on the quality of your nutrition. If you eat too fast, or do not adequately chew your food, you will miss a lot of the nutrient content and cause yourself indigestion. Digestion begins when you chew your food. If your food is not properly predigested in your mouth, much of it will not be adequately digested in your stomach. When food that's only partially digested passes through your intestines, it's likely to putrefy and ferment—causing bloating, cramps, and gas. Moreover, you will get only a limited amount of the nutrition available from the food, potentially leading to subtle forms of undernourishment. As a general rule, it's good to chew each bite of food ten to twenty times before taking the next bite.

Drink Six to Eight Glasses of Purified Water Per Day

Ample water is important to your health. One key reason is that water helps your kidneys. The main function of your kidneys is to filter out toxic waste products, both from the body's metabolism and external chemical and environmental pollutants. For the kidneys to operate properly, plentiful amounts of water are necessary to help wash away this waste. You especially need to drink ample water if you live in a hot environment, eat a lot of protein, drink alcohol or coffee, take medications, are running a fever, or have urinary problems.

The purity of the water you drink is important. Most water-purification plants focus primarily on disinfection, largely ignoring chemical contamination from industrial or agricultural wastes that find their way into ground water. Disinfection is often accomplished through chlorination, which poses additional hazards. Instead of drinking tap water directly, consider attaching a water-purification system to your tap. The two processes most commonly used for water purification are activated carbon filters and reverse osmosis. Both filter out chlorine and toxic organic molecules; however, reverse-osmosis systems will also filter out toxic metals. The downside of reverse osmosis systems is that they waste a lot of water. Activated carbon filter systems require that you replace the filter periodically. Either system is a vast improvement over plain tap water and certainly more convenient, cost-effective, and environmentally friendly than continually purchasing bottled water.

Try to limit your purchase of bottled water, as the plastic bottles tend to end up in landfills and can leach harmful substances into the water itself. If you must buy water in plastic bottles, make an effort to recycle them when possible.

Reduce Consumption of Milk and Dairy Products

The dairy industry would like you to believe that milk is the healthiest and most nutritious of all drinks. After many years, milk-moustache ads still abound in magazines. Here are the facts:

- Lactose is part of the carbohydrate component of milk. Like many people, you may be *lactose intolerant*: your stomach may not make the digestive enzyme *lactase*, which is needed to digest milk sugar (lactose). As a result, when you drink milk, you may experience bloating, excessive gas, and general intestinal distress.

- The butterfat in milk isn't good for your heart; it has a very high proportion of saturated fatty acids. Cheeses made from milk also have 50-70 percent butterfat content. If you must have milk or cheese, be sure to get the lowfat or nonfat variety.

- Casein, the protein in milk, can produce an allergic response, most frequently in the form of mucus. It is common for milk and dairy products to aggravate chronic allergic conditions such as asthma, bronchitis, and sinusitis. Milk is also known to aggravate auto-immune conditions, such as rheumatoid arthritis and lupus.

- Much of the commercial milk you drink contains residues of drugs and hormones used by the dairy industry to increase the productivity of cows. Homogenization of milk removes bacteria but not hormone residues.

In summary, it's a good idea to reduce your consumption of cow milk and milk-based products to a minimum. Cow milk is ideal for baby cows, but not for adult humans. Learn to enjoy soy milk, rice milk, or almond milk, all of which are usually available at your local grocery store.

Balance the Proteins and Carbohydrates You Eat

Until a few years ago, most nutritionists advocated eating a high amount of complex carbohydrates (for example, whole grains, pastas, bread)—as much as 70 percent of total calories. The prevailing idea was that too much fat promoted cardiovascular disease and too much protein led to excessive acidity and toxicity in the body. The ideal diet was thought to be about 15 percent fat, 15 percent protein, and 70 percent carbohydrates.

In recent years, however, evidence against the idea of eating high quantities of carbohydrates—especially simple carbohydrates by themselves—has mounted. Carbohydrates are used by the body to produce *glucose*, the sugar the body and brain use for fuel. In order to transport glucose to the cells, your pancreas secretes insulin. When you eat high levels of carbohydrates, your body produces high levels of insulin. Too much insulin has an adverse effect on some of the body's most basic hormonal and neuroendocrine systems, especially prostaglandins and serotonin.

In short, eating high amounts of cereals, chips, breads, pastas, potatoes, or even white rice, can raise your insulin levels to the point that other basic body systems are thrown out of balance. The answer is not to eliminate carbohydrates but to reduce them in proportion to the amounts of protein and fat you consume—without increasing the total number of calories in your diet. This will prevent you from ending up with a diet that is too high in fat or protein. Instead, you continue to eat fats and protein in moderation while decreasing the amount of carbohydrates you have at each meal relative to the amount of fat and protein. The optimal ratio, in terms of total calories, may be 25-30 percent protein, 25-30 percent fat, and 40-50 percent carbohydrate at each meal, with vegetable sources of protein and fat preferable to animal sources.

What to Do When You Eat Out

The unremitting pace of modern life requires that many of us eat lunch or dinner out. The problem is that most restaurant food, even at its best, contains too many calories, too much saturated fat, too much salt, and is often cooked in stale or rancid oils. Much restaurant food is also less fresh than what you can obtain on your own. For the most part, eating in restaurants is not optimal for taking care of your health. If you must often eat in restaurants, observe the following:

- Avoid all fast-food or junk-food concessions.

- Whenever possible, eat at natural-food or health-food restaurants that use whole, preferably organic foods.

- If natural-food restaurants are unavailable, go to high-quality seafood restaurants and order fresh fish, preferably broiled or baked. Complement this with fresh vegetables, potatoes or rice, and a salad. On the salad, avoid creamy or dairy-based dressings. Try to order wild fish—especially salmon—if available, and avoid fish containing high levels of methylmercury, such as swordfish, shark, marlin, king mackerel, and albacore tuna.

- As a general rule, when eating out have no more than one roll and one pat of butter, and minimize the amount of cream-based soups, such as clam chowder, that you consume.

- Stick with simple entrees, such as chicken or whitefish without elaborate sauces or toppings.

- Try to resist high-fat desserts.

- Don't hesitate to ask to have your food prepared according to your needs.

Let Change Happen Naturally

As you consider these guidelines for a more conscious diet, keep in mind that it isn't necessary to adopt all of them at once. Try just one or two that you feel most drawn to at first. Upgrade your diet at your own pace. If you want to make a difference not just for your own personal health, but for the benefit of the planet, seek to eat a more vegetarian diet based on locally grown produce.

Moving from a Meat- to a Plant-Based Diet

One of the most important practical things you can do to help the earth is to move your diet in the direction of vegetarianism. This may be easier to do in steps, rather than all at once. For example, you could try giving up red meat or selected dairy products first. These two steps alone will benefit both your health and the planet.

Why should you move away from a meat-based diet and toward a plant-based one?

Because meat production—particularly the production of beef, pork, and poultry—adversely impacts the environment in many ways. Furthermore, the meat industries are notoriously cruel and inhumane in the way they raise and slaughter animals intended for human consumption. A growing worldwide movement for humane treatment of animals, represented by organizations such as People for the Ethical Treatment of Animals (PETA), is beginning to have some impact on the meat and poultry industries. The following are six global problems that arise from meat production (the problems and statistics mentioned come from John Robbins's highly informative *The Food Revolution* (2001)):

Water Depletion

The largest percentage of water used in the United States is not for people or industry but for the production of grain for livestock. Some estimate that 50 percent of the total water used in the United States goes toward the production of grain. The amount of water required to produce one pound of different foods is highly revealing (figures according to soil and water specialists at the University of California Agricultural Extension (Robbins 2001)):

1 lb. lettuce – 23 gallons

1 lb. tomatoes – 23 gallons

1 lb. wheat – 25 gallons

1 lb. carrots – 35 gallons

1 lb. apples – 44 gallons

1 lb. chicken – 815 gallons

1 lb. pork – 1,630 gallons

1 lb. beef – 5,214 gallons

Degradation of Public Land in the American West

Currently, 70 percent of land in American western national forests and 90 percent of Bureau of Land Management land is grazed by livestock for private profit. According to Ted Williams, an environmental author, "Although cattle grazing in the west has polluted more water, eroded more topsoil, killed more fish, displaced more wildlife, and destroyed more vegetation than any other land use, the American public pays ranchers to do it" (Robbins 2001, 248).

Destruction of the Earth's Rainforests

Home to half of all the species on Earth, and a large proportion of the planet's oxygen supply, rainforests provide numerous vital benefits. In particular, they provide a "sink" for absorbing much of the world's excess carbon dioxide emissions. Yet despite all their beauty and importance, they are being destroyed at an alarming rate. One of the primary reasons why tropical rainforests are cleared is to create more grazing land for cattle, in order to produce beef for export to other countries. To date, two-thirds of the Central American rainforest has been cleared, and close to one-third of the enormous Amazon rainforest. The current rate of destruction is approximately one football field per second! Having taken millions of years to develop, rainforests, once destroyed, can never be re-established. Norman Myers sums up the situation in *The Primary Source: Tropical Forests and Our Future* (1984): "We are seeing the "hamburgerization" of the forests" (Robbins 2001, 255).

Global Warming

Fossil fuels, the burning of which is the primary source of global warming, are used in quantity to produce beef. The following statistics, again quoted from John Robbins's *The Food Revolution*, tell the story:

- Calories of fossil fuel expended to produce one calorie of protein from corn or wheat: 3 cal.

- Calories of fossil fuel expended to produce one calorie of protein from beef: 54 cal.

- Amount of carbon emissions released by driving a typical American car in one day: 3 kilograms.

- Amount of carbon emissions released by clearing and burning enough Costa Rican rainforest to produce beef for one hamburger: 75 kilograms (266).

In other words, calorie for calorie, it takes eighteen times as much energy to produce beef as to produce corn or wheat, and one hamburger is twenty-five times worse for the environment than a day's worth of driving. A cultural shift toward a more plant-based diet would be a significant step forward in helping to reduce carbon emissions.

Loss of Biodiversity

Biologists at the American Museum of Natural History say that we are now in the midst of the sixth of Earth's great mass extinctions (269). However the current one is the most rapid one in history, even when compared to the mass die-off of dinosaurs 65 million years ago due to an asteroid's impact. Biodiversity is essential to the maintenance of Earth's ecosystems. How many species can be killed before the web of life on the planet unravels?

What we know is that 25 percent of our planet's mammalian species are presently threatened with extinction. If present climate trends continue, by 2050 up to 35 percent of all species will be threatened with extinction. What is the leading threat to species in tropical rainforests? Livestock grazing. What is the leading threat to species in the United States according to the Federal General Accounting Office? Livestock grazing (270).

Hunger

Grain that could be used to feed approximately one billion undernourished people in third world countries is instead used to feed livestock. Globally, over 40 percent of the world's grain is fed to livestock. In the United States, livestock eat twice as much grain as is consumed by the entire human population. It is simply more profitable for agribusiness corporations throughout the world to sell their grain to the livestock industry for feed than to provide for impoverished people.

According to Vandana Shiva, director of the Research Foundation for Science, Technology and Natural Resource Policy in India, we are seeing "the McDonaldization of the world" (Robbins 2001, 286). As more grain is traded globally to feed livestock, more people go hungry in the third world. While more than a billion people are suffering from malnutrition or outright starvation— with thousands dying each day—McDonald's opens an average of five new restaurants per day, four of them outside of the United States. This is an unconscionable situation.

Diet for a New Earth

The points above provide compelling reasons to shift your diet away from meat consumption toward a more plant-based diet. Not only will such a change reduce your personal risk of cardiovascular disease and cancer, it will help the planet. When enough people in developed countries move away from meat to significantly undercut the meat production industries, the health of the earth will take a major step forward.

Make Time for Relaxation

A wholesome diet enhances both your physical well-being and your psychological well-being. Taking time out for personal relaxation is just as important. Relaxation is not hard to learn, nor is it hard to practice. What many people find difficult, however, is giving it much time or energy. It often seems that work, household responsibilities, entertainment, and stimulation are more important. Going to the mall or watching sports on TV can be more compelling than meditating or practicing deep relaxation or yoga. This is not surprising. The messages we receive from childhood on have to do with achieving, accomplishing, and performing—getting it done. Our days are filled with a hundred things to do, both at work and at home. The pace at which most of us work, travel, and live is considerably faster than it has been at any previous time in human history. So it's no surprise that many people find it difficult to make time to stop and do nothing other than relax. Relaxation is often thought of as doing something distracting, such as watching TV or going to a movie. Yet true relaxation is more than mere distraction. It is slowing down to a full stop, something many people are just not accustomed to doing. Practicing relaxation requires an act of will that runs counter to both the values and rhythm of our advanced, technological world.

Genuine relaxation is stopping everything—taking time out of your daily schedule to focus just on unwinding. There are numerous ways to do this. Some people prefer formal relaxation techniques, such as progressive muscle relaxation, restorative yoga, meditation, or listening to guided visualizations. Others prefer more informal ways, such as taking a walk in nature, listening to soothing music, enjoying a twenty-minute catnap, or soaking in a bath. What is important is making the time to stop all action and just let yourself be. Many books on relaxation and stress reduction are available. If you are interested in exploring a variety of formal techniques for relaxation, *The Relaxation & Stress Reduction Workbook*, by Martha Davis, Elizabeth Robbins Eshelman, and Matthew McKay (2008), now in its sixth edition, is excellent. Whatever relaxation method you prefer, if you truly want to live more peacefully, you will make relaxation a priority on a daily basis. For relaxation to make a difference in your life, it needs to be at least as important as work, family responsibilities, and entertainment such as TV or socializing.

Pacing and Downtime

Taking a half hour out of your day for some form of deep relaxation is a good start. It will relax your body, quiet your mind, and help you access the inspiration, wisdom, and creativity deep within your innermost being. Beyond this, pacing yourself more slowly and giving yourself ample downtime are two additional ways to begin reversing unhealthy trends and living more in harmony with your physical, mental, and spiritual self.

Pacing means living your life at an optimal rate. Too much activity packed into each day without sufficient breaks can lead to exhaustion, stress, and eventual disease. Not enough activity leads to boredom and self-absorption. Many people tend to push themselves too hard, following the lead of society, in which we're all told to do more, achieve more, and excel no matter what the cost.

If you tend to rush through the activities of your day, experiment with slowing down and giving yourself a five- to ten-minute "minibreak" every hour or at least every two hours. Minibreaks can be especially helpful when transitioning from one activity to another. For example, after commuting in the morning, take a short break before going into work. After cooking a meal, take a short break before sitting down to eat it. During a minibreak, you can meditate, get up and take a short walk, do a few yoga stretches, or do anything else that helps you to reenergize, relax, and clear your mind. When you pace yourself to allow for short breaks throughout the day, you will notice a significant difference in the way you feel. In fact, you may be surprised to find that you get just as much—or even more—done, because you bring more energy and clarity to your activities.

Slowing down and giving yourself short breaks throughout the day is simple in principle, but requires commitment. It's a commitment you're likely to find well worth the effort.

Downtime involves giving yourself more extended periods of time to rest and replenish your energy. While minibreaks will help you get through your day more calmly, you still need periods of time away from work and other responsibilities. Without such periods, the stress you experience in dealing with work or other responsibilities tends to become cumulative, building without remission. Nightly sleep doesn't really count as downtime. If you go to bed feeling stressed, you may sleep for eight hours and yet wake up still feeling tense and tired. How much downtime should you give yourself? Goals to work toward are:

- One hour per day

- One day per week

- One week out of every twelve to sixteen weeks

If you don't have the option to take four weeks off from work every year (the average time off for American workers is two weeks), try to obtain at least a few days' break every three or four months, even if your time off is unpaid.

During periods of downtime, disengage from any task that you consider work, put aside all responsibilities, and don't answer the phone unless it's someone you would enjoy hearing from.

There are three kinds of downtime, each of which has an important place in developing a calmer lifestyle: rest time, recreation time, and relationship time. It's important to provide yourself with enough downtime so that you can enjoy all three. Often recreation and relationship time can be combined. However, it's important to use rest time for just that and nothing else.

Rest time is time dedicated solely to relaxing. It is time when you put aside all activities and just allow yourself to be. Just stop action and let yourself fully rest. Rest time can involve lying on the couch and doing nothing, quietly meditating, sitting in your recliner and listening to peaceful music, soaking in a hot tub, or taking a catnap in the middle of the workday. The key to rest time is that it's fundamentally passive—you allow yourself to stop doing and accomplishing and just be. Contemporary society encourages us to be perpetually productive, accomplishing more and more every moment of the waking day. Rest time is a necessary counterpoint. When you are under stress, an hour of rest time per day—separate from your nightly sleep—is optimal.

Recreation time involves engaging in activities that help to re-create and replenish your energy. Recreation time brightens and uplifts your spirit. In essence, it's doing anything that you experience as fun or play. Examples of such activities include puttering in the garden, reading a novel, seeing a special movie, going on a hike, taking a short trip, baking a loaf of bread, or fishing. Recreation time can be done during the workweek, but is important to have on your days off from work. Such time can be spent either alone or with someone else.

Relationship time is time when you put aside your private goals and responsibilities in order to focus on enjoying being with another person—or, in some cases, with several people. The goal of relationship time is to honor your relationships with your partner, children, extended family members, friends, pets, and so on, and forget about your individual pursuits for awhile. If you have a family, relationship time needs to be allocated equitably between time alone with your spouse, time alone with your children, time when the entire family gets together, and time with friends. If you're single (unmarried) with a partner, time needs to be judiciously allocated between time with your partner and time with friends.

When you slow down and make time to be with others, you are less likely to neglect your own basic needs for intimacy, touching, affection, validation, and support. Meeting these basic needs is absolutely vital to your well-being. Without sufficient time devoted to important relationships, you will likely suffer—and the people you care about will as well.

How can you allow for more downtime (all three kinds) in your life? It requires a genuine commitment to leading a simpler lifestyle, regardless of what the neighbors, your friends, and the rest of the world may be doing. While deliberately making time for rest, recreation, and relationships may be challenging at first, it tends to become easier and more rewarding as time goes on. For some people, committing to more downtime translates into a decision to make earning money less important and living a simpler, more balanced lifestyle more important. Before thinking about leaving your present job, however, consider how you can shift toward placing more emphasis on the *process* of life—how you live—as opposed to accomplishments and productivity—what you actually do—within your current life situation.

Exercise

Just as with diet and relaxation, regular physical exercise is critical to both your physical and emotional well-being. This probably
seems obvious, as exercise has been so much a part of modern
culture for the past few decades. Yet this hasn't always been so. Up
until the twentieth century, the idea of making time for daily exercise would have seemed strange indeed. For a majority of people,
basic survival depended on frequent physical activity. In times
past—and in developing countries to this day—people usually
walked long distances to obtain supplies and exerted themselves
to provide for basic needs such as food, warmth, and clothing.
Not so in modern technologically advanced countries, where we
sit while we work, sit while we travel, and sit during much of our
leisure time in front of TVs or computers. Being overweight is not
a problem in some parts of the world but affects more than 60
percent of adult Americans. Along with our sedentary lifestyle
come a variety of chronic, stress-related diseases, especially cardiovascular diseases. The human body evolved over the past million
years in a physically demanding environment. It functions best
when it's frequently used.

Regular physical activity counteracts a predisposition to stress
and will help you to feel calmer throughout the day. Any form of
stress produces a state of physiological activation that prepares the
body for a fight-or-flight response. This increased nervous system
arousal and adrenaline naturally seek an outlet in physical activity. When we do nothing in response to this state of activation, the
energy implodes, often pushing up the level of internal physiological activation to even more intense levels. One way to curtail such
a reaction is to become physically active, especially when you feel
in a state of high stress. In fact, we are prewired to do just this. If
you find yourself feeling tense in a situation where you ordinarily can't move much (such as standing in line at the grocery store,
eating in a restaurant, or driving on the freeway), give yourself
permission to do so as soon as you can. Channel the activation in
your body into outward activity rather than absorb it.

If you have decided you would like to get more exercise,
consider whether you are fully ready to do so. Certain physical
conditions limit the amount and intensity of exercise you should
undertake. If you aren't accustomed to exercising (and especially

if you have chest pains, diabetes, or high blood pressure), be sure to consult with your physician before beginning any exercise program. Your physician can recommend a program of restricted or supervised exercise appropriate to your needs.

Begin to exercise gradually. If you are very out of shape, you may want to start with twenty to thirty minutes of walking on a daily basis. Gradually build up to more vigorous levels of exercise. For example, you could start with two to three minutes of jogging or cycling, and then gradually increase the duration of your daily exercise a minute at a time, remembering to stop and rest whenever you feel winded.

Choosing an Exercise Program

There are many types of exercise to choose from. Which forms of exercise you select depends upon your objectives. For many people, aerobic exercise is very effective in reducing the effects of stress. Common forms of aerobic exercise include running, cycling, brisk walking, jumping rope, rowing, stationary cycling, freestyle swimming, and various classes at your local gym or health club. Aerobic exercise requires sustained activity of your larger muscles. It reduces skeletal muscle tension and increases cardiovascular conditioning—the capacity of your circulatory system to deliver oxygen to your tissues and cells with greater efficiency.

Beyond aerobic fitness you may have other objective in taking up exercise. Mindful exercise, such as hatha yoga or tai chi, will enhance your energy and help you to feel more free and grounded in your body. Regular practice of yoga or tai chi is particularly potent in unifying body, mind, and spirit, and can enhance your connection with your innermost self. If increased muscle strength is important, you may want to include weight lifting or isometric exercises in your program. (Caution: if you have a heart condition or angina, you should probably not engage in weight lifting or bodybuilding.) If socializing is important, then racquetball, golf, or team sports such as basketball or soccer may be ideal for you. Team sports can be exciting and fun, however placing too much emphasis on competition can become an ego drama and may run counter to the values of cooperation and interrelationship that are part of the emerging new planetary consciousness. Exercise that involves stretching, such as dancing or yoga, is ideal for developing muscular flexibility. If you want to lose weight, jogging and cycling are probably most effective. Finally, if you just want to get out into nature, you may want to try hiking. Rigorous hiking—such as that done by the Sierra Club—can increase both strength and endurance.

Many people find it helpful to vary the type of exercise they do. Alternating between two or more different forms of exercise is sometimes referred to as cross-training. Cross-training helps you to develop a more balanced state of fitness by exercising different muscle groups. Popular combinations involve doing an aerobic type of exercise, such as jogging or cycling three to four times a week, and either a social exercise, such as golf, or a bodybuilding exercise twice a week. Maintaining a program of two distinct types of exercise can also prevent either from becoming too boring.

Exercise should be interesting and fun; it's important that you make it interesting early on so that you keep it up. There are several ways to do this. If you're not limited to being indoors, try to get outside, preferably into an attractive natural setting, such as a park. If you're doing a solo type of exercise, such as swimming, cycling, or jogging, see if you can find someone to accompany you at least sometimes. When you need to exercise indoors because of personal limitations or weather, play music or watch a video while you are on your stationary bike or treadmill. You can also take a portable audio player with you when running or cycling outside.

Guidelines for Starting an Exercise Program

If you haven't been exercising, it's important not to start off too fast or too hard. Doing so can result in burning out too soon and abandoning the idea of maintaining a regular exercise program. When beginning an exercise program, stick to the following guidelines:

- Approach exercise gradually. Initially set only limited goals, such as exercising for ten minutes (or to the point of being winded) every other day for the first week. Then add five minutes to your workout time each successive week until you reach thirty minutes.

- Expect exercise to be somewhat difficult at first. Aches and pains are normal if you are out of shape; they will pass. After some practice, you will come to enjoy exercise more than you do at first. An important principle to keep in mind when you feel too tired for exercise is that exercise creates energy. Exercising when you feel tired will often give you added energy.

- Give yourself a one-month trial period. Make a commitment to stay with your program for one month, despite aches and pains, inertia, or other resistance. By the end of the first month, you may have started to experience sufficient benefits to make the exercise self-motivating. Be aware that achieving a high level of fitness after being out of shape takes three to four months.

- Try to focus on the *process* of exercise rather than the product. See if you can get into the inherently enjoyable aspects of the exercise itself. If jogging or cycling is what you like, it helps to have a scenic environment. Focusing on competition with others—or yourself— may be useful for competitive sports, but is less so for personal healing and peace.

- Warm up. Just as your car needs to warm up before you begin driving, your body needs to gradually warm up before engaging in vigorous exercise. This is especially important if you are over forty. Stretching is probably not the best warm-up; a better warm-up is a few minutes of a slow-motion, low-intensity form of whatever exercise you're doing.

- After vigorous exercise, it's important to give yourself a few minutes to cool down. Walking around for two or three minutes will help bring blood back from peripheral muscles to the rest of your body. Avoid stopping exercise suddenly.

- Avoid exercising immediately after a meal; wait for an hour before beginning exercise. If possible, don't eat until an hour after exercising.

- Replenish body fluids. It's a good idea to have an eight-ounce glass of water before exercising. If you work up a good sweat, have another glass of water or juice afterward.

- Avoid exercising when you feel ill or overstressed; try a deep relaxation technique instead. Trust what your body tells you regarding the pace and intensity of your exercise.

- Stop exercising if you experience any sudden, unexplainable bodily symptoms.

- If you find yourself bored by exercising solo, find someone to accompany you—or a form of exercise that requires a partner.

- Exercise needs to be of sufficient regularity, intensity, and duration to have optimum benefit. Whatever way you choose to exercise, consider engaging in it twenty minutes to an hour at least four or five times per week. The aerobic benefits of jogging can be achieved in twenty minutes; the benefits of brisk walking may require a commitment of forty-five minutes to an hour.

Conclusion

We live in a society where many people take better care of their cars and homes than they do their own bodies. The hectic pace and demands of life on an overcrowded planet contribute to a widespread stress epidemic. This stress shows up in a variety of forms: disease, obesity, addictions of all kinds, interpersonal strife, crime, and general malaise. By making a commitment to caring for your body, you take a stand for a different kind of society: one in which health, wholeness, and inner peace are valued. Making such a commitment helps the cause of peace on earth, for social peace begins with the health and inner peace of each individual. As you consider the various ideas and practices presented on conscious diet, relaxation, and exercise, think about which ones you are ready to make part of your daily life.

22

Practice Meditation

Regular practice of meditation is one of the most effective ways to cultivate peace in your life. Meditation is not only personally beneficial, it empowers you to set an example for those around you. By stilling your restless mind, you naturally feel more inclined to build peace in all of your relationships. Meditation also dovetails with the desire to make your life more simple and free of encumbrances. Ultimately, the practice of meditation will help you to let go of your conditioned mind and align with the peace, wisdom, and compassion of your innermost self. As emphasized throughout this book, this innermost aspect of yourself is directly connected with the higher intelligence of nature and the Cosmos.

Meditation was conceived in ancient times as a method for transcending human suffering and reconnecting with the spiritual dimension of life. For thousands of years Eastern philosophy has taught that the origin of human suffering lies in our automatic, conditioned thoughts and reactions. When we can instead step back and simply witness our reactive thought patterns, we are able to free ourselves from suffering. According to the Eastern perspective, meditation is the method *par excellence* for freeing us from the suffering we create in our own minds. Christian mystics have also practiced meditation throughout the centuries.

How does meditation help to free us? In brief, through the expansion of our awareness. Awareness can be defined as a pure, unconditioned state of consciousness that we can all experience. It exists deep within, beneath the conditioned patterns of thinking and emotional reactivity we've learned over a lifetime. This awareness is always available to us, but much of the time it's clouded by the incessant stream of mental chatter and emotional reactions that make up ordinary moment-to-moment experience. Only when we become very quiet and still—only when we are "just being" rather than striving to do anything—can our mind settle down and this uncluttered awareness reemerge.

To expand or enlarge your awareness is simply to allow yourself to settle down into greater degrees of it. Because awareness lies along a continuum, it's possible to enter into it by degrees. Our language, in fact, refers to these varying degrees of awareness in expressions like "small-minded" and "large-minded." Another way to understand degrees of awareness is through the concept of depth, as discussed in chapter 9. Greater awareness is associated with greater depth. Thinking that is associated with less awareness is described as shallow; that which is associated with greater awareness is described as deep. Beyond this is a state where awareness transcends thinking altogether—where you simply observe your thoughts without reacting to them. Ultimately there is no limit to the potential enlargement or depth of awareness. As your awareness grows, it can continue to enlarge or deepen indefinitely.

Remember, your deepest inner awareness is a link or bridge to the experience of a universal or cosmic consciousness. (If this sounds too impersonal, think of this in terms of God, Spirit, a Higher Power, or a personal deity such as Christ.) At a deep level, your individual awareness connects with—or flows into—a much larger awareness that has no limit, much as a drop of the ocean is continuous with the entire ocean. As you enlarge or deepen your personal awareness, you can begin to participate to a greater degree in this larger, more universal consciousness. *Remember that you do not have to do anything to enlarge your awareness; it is something that happens naturally when you become still.*

Meditation, then, is a powerful method for expanding or deepening awareness. It enables you to relax outside of conditioned patterns of thinking and feeling long enough to experience the emergence of deeper levels of your own innate awareness. Your deepest awareness or consciousness is nothing to be afraid of—it's inherently beyond (or prior to) fear itself.

When you experience expanded awareness, you feel a deep sense of peace. Out of this place of inner peace can arise other nonconditioned states such as unconditional love, wisdom, deep insight, and joy. This state of peace isn't something you need to develop. It's always there, deep inside of you, available when you become still and quiet enough to allow it to emerge. The practice of meditation is a straightforward way to do this.

Meditation practice allows you to expand your awareness to the point where it's larger than your conditioned thoughts or emotional reactions. Take fear, for example. As soon as your awareness becomes larger than your fear, you are no longer swept up by fear but able to stand outside of it and merely witness it. You identify with a part of your consciousness that's larger than the part that's constricted by fearful thoughts. As you continue to practice meditation and enlarge your awareness further, it becomes easier on an ongoing basis to observe the stream of thoughts and feelings that make up your experience. Eventually you become less prone to get stuck or lost in them.

A final benefit of meditation practice is the development of compassion toward yourself and others. The mind constantly uses its automatic thoughts and reactions to judge. Being less stuck in your reactions allows you the freedom to be less judgmental. Although feelings of shame, guilt, and self-reproach, as well as anger and judgment of others may still arise, you don't have to get stuck or lost in these feelings. Instead you can witness them, allow them to pass, and cultivate an attitude of kindness and compassion. Human beings are actually compassionate by nature when able to rise above the adverse mental/emotional conditioning they acquire over their lifetime. Practicing meditation and moving into a stance of witnessing your own mind will help you to cultivate your innate compassion.

Ultimately meditation practice is not just for your personal benefit. It empowers you to bring more peace and compassion into the world—specifically to family, friends, and others within your sphere of influence. By cultivating inner peace, you convey peace to others. Furthermore, by quieting your mind, you put yourself more in touch with sources of wisdom and guidance beyond your own ego. Such guidance comes from the larger intelligence of the universe. The guidance that comes forth may serve your personal needs, for example, by telling you what is the right job to take, or how to work out a conflicted personal relationship. However, it may also impel you to participate in something larger than yourself—to make some contribution beyond your own personal needs. Guidance you receive from this larger intelligence of the universe is not always just about you; it may call on you to serve some aspect of its higher intentions. (This idea is discussed further in the final chapter of this book, Take Action.)

Learning to Meditate

Learning to meditate involves at least four distinct aspects:

- Right attitude

- Right technique

- Cultivating mindfulness

- Maintaining a meditation practice

Right attitude describes the mindset that you bring to meditation. Such an attitude takes time and commitment to develop. Fortunately, the practice of meditation itself helps you to learn right attitude. *Right technique* involves learning specific methods of sitting and focusing your awareness to facilitate meditation. The culmination of right attitude and right technique is *mindfulness—* the ability to witness and observe the ongoing stream of your experience. *Maintaining your practice* involves making a commitment to yourself to practice meditation regularly, on a daily basis. It requires discipline at first, yet becomes easier with time as a result of the benefits inherent to meditation.

This chapter offers only a brief and simple introduction to meditation. You may already be quite familiar with meditation and have a long-standing practice. If you are relatively unfamiliar with meditation and would like further explanation and instruction, see the books by Jon Kabat-Zinn mentioned below and his CDs (available at mindfulnesstapes.com), as well as other popular books on meditation such as *Meditation for Beginners* (2004) by Jack Kornfield, *Calming Your Anxious Mind* (2004) by Jeffrey Brantley, and *8 Minute Meditation* (2004) by Victor Davich.

Right Attitude

The attitude that you bring to the practice of meditation is critical. In fact, cultivating right attitude is part of the practice.

Your success and ability to persevere with meditation will in large part be determined by the way you approach it. The following six aspects of right attitude are based on the writings of Jon Kabat-Zinn, a prominent educator in the field of meditation. If you are serious about undertaking a regular meditation practice, you may want to consult his books, *Full Catastrophe Living* (1990) and *Coming to Our Senses* (2005).

Beginner's Mind

Observing your immediate, ongoing experience without any judgments, preconceptions, or projections is often referred to as "beginner's mind." In essence, it is perceiving something with the fresh perspective you would bring to it if you were seeing it for the very first time.

Nonstriving

Almost everything you do during your day is likely to be goal-directed. Meditation is not. Although meditation takes effort to practice, in meditation there is no aim other than to just be.

Acceptance

Acceptance is the opposite of striving. As you learn to simply be with whatever you experience in the moment, you cultivate acceptance. Acceptance does not mean that you have to like whatever comes up—for example, tension or pain—it simply means you are willing to be with it without trying to push it away.

Nonjudging

An important prerequisite for acceptance (as well as for beginner's mind) is nonjudging. To practice meditation, it's important to gain some distance from the process of judging. Simply observe your inner judgments without reacting to them, least of all judging them! Instead, cultivate a suspension of judgment: watch whatever comes up, including self-judging thoughts.

Trust

Another important attitude to bring to meditation is a basic trust in yourself. Honor your own instincts, reactions, and feelings, regardless of what any authority or other people may think or say. It's you who are responsible for your experience and no one else. To fully embrace that experience, you need to trust it. Trusting you own insight and wisdom will help you to develop compassion toward yourself as well as others.

Commitment and Self-Discipline

A strong commitment to work on yourself, along with the discipline to persevere, is essential to establishing a meditation practice. While meditation is very simple in theory, it's not always easy in practice. Learning to value just being on a regular basis requires a strong commitment in the midst of a society strongly oriented toward doing. Few of us grow up with values that honor nonstriving. So learning to stop goal-directed activity, even for just thirty minutes per day, requires commitment and discipline. The commitment is similar to that required by athletic training. Athletes don't practice only when they feel like it, when they have enough time to fit it in, or when other people are willing to keep them company. A commitment to training requires athletes to practice every day, regardless of how they feel or whether there is any immediate sense of accomplishment.

To establish a meditation practice, it's best to meditate whether you feel like it or not—whether it's convenient or not—six or seven days per week, for at least two months. (If you find you're unable to meditate that often at first, don't chastise yourself, just do your best.) At the end of this time, if you've practiced regularly, the process is likely to be a habit—one that is sufficiently self-reinforcing to make continuing your practice easier. The experience of meditation varies from session to session: sometimes it feels good, sometimes it seems ordinary, and sometimes it's difficult to meditate at all.

Though the point is not to strive for anything, a long-term commitment to regular meditation practice will transform your life fundamentally. Without changing the events that happen in your life, meditation changes your relationship to everything you experience, on a deep level. Most people feel that the hard work involved in establishing and maintaining a meditation practice is worth it.

Right Technique: Guidelines for Practicing Meditation

There is a technique to proper meditation. It's important to sit in the right fashion: upright, either on the floor or in a chair, with your back straight. There seems to be a certain energetic alignment within the body that occurs when sitting up straight that is not as likely to happen when you are lying down, although lying down is fine for other forms of relaxation. Also, it's often helpful to relax tight muscles before you meditate. Historically, the main purpose of yoga postures was to relax and energetically balance the body prior to meditation. The guidelines that follow are intended to help make your meditation practice easier and more effective:

- Find a quiet environment. Do what you can to reduce external noises and distractions. If this is not completely possible, listen to an audio recording of soft instrumental sounds or sounds from nature. The sound of ocean waves also makes a good background.

- Reduce muscle tension. If you are feeling tense, take some time (no more than a few minutes) to relax your muscles. Yoga or stretching exercises can be helpful. The following sequence of head and neck exercises may also be helpful:

Slowly touch your chin to your chest three times.

Bend your head back slowly, to stretch the back of your neck, three times.

Bend your head over to your right shoulder three times.

Bend your head over to your left shoulder three times.

Slowly rotate your head clockwise for two or three complete rotations.

Slowly rotate your head counterclockwise for two or three complete rotations.

- Sit properly. Eastern style: Sit cross-legged on the floor, with a cushion or pillow supporting your buttocks. Rest your hands on your thighs. Lean slightly forward so that some of your weight is supported by your knees as well as your buttocks. Western style (preferred by most Americans): Sit in a comfortable, straight-backed chair, with your feet on the floor and legs uncrossed, hands on your thighs (palms down or up, whichever you prefer). For both positions, keep your back and neck straight without straining to do so. Do not assume a tight, inflexible posture. If you need to scratch or move, do so. In general, do not lie down or support your head; this tends to promote sleep.

- Set aside twenty or thirty minutes for meditation (beginners may wish to start with five to ten minutes). To keep time you can set a timer—keep it within your reach—or play background music that is the right length so that you will know when you are done. If having a clock or watch available to look at makes you more comfortable, that's okay. After you have practiced for twenty or thirty minutes per day for several weeks, you may wish to try longer periods of meditation, up to an hour.

- Make it a regular practice to meditate every day. Even if you meditate for only five minutes, it's important to do it every day. It's best if you can find a set time to practice. Twice a day—upon rising in the morning and before retiring for the evening—is optimal; once a day is a minimum.

- Avoid meditating on a full stomach. Meditation is easier if you don't practice on a full stomach or when you're tired. If you are unable to meditate prior to a meal, wait at least a half-hour after eating before doing so.

- During meditation it can be helpful to close your eyes in order to reduce outside distractions. Some people, however, find they prefer to keep their eyes slightly open—just enough to see external objects indistinctly. This can reduce the tendency to be distracted by inner thoughts, feelings, and daydreams. Try this if you are having difficulty with distractibility.

- Select a focus for your attention. It doesn't matter what you choose, the point is simply to keep your attention focused. The most common devices are your own breathing cycle or a mantra. A *mantra* is simply a word or phrase that you silently repeat to keep your attention focused, such as the words "one" or "now" or a phrase such as "let it go" or "be at peace." Other common focuses include repetitive music or chants, or candle flames.

- During meditation your will find you are often distracted by extraneous thoughts, feelings, and bodily sensations. When this happens, don't judge yourself. Just gently bring your attention back to whatever you have selected as your focus. If an unpleasant thought or feeling tries to capture your attention, try reminding yourself, "This is just a thought," or "This is just a feeling." Just observe and be present with the thought or feeling without going into it. Eventually it will shift and pass. Good questions to ask to yourself occasionally are: "Can I just be the space for whatever comes up?" and "Can I just be fully present with this?"

- Distraction, boredom, restlessness, sleepiness, and impatience are common reactions during meditation. When these states come up, just notice them, allow them to be just as they are, and then return to being fully present in the moment.

- When you've finished with your practice for the day, open your eyes gently (if they've been closed) and stretch your body. Notice how you are feeling, but whether the feeling is positive or negative, don't judge it. If you feel good after your practice, refrain from setting any expectation that your next practice should be the same way. Let each practice session be a unique experience unto itself.

Ultimately, meditation practice has no goal other than just to be—to be fully aware in the present moment. However, an important benefit of regular meditation is the cultivation of *mindfulness*: the capacity to stand back and observe the ongoing stream of your experience rather than be caught up in it.

Cultivating Mindfulness

Mindfulness is paying attention, without judgment, to whatever comes up in the present moment of your experience. It is witnessing your ongoing experience just as it is, without trying to change, judge, or interfere with it. A good way to appreciate mindfulness is to realize that it encompasses all of the attitudes described in the section on right attitude: beginner's mind, nonstriving, acceptance, nonjudging, and trust. Mindfulness is not something that you have to strive to attain. By letting go and simply observing the ongoing stream of your experience without judgment, you will begin to experience mindfulness. Words cannot teach the meaning of mindfulness nearly so well as direct experience.

Compassion is a part of mindfulness. Many meditation teachers emphasize having a compassionate attitude toward your inner experience, regardless of what comes up. This may be difficult at first, since our habits of judgment and our aversion toward negative states such as fear, anger, or pain tend to be deeply rooted. As you learn to practice acceptance and nonjudgment of whatever comes up during meditation, you also begin to cultivate a more compassionate stance toward yourself. Ultimately mindfulness can change the way you deal with your experience of life in a profound way. As your practice strengthens, you can learn to relax and stay present even when fear and pain move through the present moment.

Two Exercises for Cultivating Mindfulness

While mindfulness is a general attitude of relaxed detachment— of witnessing the ongoing stream of your experience—it can be cultivated through specific exercises. Two such exercises follow. When utilizing either of these exercises, follow all of the guidelines for practicing meditation listed earlier in this chapter in the Right Technique section. (These exercises offer only a very brief introduction to mindfulness practice techniques. For a more in-depth presentation of mindfulness, see Jon Kabat-Zinn's *Full Catastrophe Living* (1990) and *Coming to Our Senses* (2005) or Jeffrey Brantley's *Calming Your Anxious Mind* (2004)).

Meditation with an Object: This is a type of structured meditation; it involves choosing a specific object or focus as an anchor for your awareness. Every time your attention wanders, you bring it back to this object. A popular focal point in many forms of mindfulness practice is the breath—experiencing your breathing cycle, preferably from your belly or your chest. Your focus could also be a mantra, a sacred phrase, the word "now," or an external object such as a candle flame or a flower. The purpose of the focus or object is to provide an anchor for your ongoing stream of experience. It becomes a point of contrast for your wandering mind, a reference point to return to every time your attention gets distracted. All the while you continue to practice the basic instruction of mindfulness, simply observing or witnessing whatever comes up in your experience with full acceptance and nonjudgment.

The tendency to become distracted during practice is inevitable. In five minutes of practice it may happen ten or perhaps fifty times. Also, you may feel the urge to stop, get up, and move around. It's very important not to judge yourself when you get distracted. Simply notice that you have been distracted and then gently bring your attention back to your object of meditation. If you don't like the fact that you're so distractible, simply notice that reaction without judgment. Be aware that there is no such thing as a good meditation session or a bad one. Often you will notice that you feel good or bad about how a particular session went. Keep in mind that the point of meditation is simply to witness your experience in the present moment, without striving to achieve anything and without evaluating how well the experience went.

Pure Awareness: In this mindfulness technique you become aware of the full field of your ongoing experience, simply observing nonjudgmentally whatever comes up in the present moment. Everything that passes though your ongoing stream of experience becomes—for a moment—the object or focus of your meditation.

Nothing is given preference or precedence over anything else. Each thought, feeling, body sensation, impulse, and external stimulus is simply witnessed as it passes though the present moment. As your attention wanders, this, too becomes yet another object of your present-centered awareness. There is no goal other than simply to be present with the full range of your experiences as they occur. Witness each element that moves into the foreground— let it become the temporary focus of your meditation, as if you were quietly observing leaves floating down a stream, one after another.

Optional: During mindfulness practice you may choose to be aware of your body sensations or emotional state apart from your thought process. Ordinarily, in most experiences, thoughts and feelings are entangled. Thoughts give rise to emotions or body sensations. For example, the thought "I am afraid" typically gives rise to some feeling of fear. Conversely, feelings and body sensations shape ongoing thoughts. If you feel frustrated and/or in physical pain, both of these conditions will tend to shape the subsequent content of your thought. It can be helpful during mindfulness practice to relax your awareness to the point that you begin to differentiate what your body is feeling from the ongoing stream of your thoughts. This will make it easier to see your thoughts as neutral, as just thoughts. As a result, you may find it easier to settle into a state of relaxed presence, free of identification with your mind.

To make progress in mindfulness practice, do it regularly. The more often you do it, the more quickly you will train your mind to be less reactive, more stable, and better able to observe. Working regularly with the resistance of your mind builds inner strength. Regular meditation practice will foster the development of the very attitudes that help facilitate the practice in the beginning: nonstriving, acceptance, nonjudgment, trust, commitment and self-discipline. Ultimately your meditation practice should have no goal. Just doing it will naturally bring about a profound shift in your way of relating to your inner experience.

Maintaining a Meditation Practice

As mentioned earlier, establishing a meditation practice requires commitment and self-discipline. Learning to meditate can be compared with learning a sport. A certain amount of training is necessary to become proficient. This means continuing to practice even on those days when you don't feel like it or find it inconvenient. Setting aside a regular time to practice for thirty to forty-five minutes each day will make this easier. Good times to practice are first thing in the morning upon awakening or before a meal such as dinner. By setting aside a regular time, you build in a place in your life for meditation.

Besides your own personal commitment and self-discipline, several other things can greatly support your practice. A local class or group that meditates regularly can be very helpful. Such a class may exist at a local hospital or college (for example, in an adult education program) in your area; additionally, some yoga centers offer meditation groups. Programs in transcendental meditation (a specific form of meditation developed by Maharishi Mahesh Yogi), are also offered in many areas. While transcendental meditation teaches only mantra meditation (using Sanskrit words), it's a good place to begin. Having the support of a group with whom you meditate regularly will help motivate you at those times when it seems hard to keep up your daily practice.

In some areas you may be fortunate to be close to a teacher who is highly skilled in the practice of meditation. If you are interested in finding a group or teacher in your area, you can contact:

Insight Meditation Society
1230 Pleasant Street
Barre, MA 01005-9701
(978) 355-4378
dharma.org

or

Spirit Rock Meditation Center
Box 169
Woodacre, CA 94973
(415) 488-0164
spiritrock.org

The Insight Meditation Society offers meditation retreats throughout the United States. A meditation retreat generally involves sitting in meditation for six to ten hours per day (with hourly breaks) for one to ten consecutive days, although a few go even longer. Retreats can be a powerful way to deepen your ongoing meditation practice, but they are not generally recommended for beginners.

Conclusion

World peace ultimately begins with each of us cultivating a more peaceful way of life. By practicing meditation, you take a stand for peace—both for yourself and for those with whom you come into contact. More than that, meditation practice is a transformative action that benefits the planet. It empowers you to move beyond the self-limiting patterns of your conditioned mind and align with the higher intelligence of the universe (or God, Spirit, Divinity, Dharma, or Tao). In so doing, you become a messenger for a compassion and wisdom that is larger than your personal ego and much needed on the earth at this time.

23

Think Larger

Thoughts shape our perception of reality. The fact that the world we perceive appears according to our thoughts about it is commonly recognized. The idea is an ancient one. The Greek philosopher Epictetus held that people are not disturbed by things but instead by their interpretation—the view they hold—of things. Today this idea is a core theme of both New Age and new thought philosophy, as well as cognitive and rational-emotive psychotherapy. It also underlies the idea explored earlier that paradigms (consensual assumptions) shape theories and observations in conventional science. Our views of ourselves, each other, humanity, and the world, are no larger or smaller than the beliefs we hold about them. If you want to change your life powerfully, work on expanding your mind.

Thinking larger is a general term that refers to a variety of practices that can empower you to shift your thinking to a larger perspective. All of these practices involve moving from a narrow to a more expanded focus. Some of them can enhance your personal well-being; others can help align you with the well-being of the planet and humanity at large. All of these practices loosen your identification with your mind and increase your awareness of just how much your thoughts shape your ongoing experience of life. By gaining skill in thinking larger—shifting to a larger perspective—you can both create clarity in your own life and participate in the larger shift in consciousness happening on the planet at this time.

Changing Your Mind

This chapter begins with three practical skills that can help you move beyond limited, self-defeating thinking: reframing, focusing on what you want rather than on what you don't want, and disidentifying with your thinking altogether. While there are many other useful practices, these three offer a good place to begin "thinking larger" in everyday situations. The latter part of this chapter will focus on inclusive thinking—thinking larger for the planet.

Reframing

To *reframe* means to put a situation in a different context, or to put a different frame around it. For example, imagine that you are stuck in traffic. One way to frame being in a traffic jam is to resist the situation and make yourself tense with self-talk such as, "I can't stand this," "I've got to get out of here." When you reframe you shift your attitude and put the whole situation in a different context. Instead of fighting the traffic, you might attempt to view it as an opportunity to settle down and relax. You could say to yourself instead, "Okay, I might as well just relax and adjust to the pace of the traffic," or "I can use this time to unwind by listening to some relaxing music."

In many cases, even when you're upset, you can find another way to look at a problem that will help to defuse it. When you change the context of a situation to make it easier to handle, you make what can be called a "cognitive shift." There are several types of cognitive shifts that can be applied to problem situations. What follows are nine common ones that you can use to change your perspective on any upsetting situation:

- Surrender to the fact that the situation is the way it is. Taking time out to relax can often help foster acceptance of situations over which you have little control. (See chapter 21 for more information on relaxing and reducing stress.)

- Acknowledge that it would be okay to lighten up about it; attempt to see some humor in it.

- Look for what the problem has to teach you—what can you learn by facing it and working through it.

- Expand your compassion for people who have similar problems.

- Realize that the problem is not likely to be as bad as your worst thoughts about it.

- Acknowledge that what's bothering you is not what really matters the most in life anyway.

- Trust that it will inevitably pass.

- Trust that problems generally work themselves out in one way or another.

- Turn everything over to God, Spirit, or a Higher Power (however you choose to define the creative intelligence of the universe).

This final way of reframing a problem situation deserves special attention in its own right.

Relinquishing a Problem to God, Spirit, or Your Higher Power

Deciding to ask for help from God, Spirit, or a Higher Power is a radical step, because it involves relying on a resource you can neither see nor fully understand. When you turn to God, or to what was referred to earlier as the creative intelligence of the universe, you are not just looking for a consoling concept or a convenient idea to comfort you. Anyone who has uttered a sincere prayer for assistance knows praying is more than simply a form of self-consolation. It is reaching out from your heart and soul for real assistance, assistance you've not been able to find to your satisfaction in anything else you have tried.

Surrendering control—letting go to an unseen force—can sometimes be a difficult step. The more afraid you are of a stressful life situation, the more you may try to struggle to exert control. To relinquish control requires humility, trust, a capacity to tolerate uncertainty, and faith. Keep these traits in mind if you choose to work with the following exercise.

Turning a Problem Over to Spirit

This exercise is intended to help you get in touch with your inner spiritual resources and obtain assistance to deal with any problem situation. Use the exercise only if it feels appropriate to you. To many readers, the following process will appear to be a variation on traditional prayer. However, you may have your own methods of prayer and meditation which you find preferable.

- Get comfortable in a seated position (you may also lie down if you prefer). Take a few minutes to become centered and relaxed.

- Bring to mind the troubling situation or person— whatever it is you are concerned about. Focus on this for several moments until you have it clearly in mind. If feelings of anxiety, hurt, or anger come up, allow yourself to just witness them, letting them pass without judgment.

- Affirm over and over, with as much conviction as you can: "I turn this over to my Higher Power (or God)," and, "I release this problem to my Higher Power (or God)."

- Simply repeat these statements slowly, calmly, and with feeling, as many times as you wish until you begin to feel better. While doing this, it is good to bring to mind the following ideas about Spirit or God:

  It is all knowing, in other words, it has wisdom and intelligence that go beyond your conscious capacity to perceive solutions to problems.

  In its great wisdom, Spirit—the creative intelligence of the universe—has a solution to whatever you're worried about.

  Even though you can't see the solution to your situation right now, you can affirm your faith that there is no problem that can't be resolved through the help of Spirit or God.

- If you are visually inclined, imagine that you're going to meet your Higher Power. See yourself in a beautiful setting of your choice, and then imagine that you see a spiritual figure approaching you. It may be indistinct at first and grow gradually clearer. You may notice that this figure exudes love and wisdom. It could be a wise old man or woman, a being of light, Jesus, Buddha, the supreme being in your particular religion, or any other presence that adequately represents your higher power.

- While in the presence of whatever comes up in your inner experience, simply find a way to ask for help. For example, you might say, "I ask for your help and guidance with _____." Keep repeating your request until you feel better. You may want to listen to see if your Higher Power has an immediate answer or an insight to offer you about your request. It is quite all right, though, simply to make your request and ask for help without getting an answer. The key to this part of the process is an attitude of genuine humility. By asking for help from God or Spirit, you relinquish some of your conscious control of the situation, and exercise a willingness to trust.

Give this process time. It may be necessary to persist with it for as long as half an hour to forty-five minutes in order to feel a genuine spiritual connection and a deep trust that the problem you're worried about can truly be resolved. After completing this process, if concern about your difficulty comes back the next day, simply repeat the exercise every day until you start to feel more at peace. To many readers, the above process will appear to be a variation on traditional prayer.

Focus on What You Want Instead of What You Do Not Want

When you work with your thinking, it is fundamental to focus on what you want instead of what you do not want. A basic principle of consciousness is that we tend to draw to us what we focus on (the so-called law of attraction). If you tend to focus often on what you do not want in your life—problems and difficulties— you tend to attract more of the same to yourself. To the extent you are willing and able to focus on what you do want, you will tend to draw more of that to yourself.

There are many ways to shift out of a negative attitude into a more positive one. Reframing the situation, as described above, is one way. Another way is to do something physical that makes you feel good, such as exercising, resting, meditating, getting hugged, or nourishing yourself with good food. It is much easier to cultivate constructive thinking when your body is relaxed and comfortable. The more relaxed you are, the easier it is to let go—to break the loop of conditioned negative thoughts.

The Power of Intention

Once you have shifted your mental frame of reference to what you want, you can help bring it about by consistently visualizing or affirming it. Whether it's greater prosperity, a harmonious relationship, or physical health, when you intend or ask for something with focus and sincerity, it tends to come to you. It is most likely to come about when what you intend is for your own highest good and doesn't conflict with anyone else's highest good.

How does intention work? As discussed throughout this book, all consciousness is interconnected at the deepest level. Thus if you hold an intention for good health in your mind, you will tend to resonate or align with that same idea in universal consciousness. What is an "idea in universal consciousness?" Traditional metaphysics has used a variety of terms for this concept, ranging from Platonic forms to angels embodying certain virtues. For our purposes, think of the universal field of consciousness not as a boundless void, but as holding specific ideas, just like our own minds. (Keep in mind that this view of cosmic consciousness is a metaphor or analogy for describing something beyond our full comprehension.) In terms of the model of consciousness described in chapter 10, universal ideas are aspects of the causal and celestial fields.

Consciousness, whether at a personal or cosmic level, is not static. Philosophers from Plato and Plotinus down to Whitehead have noted that it has a tendency to creatively manifest ideas into physical form. Again, if you hold a positive intention about health in your mind, your own consciousness aligns with the larger idea of health (harmony) in the universal consciousness. Thus you join that "place" in the universal field of consciousness where health is manifesting or coming about, which gives enormous force to your intention. Your whole life then becomes about being healthy rather than about being ill or sick.

The power of intention does not work indiscriminately. What you intend is more powerful and has a greater chance of coming about if it's aligned with your authentic self—your soul—rather than self-centered ego needs. Keep in mind that there can be limits to the power of intention, because your intentions do not occur in isolation but are deeply interrelated with everyone else's intentions. You are less likely to receive something you ask for when it interferes with someone else's well-being. Nor does the law of attraction govern everything that happens in the world; there are other laws that operate along with it, including the laws of physics and the law of karma.

For an intention to manifest, it's best to hold it deeply in your innermost heart and soul. When you do so, your mind lines up with a consciousness much larger than yourself—what was described in chapter 9 as the supraconscious mind. That is why heartfelt prayer can be powerful in effecting positive changes. When you ask for something sincerely from your heart, you connect with larger forces that can empower you to bring it about more easily.

When many people hold an intention, there is an even larger effect on collective consciousness than can be achieved by one person. For example, if many people pray for peace on earth at the same time, a large force for peace is realized in the collective consciousness of humanity. If we are all interconnected as one, the implications of this are quite significant. Theoretically, if enough people were to consistently maintain a positive intention for peace, war and conflict on the planet could disappear.

Holding an intention is a skill that can be learned. Though the idea is very old, scores of recent books describe how to creatively manifest goals. Some of the best-known of these are *Creative Visualization* (2002) by Shakti Gawain, *The Power of Intention* (2004) by Wayne Dyer, and the very popular book and movie, *The Secret* (2006). Manifesting intentions is also taught in New Thought churches such as Unity and the Church of Religious Science.

Disidentify with Your Thoughts

The ultimate step in working with your thoughts is to learn to disidentify with them. Most of our life is spent identifying with the thoughts and feelings that continually stream through our minds. The problem is that we mostly believe our thoughts, even when they are false or illusory. We become absorbed in the drama our mind creates, as if we were hypnotized. Only infrequently do we stop and recognize that the contents of our awareness are just thoughts or just feelings—superficial and transient states that do not make up our innermost self or being, which is always still and at peace. The goal of contemplative practices throughout the world's religions is to step out of the chattering mind and reclaim our connection with the still point of inner awareness that lies deep inside. As discussed in the previous chapter, regular practice of meditation is one of the most potent ways to learn to disidentify with your thoughts.

When you disidentify with your thoughts, you not only free yourself from the conditioned and often negative patterns of your own thinking, you align with your innermost self. This in turn connects you to the greater intelligence of the universe. As Einstein once said, a problem may not be solvable at the level of the problem itself. The mindset in which you set up the problem may be incapable of providing the answer to it. However, by connecting with the guidance and wisdom of your innermost or transpersonal self, your consciousness may expand to a level where the solution becomes clear. When we relax and get our ego (mind) out of the way, our consciousness begins to rediscover its essential connection with the larger consciousness of the universe. If you're interested in reading more about disidentifying with your mind, a good book to start with is *A New Earth* by Eckhart Tolle.

Inclusive Thinking

Inclusive thinking may be defined as expanding your mental perspective to embrace the entire planet. It means you think beyond your own personal needs (or the needs of your immediate family) to the needs of the earth and humanity at large. For example, when you throw away the trash, you think about what items can be recycled in order to preserve the planet's resources. When you see poverty in Africa on TV, or simply homeless people in your community, you think compassionately about their plight. When you see lights on in a room you're not using, you turn them off—not just to reduce your electric bill, but so that you can reduce your personal carbon emissions. Basically you think more broadly about the earth's situation in your practical, day-to-day activities. You begin to identify yourself not just by your vocational and family roles, or not just by the city, state, or country you live in, but as a planetary citizen—a member of the earth's community.

How do you shift your thinking and consciousness to a global perspective? There are several ways. Perhaps you've already begun to embrace some of the ideas presented earlier in this book. If you believe that the earth—and indeed the entire universe—is actually some type of conscious being, then you will begin to think of it as worthy of awe, respect, and even reverence. You will feel a genuine concern about the damage that industrial civilization has done to the earth's atmosphere, forests, oceans, and biodiversity. Such a concern will then motivate you to do something for the earth.

If you believe that all human beings are deeply interconnected—that there is one collective consciousness—then you will think beyond differences of race, religion, nationality, or ethnicity. The way you think expands as you realize that people in Uganda are people just like yourself, born into a situation where they do not have the same opportunities for basic survival—food, sanitation, health care, and education—that you take for granted. So you begin to feel compassion for them and are naturally motivated to contribute to organizations that will help them. Just because they live on the opposite side of the globe, doesn't mean you forget or ignore them. As your mind expands to embrace global thinking, the globe itself starts to shrink.

Perhaps you don't really believe the ideas presented in this book—that the earth is a type of conscious being or that all of humanity is united in a single consciousness. That's fine, it doesn't matter. Certainly it's not necessary to hold these beliefs to begin to think larger about the concerns of the planet. You may simply be struck by the difficulties that the earth and humanity are facing and want to do something to help. One day you may start to feel that there is more to life than just your personal, material, and emotional needs, and that you would like to give something back. Or perhaps you recognize that your own future well-being is intimately tied up with the well-being of the earth. Self-interest and the earth's needs are woven together, part of the same cloth. The future economic and political stability of developed countries will become increasingly dependent on the integrity of the earth's environment as well as the welfare of people in developing nations. So it's unnecessary to accept the worldview shifts described earlier in this book in order to think globally.

It may be that your mind expands simply by coming into contact with friends and acquaintances who have already made the shift to global thinking. Or it may expand as the result of seeing programs on TV or reading magazine articles that deal with environmental and social problems. Perhaps a book such as *An Inconvenient Truth* (2006) by Al Gore, *Plan B3.0* (2008) by Lester Brown, *The End of Poverty* (2005) by Jeffrey Sachs, or *Giving* (2007) by Bill Clinton (to name just a few) will help you to enlarge your perspective.

So there are many ways your thinking may shift to a more global, inclusive point of view. Once you make the shift, you never view your life in quite the same way. You begin to see how what you think, value, and do in your daily life fits into the fabric of the whole planet. Your life becomes part of the solution to the earth's difficulties rather than part of the problem. Instead of merely focusing on your own interests and needs, you start to care about the earth and its people.

Conclusion

Thinking larger means moving outside of the habitual beliefs and mindsets that define your perception of yourself, others, and the world. The various strategies described in this chapter provide a brief introduction to doing just this—both for your own peace of mind as well as for the benefit of the planet. In a sense, this entire book is about expanding your worldview to embrace the evolutionary shift in consciousness needed by humanity at this time. *The core shift is simply to move beyond self-interest to a concern for others and the world.* When you recognize the degree to which your own welfare and that of the planet are deeply interrelated, such a shift in consciousness becomes natural.

24

Take Action

Taking action to help the planet is a practice in self-transcendence. By taking concrete steps to do something for the earth and humanity, you move beyond the sphere of your own personal needs and interests. As you do so, you add a dimension of meaning and purposefulness to your life. No matter what your perception of the earth's future—optimistic, guarded, or pessimistic—you experience the satisfaction that you are doing something that makes a difference. In whatever small way, your life becomes part of the global shift needed for humanity to prevail in the difficult decades ahead.

There are two ways to make a difference:

- Changing your lifestyle and personal habits

- Making a specific contribution of your time, energy, or money to help environmental and/or social causes

Lifestyle Changes

There are three broad lifestyle changes you can make, the first two of which were described in previous chapters.

Reduce Your Energy Consumption

Besides saving you money, using less energy (primarily electricity, natural gas, and fuel) reduces your personal carbon footprint.

In this category there are many possible changes, such as driving a high-mileage vehicle, driving and flying less, buying Energy Star–rated appliances, or installing a solar water-heating system on the roof of your house. (See the section, "Simplicity and the Planet," in chapter 19 for a more complete list.)

Reduce Meat Consumption and Move Toward a More Plant-Based Diet

Consuming less meat does not mean that you have to become a strict vegetarian. However, whatever you can do will make a difference. By eating less meat, you give less of your money to the meat-production industries that consume enormous amounts of water, contribute to deforestation, are carbon intensive, and treat millions of animals in ways that are often inhumane and torturous. (See the section, "Conscious Diet," in chapter 21 for more information.)

Conserve Earth's Resources by Reducing Overall Consumption and Recycling

There are numerous ways to conserve resources. For example, you can use less paper by stopping junk mail and buying recycled copy paper. You can recycle plastic, glass, metal, and paper either at your curb or by taking it to your local recycling center. Using fewer of the earth's resources is often referred to as reducing your ecological footprint, in contrast to reducing your carbon footprint by using less electricity and fuel. Detailed guidelines for conserving important resources as well as recycling are presented in this chapter.

Of these various changes in personal habits and lifestyle, which ones are likely to have the greatest impact? It turns out that the first two will have a significant impact on reducing personal carbon emissions, while the latter will help save water and trees as well as diminish the air and water pollution caused by landfills. With regard to personal carbon dioxide emissions, several studies have come up with the following average percentages of total carbon output: (See the websites of the Natural Resources Defense Council and the Union of Concerned Scientists at nrdc.org and ucsusa.org for further information.)

- 30-35 percent due to driving vehicles.

- 35-40 percent due to household operations (heating, air conditioning, lighting, appliances, and electronic devices) which frequently use electricity generated by fossil fuel–burning power plants.

- 12-15 percent due to meat consumption (fossil fuels used in the process of producing and transporting meat).

- The remaining 20 percent is due to a wide variety of personal items and services, ranging from yard care to jet travel.

So it appears that just three personal activity areas—transportation, household operations, and food—account for roughly 80 percent of a person's carbon emissions. Making lifestyle changes in these areas will have the largest effect in reducing global warming as well as air pollution. Each of us could have a significant impact by: changing the kind of car we drive (for example, from an SUV to a hybrid or compact car) as well as some of our driving habits (using bicycles or public transportation when possible; combining errands to make fewer trips); reducing power used in heating and cooling our homes (turning our thermostats 2 degrees down in the winter and 2 degrees up in the summer); using energy-efficient appliances and lighting (Energy Star–rated appliances and compact fluorescent bulbs); and moving away from a meat-based diet toward a plant-based one, as well as buying produce at local farmers' markets whenever possible.

Reduce Your Ecological Footprint

Reducing your personal carbon emissions is important for mitigating global warming, but what can you do to help save precious planetary resources such as water and forests? In many parts of the world water is already being rationed, and a study reported by the Worldwatch Institute predicts nearly three billion people will be facing water shortages within twenty years (Renner 2005). As for forests, one third of the Amazon rainforest is now gone, and, worldwide, virgin forests are presently being cleared at the rate of one football field–sized area per second! (Robbins 2001, 255)

To reduce your ecological footprint it's important to conserve resources and recycle whatever you use, sending as little as possible to a landfill. This typically involves some thoughtfulness and effort. For example, you may be used to leaving the water running while you brush your teeth rather than turning it off. Or you may be used to tossing plastic bottles in the trash rather than recycling them. Choosing to live sustainably rather than wastefully requires a shift in values and a genuine commitment. At first it may seem cumbersome, but with practice new habits will start to take hold. As you read through the following guidelines about conservation and recycling, consider which ones you are ready to take action on now. Even a few small steps toward helping the planet will empower you to feel you're part of the solution rather than the problem—and help overcome humanity's wasteful and dysfunctional relationship with the earth.

Conserving Water

Numerous small changes in personal habits can help conserve water; for example:

- Try taking a shorter shower. Every two minutes less you spend in the shower can save up to ten gallons of water. You can also install low-flow showerheads.

- Turn off the faucet while you brush your teeth or shave. This will save a gallon or two of water a day, which adds up over months and years.

- Minimize pre-rinsing your dishes before you put them into the dishwasher

- If you have a garden, install a drip irrigation system. This will save up to 70 percent of the water you use by sprinkling. In a few years your savings in water will offset your installation cost.

- If you water your lawn in the summer, do so in the early morning or evening to reduce evaporation. Except during extreme heat, you only need to water your lawn once per week.

- If you have your own swimming pool, you can substantially reduce water loss due to evaporation by covering it when you're not using it.

- While traveling, use the same bed sheets and towels throughout your stay. By doing so, you will save up to two hundred gallons of water per day.

Saving Forests

To save the earth's forests, reduce your consumption of paper, recycle the paper products you do use, and buy only recycled paper.

- As mentioned in chapter 19, you can save a lot of paper by reducing your junk mail. Go to dmachoice .org and follow prompts to reduce your junk mail. It only costs a dollar.

- Most health-food stores and many grocery stores offer paper towels, napkins, and toilet paper made from recycled paper. They may cost slightly more, but you'll be doing the earth a big favor.

- Use ceramic rather than paper plates. Biodegradable plates are now available in some places.

- Buy recycled copy paper at your local office supply store.

- When possible at school or work, make double-sided rather than single-sided copies.

- Use ceramic mugs rather than paper cups for coffee and tea at work and home.

- When asked, "Paper or plastic?" at the grocery checkout counter, say "Neither." Use reusable cloth or

canvas bags and save considerable paper as well as
plastic.

- When eating out, use one napkin instead of grabbing
a bunch of them

- Pay your bills online or arrange automatic debits to
your bank account, to reduce the monthly deluge of
paper bills

- Recycle, recycle, recycle. Instead of trashing paper at
home (including newspapers, magazines, paper pack-
aging, junk mail, and paper towels) separate them
out for recycling, either at your curb or at your local
recycling center.

Recycling

Consumer recycling has been around for about thirty years,
and in some progressive American cities, recycling accounts for
as much as 50 percent of the municipal solid waste stream. On
the other hand, the national recycling rate has stagnated, staying
at about 30 percent since the 1990s, a figure well below rates of
several European countries. Opposition to recycling consistently
comes from corporate groups such as the timber and mining companies, and in tough economic times, cities often curtail curbside
recycling programs.

If you do not have curbside recycling in your community, find
out where you can take used paper, plastic, glass, and metal items to
be recycled. Because of the global problem of disappearing forests,
recycling paper has the highest priority. This includes newspapers
and magazines, junk mail, office paper, cardboard, and paper bags.
Typically paper should be free of food, plastic, wax, rubber bands,
clips, and tape. After paper, recycle aluminum cans, plastic con-
tainers, plastic bottles, and clear glass bottles. Check with your
local recycling program for specific guidelines, as these can vary
from one city to another.

Recycling helps reduce the amount of trash that ends up in
landfills. Landfills have become a serious environmental hazard.
Worldwide, they take up a space about the size of the state of
Pennsylvania. The highest point on the east coast of the United

States from satellite cameras is a landfill. Burning the contents of landfills releases toxins into the air. Letting the contents sit in the earth results in leaching of toxins into the groundwater. Some landfill contents—such as Styrofoam and some metals—will be around for more than a thousand years. Recycling not only helps to conserve environmental resources, it reduces the greenhouse gases and pollution produced by both mining operations and plastic manufacturers.

Reduce Electronic Waste

The unmanaged disposal of electronic devices has caused landfills to grow by leaps and bounds in recent years. For example, more than 100 million cell phones end up in landfills *per year*. Add to that about 50 million computer monitors. Electronic devices contain heavy metals such as lead, mercury, and zinc that can end up in the air or groundwater. Used batteries contain lithium, which isn't any healthier. Since the typical American household contains dozens of electronic devices—many of which contain batteries—the prospect of trashing all of these devices over the next few decades is not a pretty picture for the environment. Extrapolate this to the entire globe and there is a serious environmental hazard in the making.

To oppose this trend, consider either storing used electronic devices or giving them to friends or charities. Alternatively, look up resources for electronic waste disposal in your phone directory or online, and take used items to a local site once or twice a year. In some cases, you may even receive a tax deduction or hard cash for doing so.

Reuse Kitchen Waste

If you have a garden, consider using kitchen waste (fruits, vegetables, coffee grounds) to create a compost site in your yard. This will help fertilize your garden and keep food waste out of landfills.

Contribute Your Time or Money to Make a Difference

Becoming part of the present planetary shift begins with changing your own personal habits. Beyond this, you can give to others. There are a variety of ways you can directly contribute money and/or time to help the earth and humanity make a shift to a more sustainable, prosperous, and peaceful future. Some, but by no means all of these changes include:

- Help socially disadvantaged people, locally or globally

- Offer your time and/or money to environmental non-profit organizations

- Invest in socially responsible companies and funds

- Educate yourself and others about global issues

- Take political action

As you read about these various options, consider which ones you are willing to embrace either today or in the near future.

Help the Socially Disadvantaged, Locally and Globally

All human beings, regardless of their national, racial, ethnic, or socioeconomic status, have an equal, inalienable right to life, health, the fulfillment of basic needs, and the free pursuit of their own destiny. Since ultimately we are all one in consciousness, living in alignment with the natural order is to live in a way that does not interfere with any other human being's basic rights. At depth, what you do to others you do to yourself. The emerging worldview calls on each of us to honor all human beings, regardless of their race, ethnic group, religion, nationality, educational or socioeconomic status. This is what it means to be a global citizen.

On a practical level, we can reach out to people who are impoverished, homeless, hungry, in threat of disease, or otherwise socially disadvantaged. This includes both committing to help needy people in our own communities as well as contributing to organizations that strive to help people around the globe. In the words of performer and humanitarian Bono, "We can be the generation that no longer accepts that an accident of latitude determines whether a child lives or dies—but *will we be that generation*?" (Sachs 2005, xiv.) There are at least two ways you can begin to help others in your own community or elsewhere: volunteering your time and making a financial contribution.

Volunteer Locally

You could, for example, spend an hour or two a week volunteering for organizations that help people who are challenged by poverty, hunger, or homelessness. Other organizations assist people challenged by mental or physical disabilities, substance abuse, or age and infirmity. If you don't know where to start, try doing an Internet search for volunteer opportunities in your city or county. Your church may also offer opportunities to be directly involved with people in need. Another good resource is the website volunteermatch.org, which allows you to enter your zip code to obtain a list of opportunities in or nearest your area.

Make a Financial Contribution

Perhaps the simplest way to make a difference is to make a financial contribution. The Internet has made this much easier than it used to be. Instead of mailing in your donation, you can simply go to the websites of your favorite organizations and make contributions using your credit card.

How much should you give? Through their widely known foundation, Bill and Melinda Gates have contributed about a third of their total assets ($35 billion) to a broad range of global issues, including education and health care, preventable diseases, and extreme poverty, both in the United States and many third world countries. Former President Bill Clinton holds a fundraising event each September that has managed to raise almost $10 billion for similar causes as well as climate change and social justice issues. For the vast majority of us with lesser means, donations might range from 1 to 10 percent of annual income after taxes. If you wish to make a difference for the world through a financial contribution, take time to reflect on what annual amount makes sense for you. Keep in mind that it's tax deductible.

Countless nonprofit organizations deal with problems relating to poverty, hunger, disease, and social injustice, all with websites. Some of the better-known ones include:

American Institute for Philanthropy (charitywatch.org)

Bill and Melinda Gates Foundation (gatesfoundation.org)

Bread for the World (bread.org)

Care International (care.org)

Center for Global Development (cgdev.org)

The Clinton Foundation (clintonfoundation.org)

Doctors Without Borders (doctorswithoutborders.org)

InterAction (interaction.org)

One World (oneworld.net)

Oxfam International (oxfam.org)

UNICEF (unicefusa.org)

World Resources Institute (wri.org)

To learn more about the wide range of opportunities available for giving, consider reading books on the subject such as *Giving: How Each of Us Can Change the World* (2007) by Bill Clinton, *How to Save the World in Your Spare Time* (2007) by Elizabeth May, or *A Kid's Guide to Giving* (2006) by Freddi Zeiler (this last book also contains many good ideas for adults).

Contribute to Environmental Organizations

The first part of this chapter described lifestyle changes that can help the environment. Each of us can further help by becoming involved, through membership and/or financial contributions, with nongovernmental organizations that deal with climate change, conservation of natural resources, sustainable development, and alternative forms of energy. Some of the better-known of these organizations include:

Environmental Defense (edf.org)

Greenpeace (greenpeace.org)

Natural Resources Defense Council (nrdc.org)

Sierra Club (sierraclub.org)

World Conservation Union (iucn.org)

World Resources Institute (wri.org)

World Wildlife Fund (worldwildlife.org)

Also consider getting involved with local environmental groups that focus on causes such as preserving natural habitats or working with municipal utility companies to purchase wind and solar-based energy.

Socially Responsible Investing

Socially responsible investing involves considering the social and environmental consequences of where you invest your money. Each of us can refrain from investing in companies that create hazards to human health, either through their products—such as tobacco and alcohol—or through pollution. More generally, we can avoid investing in companies whose practices harm forests, animals, or human life, such as defense contractors and companies that test animals. We can also avoid companies that exploit workers, whether in third world countries or elsewhere.

Three different approaches are commonly utilized in socially responsible investing: screening, shareholder advocacy, and investing in local communities.

Screening

Most socially responsible investors start by screening stocks. Screening involves avoiding companies that harm the environment or people while seeking out those companies that exhibit consciousness about the environment and/or the need for renewable energy. Socially responsible investors often also screen with regard to a company's human rights record and labor practices.

If you would like to invest in socially responsible companies, you may want to consider socially responsible mutual funds (professionally managed portfolios of companies). Most of these funds screen out negative companies, while a few do positive screening as well—that is, they also seek out good companies. In order to maintain good financial performance, very few of the funds consist *only* of environmentally progressive, socially conscious companies. Some of the better-known socially responsible funds are Calvert Funds, Domini Social Equity Fund, Portfolio 21, and the Winslow Growth Fund. SocialFunds.com offers an extensive list of socially responsible funds along with a brief description of the screening criteria each fund uses.

Shareholder Advocacy

Shareholder advocacy is using your position as a shareholder to encourage a company to take specific actions. In conjunction with other shareholders, you can attend annual shareholder meetings, ask questions at the meetings, and vote on various issues put before shareholders. With a certain minimum investment, you can propose a nonbinding corporate resolution—a shareholder resolution for company policy change. With the help of other shareholders, such resolutions can get a company to at least pay attention to public sentiment about environmental issues. For example, in 1999, long-standing shareholder advocacy efforts pressured Home Depot to stop sales of old-growth wood products from ancient trees.

Community Investment

In terms of socially responsible investing, community investment is investing capital in communities where ordinary financial services and loans are hard to come by. Both in the United States and around the world, community investing allows you to make micro-loans to low-income individuals who are trying to start a small business. For example, through an organization known as Kiva (kiva.org), you can make loans to individuals attempting to start grassroots businesses in developing countries.

Useful Resources

Useful resources on socially responsible investing are available from the Social Investment Forum (socialinvest.org), SocialFunds.com, Co-op America's *Real Money* bimonthly newsletter and website (realmoney.org), and Socially Responsible Investing-World Group (sriworld.com).

Educate Yourself About Global Issues

Another way to make a difference is to educate yourself about global issues and then spread the word to your friends. Some of the most important global issues today are climate change, diminishing resources (especially oil, food, and water), loss of biodiversity, deforestation, overpopulation, poverty, hunger, disease, and inadequate education. While most of these issues were touched upon briefly in chapter 1, a full discussion of any one of them would require a book-length treatment. To educate yourself about global problems, consider starting with the annual reports of the Worldwatch Institute. An independent research organization based in Washington, D.C., every year the Worldwatch Institute produces a report on the state of the world, focusing on many of the major problems the earth faces. Its discussions are balanced and thorough, describing the complex interrelationships among problems such as global warming, poverty, hunger, and increasing competition for fossil fuels and food, as well as the prospects for future wars over strained resources. To find out more, visit worldwatch.org.

Also, you can read books that focus on global concerns. Three that are good to start with are *An Inconvenient Truth* (2006) by Al Gore, *Plan B3.0* (2008) by Lester Brown, and *The End of Poverty* (2005) by Jeffrey Sachs. (A more extensive list can be found under Global Issues in the resources section located at the back of this book.)

Take Political Action

Each of us can support candidates at the local, state, and federal level who are pro-environment. The League of Conservation Voters maintains a website (lcv.org) that evaluates the environmental credentials of political candidates at the federal, and, in some cases, state level. You can also contact your state congresspeople regarding your views on key issues such as global warming, habitat protection, animal rights, promotion of energy-saving technologies, or whatever issues interest you. Let your elected representatives know that a world that spends a trillion dollars every year on defense (half of this is spent by the United States) is out of touch with a situation where the future of civilization is in question. The Worldwatch Institute estimates that investing about one-fifth of this budget each year would be sufficient to solve all of the problems Earth and humanity are presently facing (Renner 2005).

Many environmental organizations, such as the Natural Resources Defense Council and the Sierra Club, have petitions you can sign to take a stand on a wide variety of environmental concerns. Making a difference with your vote or signature often involves little more than the click of a mouse. Consider making a start today—taking action right now—by going to the websites of any of the various environmental organizations listed above.

Conclusion

This chapter has enumerated a variety of actions each of us can take to make a difference. None of us can solve the immense problems the earth and its people face alone. Yet each of us, by engaging in a few simple actions to help the environment and disadvantaged people, can make a contribution and potentially influence others we know to do the same. The next two decades will tell how serious the earth's situation has to become before large numbers of people feel compelled to shift both the way they think and how they live their lives. There is still hope for the planet if enough of us can come together to make an impact on societal consensus—to actually bring about a global shift in attitudes, values, and actions that is needed to redirect humanity toward balance and unity.

Conclusion

It is often said that the fate of humanity rests in the hands of those government leaders who have the ultimate decision-making power to affect the numerous crises our planet faces. Climate change, for example, may be mitigated if the American government implements and maintains a viable carbon cap-and-trade system for industry, taxes consumer energy use, and undertakes an almost warlike "surge" to develop carbon-free energy alternatives. Even more helpful would be if America were to pass on such incentives and technological innovations to the nations with the largest future role in climate change: China and India.

No doubt such pronouncements are true. Government leaders, together with multinational corporations and global political organizations such as the United Nations, have the largest role to play in creating a new planetary civilization based on sustainability, stewardship of the earth, and international cooperation.

Creating a more sustainable and cooperative world order is doable. The question is whether it will be done—whether the political will exists to get it done—in time to avert worldwide catastrophe. Without a widespread shift in consciousness, it is more likely that humanity will wait until the curtain begins to descend. Then nations will rush to implement draconian measures in an atmosphere of increasing environmental, economic, and social chaos.

Such a catastrophe may be averted if the emerging global shift reaches a critical mass in time. This is where we come in. Governments and multinational corporations may seem remote, all-powerful, and far away. Yet if all human consciousness is interconnected, then each of our personal contributions to the global shift makes a difference. As more of us change, governments and corporations will be influenced to change as well.

The global shift needed at this time begins with you. To be a part of the shift, first work on your own personal healing and inner peace. Such healing can come in countless ways: cultivating skills in communication, forgiving others, eating a more conscious diet, simplifying your life, practicing meditation, or reframing your attitude about a long-standing challenge. When implementing healing practices, remember that help is available—from books, magazines, and Internet-based media, as well as from healing practitioners, friends, and unseen sources. Working on your own healing is not self-centered; it is an important way to engage in the emerging global shift.

As you cultivate healing and inner peace for yourself, you step into a larger stream—the stream of larger and evolving fields of consciousness: the consciousness of humanity, the planet, and the Cosmos at large. Healing yourself means, among other things, that you learn to loosen, then relinquish, conditioned mental and emotional patterns that limit contact with your authentic self—your innermost being that is naturally aligned with the larger creative intelligence of the Cosmos. Healing yourself opens you to inspiration, guidance, and empowerment from the Cosmos at large (or God, if you prefer). Then your life comes to be about more than just your own personal needs. It becomes natural to reach out beyond yourself to do something to help the environment or impoverished peoples. It's not about just you anymore—you've become a part of the larger planetary shift. As you begin to move along with this shift, don't worry about what other people are doing or whether you're doing enough. Just listen inwardly and get in touch with the work that is yours to do.

It's likely that humanity's rite of passage over the next few decades will be neither comfortable nor easy. Much of what is out of balance in the world has to go—it's just not working anymore. As a part of humanity, your own personal shift may not be easy either, though this will be influenced largely by your degree of resistance. Resistance arises out of fear of change; when you trust the process of your life enough to release resistance, change comes more easily. If the changes you need to make appear challenging, embrace them and see them as doable, especially when you know you have help. Remember to get support when you need it. If, in coming years, the world around you seems to career toward increasing discord and chaos, it will become increasingly critical that you hold peace and clarity in your own mind and heart. That way you can continue to be a force for reconciliation and constructive action no matter what happens. In doing so, you also become an example to others.

Despite our differences, we are all in this together. No act of kindness or compassion goes unnoticed. To change the world, take compassionate action within your immediate sphere of influence. To change yourself, start by being still and making time just to listen. Listen to what your higher wisdom has to say about how you can deepen your participation in the global shift—through personal healing, changing your worldview, or finding ways to help others and the environment. This is how you can both heal yourself and help to heal humanity. At their deepest level, the two are joined and ready to awaken to a new world.

Resources and
Further Reading

Global Crisis

Brown, Lester R. 2008. *Plan B 3.0: Mobilizing to Save a Civilization.* New York: Norton.

Gore, Al. 2006. *An Inconvenient Truth: The Planetary Emergency of Global Warming and What We Can Do About It.* Emmaus, PA: Rodale Press.

Sachs, Jeffrey. 2005. *An End of Poverty: Economic Possibilities for Our Time.* New York: Penguin.

Worldwatch Institute. 2008. *State of the World 2008.* New York: Norton. (Published annually since 1984, these reports provide encyclopedic knowledge about global issues and proposed policy, economic and technological solutions.)

New Paradigm

Elgin, Duane. 2000. *Promise Ahead: A Vision of Hope and Action for Humanity's Future.* New York: Quill.

Gerber, Richard. 2001. *Vibrational Medicine: The #1 Handbook of Subtle-Energy Therapies.* Rochester, VT: Bear & Company.

Laszlo, Ervin. 2004. *Science and the Akashic Field: An Integral Theory of Everything.* Rochester, VT: Inner Traditions.

de Quincey, Christian. 2002. *Radical Nature: Rediscovering the Soul of Matter.* Montpelier, VT: Invisible Cities Press.

Radin, Dean. 2006. *Entangled Minds: Extrasensory Experiences in a Quantum Reality.* New York: Pocket Books.

Tarnas, Richard. 2006. *Cosmos and Psyche: Intimations of a New World View.* London: Viking UK.

Wilber, Ken.1996. *A Brief History of Everything.* Boston, MA: Shambhala.

Two magazines which offer excellent articles on various aspects of the emerging worldview and its implications for humanity are *Kosmos Journal* and *Shift* (the latter is published by the Institute of Noetic Sciences, co-publisher of this book). For more information, see kosmosjournal.org and noetic.org.

Transformative Practices

Simplify Your Life

Elgin, Duane. 1993. *Voluntary Simplicity.* New York: William Morrow.

Fanning, Patrick, and Heather Garnos Mitchener. 2001. *The 50 Best Ways to Simplify Your Life.* Oakland, CA: New Harbinger Publications.

Build Peace in All Relationships

McKay, Matthew, Martha Davis, and Patrick Fanning. 1995. *Messages.* Oakland, CA: New Harbinger Publications.

Rosenberg, Marshall. 2003. *Nonviolent Communication: A Language of Life.* Encinitas, CA: Puddle Dancer Press.

Care for Your Body

Pollan, Michael. 2007. *The Omnivore's Dilemma: A Natural History of Four Meals*. New York: Penguin.

Robbins, John. 2001. *The Food Revolution: How Your Diet Can Help Save Your Life and Our World*. Boston, MA: Conari Press.

Practice Meditation

Brantley, Jeffrey. 2004. *Calming Your Anxious Mind*. Oakland, CA: New Harbinger Publications.

Kabat-Zinn, Jon. 1990. *Full Catastrophe Living*. New York: Delta.

Kabat-Zinn, Jon. 2005. *Coming to Our Senses: Healing Ourselves and the World Through Mindfulness*. New York: Hyperion.

Kornfield, Jack. 1993. *A Path with Heart*. New York: Bantam.

Kornfield, Jack. 2004. *Meditation for Beginners*. Boulder, CO: Sounds True.

Think Larger

Hay, Louise. 1987. *You Can Heal Your Life*. Carlsbad, CA: Hay House.

Tolle, Eckhart. 1999. *The Power of Now*. Novato, CA: New World Library.

Tolle, Eckhart. 2005. *A New Earth*. New York: Dutton.

Zukav, Gary. 1995. *The Seat of the Soul*. New York: Simon & Schuster.

Take Action

Clinton, Bill. 2007. *Giving: How Each of Us Can Change the World*. New York: Knopf.

Hawken, Paul. 2007. *Blessed Unrest*. New York: Viking.

May, Elizabeth. 2007. *How to Save the World in Your Spare Time.* Toronto: Key Porter Books.

Zeiler, Freddi. 2006. *A Kid's Guide to Giving.* Norwalk, CT: Innovative Kids.

Organizations for Making a Difference

Protecting the Environment

Environmental Defense (edf.org)

Greenpeace (greenpeace.org)

Natural Resources Defense Council (nrdc.org)

Sierra Club (sierraclub.org)

World Conservation Union (iucn.org)

World Resources Institute (wri.org)

World Wildlife Fund (worldwildlife.org)

Poverty and Social Justice

American Institute for Philanthropy (charitywatch.org)

Bill and Melinda Gates Foundation (gatesfoundation.org)

Bread for the World (bread.org)

Care International (care.org)

Center for Global Development (cgdev.org)

The Clinton Foundation (clintonfoundation.org)

Doctors Without Borders (doctorswithoutborders.org)

InterAction (interaction.org)

One World (oneworld.net)

Oxfam International (oxfam.org)

UNICEF (unicefusa.org)

World Resources Institute (wri.org)

Sustainable Living

Awakeningearth.org

Campaign Earth (campaignearth.org)

Co-op America (coopamerica.org)

Eartheasy Sustainable Living (eartheasy.com)

Lighterfootstep.com

Northwest Earth Institute (nwei.org)

The Simple Living Network (simpleliving.net)

Responsible Investing

Co-op America's Real Money Newsletter (realmoney.org)

Socialfunds.com

Social Investment Forum (socialinvest.org)

Transforming Culture & Consciousness

Center for Conscious Evolution (evolve.org)

Emergent Mind (emergentmind.org)

Foundation for Global Community (globalcommunity.org)

Institute of Noetic Sciences (noetic.org)

Kosmos Journal (kosmosjournal.org)

WiserEarth (wiserearth.org)

References

Assagioli, Roberto. 1975. *Psychosynthesis: A Manual of Principles & Techniques.* New York: Viking Press.

Barbour, Ian G. 1997. *Religion and Science: Historical and Contemporary Issues.* New York: HarperSanFrancisco.

Bohm, David. 1980. *Wholeness and the Implicate Order.* London: Routledge.

Brown, Lester. 2008. *Plan B 3.0: Mobilizing to Save Civilization.* New York: Norton.

Capra, Fritjof. 1975. *The Tao of Physics.* Berkeley, CA.: Shambhala.

Church, Dawson, and Geralyn Gendreau, eds. 2004. *Healing Our Planet, Healing Our Selves: The Power of Change Within to Change the World.* Santa Rosa, CA.: Elite Books.

Clinton, Bill. 2007. *Giving: How Each of Us Can Change the World.* New York: Knopf.

Elgin, Duane. 1993. *Voluntary Simplicity: Toward a Way of Life That Is Outwardly Simple, Inwardly Rich.* Rev. ed. New York: William Morrow & Co.

———. 2000. *Promise Ahead: A Vision of Hope and Action for Humanity's Future.* New York: William Morrow & Co.

Esty, Daniel. 2008. Foreword. In *State of the World 2008: Innovations for a Sustainable Economy*, Worldwatch Institute, xiv. New York: Norton.

Gerber, Richard. 2001. *Vibrational Medicine: The #1 Handbook of Subtle-Energy Therapies*. Rochester, VT.: Bear and Company.

Gilbert, M., ed. 2008. *The 2008 Shift Report: Changing the Story of Our Future*. Petaluma, CA: Institute of Noetic Sciences.

Gilbert, M., and D. Powell, eds. 2007. *The 2007 Shift Report: Evidence of a World Transforming*. Petaluma, CA: Institute of Noetic Sciences.

Gore, Al. 2006. *An Inconvenient Truth: The Planetary Emergency of Global Warming and What We Can Do About It*. Emmaus, PA.: Rodale Books.

Greene, Brian. 1999. *The Elegant Universe: Superstrings, Hidden Dimensions, and the Quest for the Ultimate Theory*. New York: Norton.

Grunwald, Michael. 2008. The clean energy scam. *Time Magazine*, April 7.

Harman, Willis. 1990. *Global Mind Change: The New Age Revolution in the Way We Think*. New York: Warner Books.

Hartshorne, Charles. 1991. *The Philosophy of Charles Hartshorne, Library of Living Philosophers*, Vol. 20. La Salle, IL: Open Court.

Hawken, Paul. 2007. *Blessed Unrest*. New York: Viking.

Hawken, Paul, Amory Lovins, and Hunter Lovins. 2000. *Natural Capitalism: Creating the Next Industrial Revolution*. Boston, MA: Back Bay.

Hawking, Stephen. 1988. *A Brief History of Time*. New York: Bantam.

Hillman, James. 1975. *Re-visioning Psychology*. New York: Harper & Row.

Huxley, Aldous. 1945. *The Perennial Philosophy*. Repr., New York: HarperCollins, 2004.

James, William. 1902. *The Varieties of Religious Experience*. Repr., New York: Touchstone, 1997.

Judith, Anodea. 1996. *Eastern Body, Western Mind*. Berkeley, CA: Celestial Arts.

Jung, Carl Gustav. 1973. *Synchronicity.* Princeton, NJ.: Princeton University Press.

————. 1976. *Psychological Types.* Princeton, NJ.: Princeton University Press.

Kabat-Zinn, Jon. 1990. *Full Catastrophe Living.* New York: Delta.

Koestler, Arthur. 1967. *The Ghost in the Machine.* Repr., New York: Penguin, 1991.

Kuhn, Thomas S. 1970. *The Structure of Scientific Revolutions.* Chicago: University of Chicago Press.

Kunzig, Robert. 2008. Proof positive. *National Geographic Special Report: Changing Climate,* March.

Laszlo, Ervin. 2004. *Science and the Akashic Field.* Rochester, VT.: Inner Traditions.

Lovejoy, Arthur. 1960. *The Great Chain of Being: A Study of the History of an Idea.* New York: Harper & Row.

Lovelock, James. 1979. *Gaia: A New Look at Life on Earth.* Repr., New York: Oxford University Press USA, 1987.

————. 2006. *The Revenge of Gaia: Why the Earth is Fighting Back— and How We Can Still Save Humanity.* Santa Barbara, CA.: Allen Lane.

Maddox, James. 1981. A book for burning. *Nature,* September.

McKay, Matthew, Martha Davis, and Patrick Fanning. 1995. *Messages.* Oakland, CA.: New Harbinger Publications.

Monroe, Robert. 1994. *Ultimate Journey.* New York: Doubleday Books.

Motoyama, Hiroshi. 1981. *Theories of Chakras: Bridge to Higher Consciousness.* Wheaton, IL.: Theosophical Publishing House.

Murphy, Mark. 2008. The natural law tradition in ethics. *The Stanford Encyclopedia of Philosophy* (Spring).

Myers, Norman. 1984. *The Primary Source: Tropical Forests and Our Future.* New York: Norton.

Nagel, Thomas. 1998. Conceiving the impossible and the mind-body problem. *Philosophy* 73 (285): 337–352.

Nierenberg, Danielle. 2006. Population continues to grow. In *Vital Signs 2006-2007: The Trends that Are Shaping Our Future,* Worldwatch Institute, 74-75. New York, Norton.

Pirages, Daniel. 2005. Containing infectious disease. *State of the World 2005: Redefining Global Security,* Worldwatch Institute, 42-59. New York: Norton.

de Quincey, Christian. 2002. *Radical Nature: Rediscovering the Soul of Matter.* Montpelier, VT.: Invisible Cities Press.

Radin, Dean. 1997. *The Conscious Universe: The Scientific Truth of Psychic Phenomena.* New York: HarperSanFrancisco.

———. 2006. *Entangled Minds: Extrasensory Experiences in a Quantum Reality.* New York: Paraview Pocket Books.

Ray, Paul, and Sherry Ruth Anderson. 2000. *The Cultural Creatives: How 50 Million People Are Changing the World.* New York: Three Rivers Press.

Renner, Michael. 2005. Security redefined. *State of the World 2005: Redefining Global Security,* Worldwatch Institute 3-19. New York: Norton.

Robbins, John. 2001. *The Food Revolution: How Your Diet Can Help Save Your Life and Our World.* Berkeley, CA.: Conari Press.

Rosenberg, Marshall. 2003. *Nonviolent Communication: A Language of Life.* Encinitas, CA.: Puddle Dancer Press.

Sachs, Jeffrey. 2005. *The End of Poverty.* New York: Penguin.

Sheldrake, Rupert. 1981. *A New Science of Life: The Hypothesis of Formative Causation.* New York: Houghton Mifflin.

Smith, Houston. 1992. *Forgotten Truth.* New York: HarperOne.

Sorokin, Pitirim. 1941. *The Crisis of Our Age.* New York: Dutton.

Stix, Gary. 2006. A climate repair manual. *Scientific American,* September, 47.

Tarnas, Richard. 1991. *The Passion of the Western Mind: Understanding the Ideas That Have Shaped Our World View.* New York: Ballantine Books.

———. 2006. *Cosmos and Psyche: Intimations of a New World View.* New York: Viking.

Teilhard de Chardin, Pierre. 1959. *The Phenomenon of Man.* New York: Harper and Row.

Tolle, Eckhart. 2005. *A New Earth.* New York: Dutton.

Toynbee, Arnold. 1947. *A Study of History.* Oxford, UK: Oxford University Press.

Whitehead, Alfred North. 1967. *Adventures of Ideas.* Repr., New York: Free Press.

Wilber, Ken. 1977. *The Spectrum of Consciousness.* Wheaton, IL.: Quest Books.

———. 1996. *A Brief History of Everything.* Boston: Shambhala.

———. 1998. *The Marriage of Sense and Soul: Integrating Science and Religion.* New York: Random House.

Woodhouse, Mark B. 1996. *Paradigm Wars: Worldviews for a New Age.* Berkeley, CA.: North Atlantic Books, Frog Ltd.

Zukav, Gary. 1979. *The Dancing Wu Li Masters.* New York: William Morrow & Co.

Edmund J. Bourne, Ph.D., is a psychologist in northern California specializing in the treatment of anxiety disorders and related problems. He is author of several books, including the bestselling *Anxiety & Phobia Workbook,* that have reached hundreds of thousands of people throughout the world. He welcomes comments and feedback, which can be sent to edbourne@GLOBALSHIFT NOW.com.

Foreword writer **Matthew Gilbert** is director of communications at the Institute of Noetic Sciences and editor-in-chief of *Shift,* its quarterly publication. He is author of *The Workplace Revolution* and *Communication Miracles at Work.* He lives in the San Francisco Bay Area.

About the Institute of Noetic Sciences (IONS)

Noetic Books is an imprint of the Institute of Noetic Sciences, which was founded in 1973 by Apollo 14 astronaut Edgar Mitchell. IONS is a 501(c)(3) nonprofit research, education, and membership organization whose mission is advancing the science of consciousness and human experience to serve individual and collective transformation. "Noetic" comes from the Greek word *nous*, which means "intuitive mind" or "inner knowing." The Institute's primary program areas include consciousness and healing, extended human capacities, and emerging worldviews. The specific work of the institute includes the following:

- Sponsorship of and participation in original research

- Publication of the quarterly magazine *Shift: At the Frontiers of Consciousness*

- The monthly membership program, Shift in Action, and its associated website, www.shiftinaction.com

- Presentation and cosponsorship of regional and international workshops and conferences

- The hosting of residential seminars and workshops at its on-campus retreat facility, located on 200 acres thirty minutes north of San Francisco

- The support of a global volunteer network of community groups

IONS also publishes *The Shift Report*, a now bi-annual publication that charts shifts in worldview across a wide range of disciplines and areas of human activity. Information on these reports can be found at *www.shiftreport.org*. More information about Noetic Books is available at *www.noeticbooks.org*.

To learn more about the Institute and its activities and programs, please contact

Institute of Noetic Sciences
101 San Antonio Road
Petaluma, CA 94952-9524
707-775-3500 / fax: 707-781-7420
www.noetic.org